Life

SECOND EDITION

PAUL DUMMETT

JOHN HUGHES

HELEN STEPHENSON

Australia • Brazil • Mexico • Singapore • United Kingdom • United States

Contents

Unit	Grammar	Vocabulary	Real life (functions)	Pronunciation
7 Customs and behavior pages 81–92	zero and first conditionals time linkers *usually, used to, would, be used to,* and *get used to*	raising children: verbs food word focus: *same* and *different* weddings wordbuilding: word pairs	describing traditions	/juː/ and /uː/ the letter *s*
VIDEO: Eating insects page 90 ▶ REVIEW page 92				
8 Hopes and ambitions pages 93–104	second, third, and mixed conditionals *wish* and *if only*	word focus: *make* and *do* wordbuilding: noun suffixes strong feelings word focus: *better*	discussing preferences	contracted or weak forms /ʃ/ and /tʃ/ *do you, would you*
VIDEO: What would you do if money didn't matter? page 102 ▶ REVIEW page 104				
9 The news pages 105–116	verb patterns with reporting verbs passive reporting verbs	reporting verbs positive adjectives wordbuilding: forming adjectives from verbs word focus: *word*	reporting what you have heard	the schwa
VIDEO: News: the weird and the wonderful page 114 ▶ REVIEW page 116				
10 Talented people pages 117–128	articles: *a/an, the,* or zero article? relative clauses	careers wordbuilding: verb (+ preposition) + noun collocations the senses word focus: *self* personal qualities	describing skills, talents, and experience	linking vowels difficult words
VIDEO: Queen of Egypt page 126 ▶ REVIEW page 128				
11 Knowledge and learning pages 129–140	*could, was able to, managed to,* and *succeeded in* future in the past	education wordbuilding: homonyms word focus: *learn*	getting clarification	contrastive sentence stress linking in question forms
VIDEO: Paraguay shaman page 138 ▶ REVIEW page 140				
12 Money pages 141–152	focus adverbs: *only, just, even* causative *have* and *get*	money services wordbuilding: *the* + adjective business words	negotiating	focus adverbs /ʃ/, /tʃ/, /ʒ/, and /dʒ/ long vowel sounds
VIDEO: The Farmery page 150 ▶ REVIEW page 152				

COMMUNICATION ACTIVITIES page 153 ▶ GRAMMAR SUMMARY page 168 ▶ AUDIOSCRIPT page 185

Listening	Reading	Critical thinking	Speaking	Writing
someone describing the customs on the Tokyo subway an excerpt from a radio program about the diet of the indigenous people of northern Alaska	an article about the "tiger mother" approach to parenting a blog about personal space and turn-taking	questions and answers	traditional rules of behavior food and eating habits turn-taking in conversations	text type: a description writing skill: adding detail
someone talking about an unusual mural eight explorers describing superpowers they wish they had	an article about the first human computers an article about Madagascar's unique environment	emotive language	ambitions wishes strong feelings	text type: an online comment writing skill: giving vivid examples
a radio news report about the parents of Chinese university students three good-news stories reported on the television news	an article about an iconic image an article about the power of the press	different perspectives	something true that happened to you good-news stories the media	text type: a news article writing skill: using quotations
a description of a mahout's job someone talking about an extraordinary career a description of a man with an unusual talent	an article about an extraordinary career an article about a woman who was king	examining the evidence	a career path superhuman abilities job descriptions	text type: a personal profile writing skill: using *with*
a parent talking about a children's museum a talk by a psychologist on memory	an article about an innovative school an article about how animals think	explaining ideas	learning experiences making excuses types of learner	text type: an email about a misunderstanding writing skill: linking contrasting ideas
two people talking about the standard of living an interview with a professor about the growing service economy	an article about Norway's riches an article about a new business trend	opinion words	the economy in your country getting things done new business ideas	text type: a short report writing skill: key phrases in report writing

Life around the world—in 12 videos

Unit 7 Eating insects
Discover why eating insects could be good for you, and why one man is on a mission to change our tastes.

Unit 1 Lady Liberty and Ellis Island
The gateway for immigrants to the United States.

Unit 3 3D-printed prosthetic limbs
Discover how 3D printing is revolutionizing prosthetics.

Unit 12 The Farmery
Learn about how one farm is trying to do things differently to benefit the local community.

Unit 4 Making plants into art
Learn about the work of the topiary artist Pearl Fryar.

Unit 2 How not to climb a mountain
A climber talks about how one climb went wrong.

Unit 11 Paraguay shaman
Find out why it's essential to record plants from the rain forests of Paraguay before they disappear.

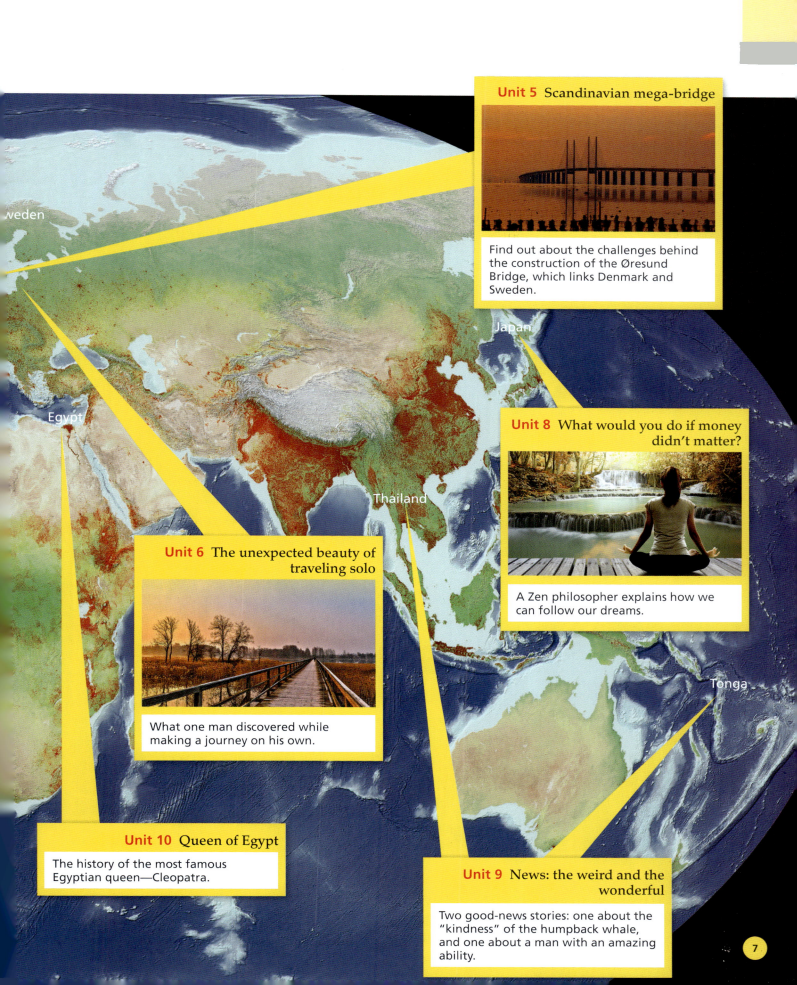

Unit 5 Scandinavian mega-bridge

Find out about the challenges behind the construction of the Øresund Bridge, which links Denmark and Sweden.

Unit 8 What would you do if money didn't matter?

A Zen philosopher explains how we can follow our dreams.

Unit 6 The unexpected beauty of traveling solo

What one man discovered while making a journey on his own.

Unit 10 Queen of Egypt

The history of the most famous Egyptian queen—Cleopatra.

Unit 9 News: the weird and the wonderful

Two good-news stories: one about the "kindness" of the humpback whale, and one about a man with an amazing ability.

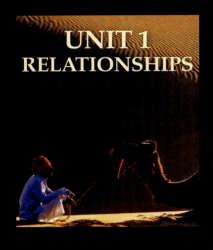
UNIT 1
RELATIONSHIPS

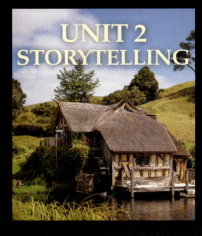
UNIT 2
STORYTELLING

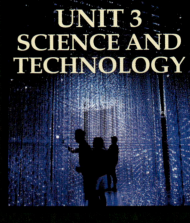
UNIT 3
SCIENCE AND TECHNOLOGY

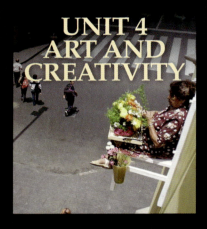
UNIT 4
ART AND CREATIVITY

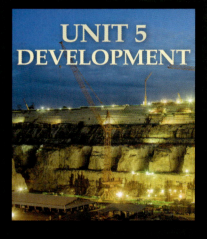
UNIT 5
DEVELOPMENT

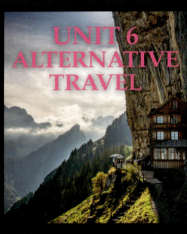
UNIT 6
ALTERNATIVE TRAVEL

UNIT 7
CUSTOMS AND BEHAVIOR

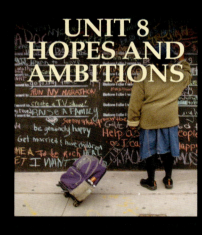
UNIT 8
HOPES AND AMBITIONS

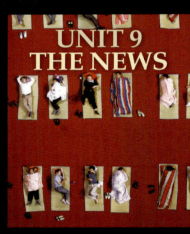
UNIT 9
THE NEWS

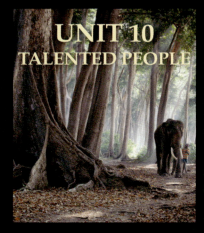
UNIT 10
TALENTED PEOPLE

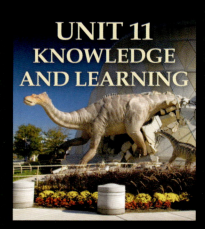
UNIT 11
KNOWLEDGE AND LEARNING

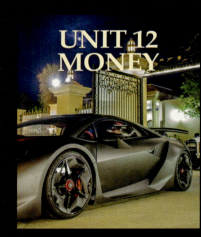
UNIT 12
MONEY

Unit 7 Customs and behavior

A crowded Tokyo subway train during evening rush hour

FEATURES

82 Cruel to be kind

The "tiger mother" approach to parenting

84 A matter of taste

The diet of the indigenous people of northern Alaska

86 Cultural conventions

Understanding personal space and turn-taking

90 Eating insects

A video about Americans with an unusual taste for insects

1 Work in pairs. Look at the photo and the caption. What rules or customs do people follow in this situation? Make a list of polite/thoughtful behavior and a list of rude/inconsiderate behavior.

2 ▶ 58 Listen to someone describing customs on the Tokyo subway. Work in pairs and answer the questions.

  1 Did the speaker mention any of your ideas from Exercise 1?
  2 Which customs or behaviors are unique to the Tokyo subway?

3 Look at the rules of behavior (1–4) for students attending college lectures. Complete the sentences with these words.

| chew | interrupt | raise | show | stare |

  1 Don't _____ the lecturer. _____ your hand first if you have a question.
  2 Be attentive. By all means take notes, but don't just sit and _____ at your laptop screen.
  3 Don't eat food or _____ gum during a lecture or seminar.
  4 Be polite, respectful, and _____ consideration to other students.

4 Work in pairs. Do you agree with the rules of behavior in Exercise 3? Are there any more rules you would add?

7a Cruel to be kind

Reading

1 Work in pairs. Which of these things (1–6) do you think should be:
- controlled strongly by parents;
- controlled a little by parents; or
- left to the child to decide? Give reasons.

1 watching TV
2 practicing a musical instrument
3 going out to play with friends
4 doing homework
5 choosing which subjects to study in school
6 choosing activities outside school (e.g., sports, hobbies)

2 Read the article. Work in pairs and answer the questions (1–3).

1 What is a "tiger mother"?
2 What are a tiger mother's attitudes to the first four things in Exercise 1?
3 What are the results of Amy Chua's "tiger mother" parenting?

Vocabulary raising children: verbs

3 Work in pairs. Look at the pairs of verbs in **bold**. The first verb in each pair is from the article. Discuss the differences in meaning between the verbs in each pair. Use a dictionary if necessary.

1 **bring up** and **educate** children
2 **praise** and **reward** good behavior
3 **give in to** and **spoil** your children
4 **encourage** and **force** your children to do something
5 **punish** and **shame** someone
6 **rebel against** and **disobey** your parents

CRUEL TO BE KIND

▶ 59

Is there a right way to bring up children? Some parents read books to find an answer, some follow their instincts. Whatever they do, a doubt always remains: "When my children have grown up, will I have any regrets about my parenting?"

But "doubt" is not in the vocabulary of Amy Chua, a successful lawyer, professor, and author of *Battle Hymn of the Tiger Mother*, a guide to bringing up children. According to Chua, most mothers are too soft on their children. They praise them for every effort, even if the result is coming last in a race or playing a piano piece badly. Often, when their children ask to go out and play rather than do their homework, the parents just give in to them.

The tiger mother's approach—described by Chua as "the Chinese way"—is very different. Tiger mothers accept nothing less than "A" grades in every subject; if the child fails to achieve this, it simply shows they have not worked hard enough. Tiger mothers encourage their children not with praise, but with punishment. "Unless you learn this piano piece," Chua told her daughter, "I will donate your doll house to charity." She even rejected her daughter's homemade birthday card because it had been drawn in a hurry.

But Chua says that this is a more honest and direct approach. If her child has been lazy, she says, she will punish them—that is the tiger mother's way. In the same situation, other parents usually tell their children not to worry: If they keep trying, they will do better next time.

A strict routine of work before play, no TV or video games, plus constant nagging—it doesn't seem much fun for the children. But perhaps it works. Chua's daughters have not rebelled against her. They attend Ivy League colleges now, and are proficient at violin and piano. Chua is convinced that as long as she continues to push them, they will have successful careers.

Amy Chua (middle) with her two daughters

Grammar zero and first conditionals

> ▶ **ZERO and FIRST CONDITIONALS**
>
> **Zero conditional**
> *If* the child **fails** to achieve this, it simply **shows** they have not worked hard enough.
> *When* their children **ask** to go out and play rather than do their homework, the parents just **give** in to them.
>
> **First conditional**
> *If* they **keep** trying, they **will do** better next time.
> *If* her child **has been** lazy, she **will punish** them.
>
> ***unless*** or ***as long as***
> *Unless* you **learn** this piano piece, I **will donate** your doll house to charity.
> *As long as* she **continues** to push them, they **will have** successful careers.

For more information and practice, see page 168.

4 Look at the grammar box above. Work in pairs and answer these questions.

1 Which tenses or verb forms are used in zero and first conditional sentences?
2 Which type of conditional do we use to talk about:
   a a fact or something that is generally true?
   b a particular possible future situation?
3 In which sentences can you use either *if* or *when* with a similar meaning?
4 How are the words *as long as* and *unless* different in meaning from *if*?

5 Circle the correct options to complete these zero and first conditional sentences.

1 If Charlie *continues / will continue* drinking soda all the time, it *will ruin / ruins* his teeth.
2 Some children *become / will become* very confused if they *won't / don't* have an established routine.
3 If a child *will be / is* misbehaving, it *will be / is* important to understand why.
4 When parents *will be / are* too strict, it *is / will be* natural for some children to rebel against them.
5 When I *will have / have* children, I *will try / try* to be the kind of parent that praises, not punishes.

Grammar time linkers

> ▶ **TIME LINKERS**
>
> Time linking words (*when, as soon as, before, after, while, until*) can be used in sentences about the future.
> *When* my children **have grown** up, will I **have** any regrets about my parenting?

For more information and practice, see page 168.

6 Look at the grammar box about time linkers. Circle the correct option to complete the rule below.

In a sentence about the future where two clauses are connected by a time linking word, we use a *present / future* verb form after the time linking word.

7 Look at the prompts. Write complete sentences about the future using appropriate verb forms.

1 I / go and get / some milk / before / the store / close.
2 She / stay / in her current job / until / she / find / a better one.
3 She / meet / us / after / she / finish / work.
4 As soon as / everyone / board / the plane, / we / be / able to leave.
5 I / have / to take the bus to work next week / while / the car / be / repaired.
6 Dinner / be / ready for you / when / you / get / home.

8 Circle the best options to complete the sentences.

1 I'll continue to live at home *as long as / until* I find a reasonably priced apartment to rent.
2 My dad says he'll teach me how to drive *while / as long as* I pass all my exams.
3 *Unless / If* you do as you're told, we won't be going to the festival on Saturday.
4 I'm sure you'll be able to watch the game *while / until* you're waiting at the airport.
5 I think he'll change his mind about going to college *until / after* he has had time to think about it.
6 Los Angeles is a great place to live *before / if* you have a car and plenty of money.

9 Below are expressions commonly said by adults either to or about children. Complete them in your own words. Then compare your sentences with a partner.

1 "If you don't finish your dinner, …"
2 "Children only appreciate how difficult it is to be a parent when …"
3 "If you do well in your exams, …"
4 "It's fine for children to live at home until …"

Speaking *myLife*

10 Work in small groups. Think of four traditional rules of behavior that parents have given to children. Then discuss which are still good rules, and which you think are old-fashioned or no longer appropriate.

*"Don't speak until you are spoken to." I think this rule is old-fashioned and wrong because if you **tell** your children not to speak, they **won't develop** good communication skills.*

Unit 7 Customs and behavior

7b A matter of taste

Listening

1 Work in pairs. What is the strangest thing you have ever eaten? Why did you eat it? What did it taste like?

2 ▶ 60 Listen to an excerpt from a radio program about the diet of the indigenous people of northern Alaska. Work in pairs and answer the questions.

1 What kind of food forms their traditional diet?
2 What is surprising about their diet?

3 ▶ 60 Listen to the excerpt again. Circle the correct option (a, b, or c) to complete each sentence.

1 In less _____ countries, people don't eat so much meat.
   a well-off
   b cold
   c populous
2 In northern Alaska, there aren't many _____ available to eat.
   a dairy products
   b small animals
   c plants
3 The speaker has been told that whale skin is very _____ .
   a nutritious
   b delicious
   c tough
4 Harold Draper says that what is important is eating the right _____ .
   a nutrients
   b foods
   c vitamins
5 Since Alaska Natives have started eating more processed foods, they have had more _____ problems.
   a health
   b financial
   c social

4 Work in pairs. Are you surprised by the Alaska Native diet? Why or why not? Do you think we should eat less processed food? What would you miss most if this were the case?

Grammar usually, used to, would, be used to, and get used to

▶ USUALLY, USED TO, WOULD, BE USED TO, and GET USED TO

usually + simple present
1 We **usually eat** fruit to get more vitamin C. ____

used to + base form of the verb
2 Heart conditions among Alaska Natives **used to be** about half the number in the wider population of North America. ____
3 They **didn't use to have** a so-called balanced diet. ____

would + base form of the verb
4 They **would cook** the meat in seal oil. ____

be used to + noun or -ing
5 On the whole, we **are used to eating** a range of foods. ____

get used to + noun or -ing
6 We **have gotten used to eating** certain foods in order to get each nutrient. ____

For more information and practice, see page 168.

5 Look at the sentences in the grammar box. Match the phrases in **bold** (1–6) with the descriptions below (a–e).

a a repeated past action, habit, or situation that no longer happens (two phrases)
b a repeated action or habit (not a state or situation) in the past
c a habit or action that happens regularly or is generally true
d something that seems or seemed normal (not strange or difficult)
e a new thing that people adapt to or that becomes normal

6 Circle the correct options to complete the paragraphs about eating habits.

A Fifty years ago, people in the US ¹*used to sit / got used to sitting* down for meals with their families each evening. Families nowadays ²*get used to eating / usually eat* together no more than three times a week, because busy lives, work, and TV get in the way. But it is believed that if more families could ³*be used to dining / get used to dining* together again, it would strengthen family relationships.

B When I was young, I ⁴*was used to eating / used to eat* a lot of candy. Every Saturday, my sister and I ⁵*would go / got used to going* to the store and spend our allowance on chocolate, gum, and all kinds of things that were bad for our teeth.

7 Complete these sentences with *usually, used to, would, get used to,* or *be used to.* Where there is a verb in parentheses, put it in the correct form.

1. We ___used to eat___ (eat) out a lot, but restaurants are so expensive these days that we don't anymore.
2. I go to that café a lot. I _____ (order) the salmon when I go there.
3. I _____ (take) sugar in my coffee, but now I drink it without sugar. It took a little while to _____ the taste, but now it feels normal.
4. When I was little, if I didn't like some food on my plate, I _____ (hide) it in my napkin when no one was looking and put it in my pocket.
5. When I was staying with my grandparents, we _____ (have) dinner at six o'clock every evening. It was strange, because I _____ (eat) dinner much later.

8 Are any of the sentences in Exercise 7 true for you? How is your experience different? Discuss with a partner.

9 Pronunciation /juː/ and /uː/

a ▶ 61 Look at the words in **bold** below. The letter *u* (underlined) is pronounced /juː/. Listen to the sentences and repeat.

1. I <u>u</u>sually eat a big breakfast.
2. Did you <u>u</u>se to eat a big breakfast?
3. I'm not <u>u</u>sed to eating a lot of meat.

b Work in pairs. Practice saying these words with the /juː/ sound (underlined).

| reg<u>u</u>lar | c<u>u</u>cumber | f<u>u</u>ture | h<u>u</u>man |
| c<u>u</u>te | rep<u>u</u>tation | h<u>u</u>ge | val<u>u</u>e |

c ▶ 62 In these words, there is no /j/ sound before the /uː/ sound. Practice saying the words. Then listen and check. Which sounds come before /uː/?

| fr<u>u</u>it | j<u>u</u>ice | J<u>u</u>ne | j<u>u</u>nior | r<u>u</u>le | tr<u>u</u>e |

Vocabulary and speaking food and eating habits *my*Life

10 ▶ 63 Work in pairs. Look at these food items. Put each food item in the correct category in the chart. Then listen and check your answers. Think of two more food items for each category.

mustard	cucumber	beef	lettuce
apple	ketchup	lamb	muesli
raspberries	cheese	tuna	butter

1 Fruit and vegetables	
2 Dairy products	
3 Breakfast cereals	
4 Sauces	
5 Meat and seafood	

11 Find out about your classmates' eating habits. Ask three classmates questions about these areas and take notes.

- **Meals:** times, who they eat with, what they eat
- **Fast food:** how often and what
- **Fruit and vegetables:** which and how much
- **Candy:** which, when, and how often
- **Eating habits in general:** have they changed?

12 Work in pairs. Compare your notes from Exercise 11 and make conclusions using *usually, used to,* and *get used to.*

*Most people don't **usually** eat a big breakfast.*
*Mary **used to** eat dinner with her family every night, but now she **usually** buys fast food.*
*Scott is trying to **get used to** cooking for himself.*

7c Cultural conventions

Reading

1 Work in pairs. Imagine you are at a job interview. Discuss what you would do.

   1 **Clothes:** dress professionally or casually?
   2 **Posture:** sit forward or lean back?
   3 **Distance:** be close to the interviewer or not?
   4 **Voice:** speak loudly, softly, or confidently?
   5 **Eye contact:** keep strong eye contact or not?
   6 **Body language:** fold arms or keep hands down?

2 Read the first paragraph of the blog. What do the terms "personal space" and "turn-taking" mean?

3 Read the rest of the blog. Which of these statements (a–c) best summarizes the author's findings about personal space and turn-taking?

   a There are cultural differences in these areas, but they are not significant.
   b More scientific evidence is needed to support claims of cultural differences.
   c The differences in these areas are small, but need to be resolved to improve communication between different cultures.

4 Work in pairs. Answer these questions.

   1 What do you think is meant by "contact" and "non-contact" cultures?
   2 What does Edward Hall think we risk if we fail to understand differences in personal space?
   3 According to the author, what is missing from the research done so far into personal space?
   4 What do the two stories about turn-taking in Nordic countries tell us?
   5 What is the average time that people anywhere in the world take to respond in conversation?

5 Work in pairs. Underline words or phrases in the blog that mean the following:

   1 made bigger than it really is (paragraph 1)
   2 proof based on personal stories/accounts (paragraph 3)
   3 a line on which we measure things (paragraph 4)
   4 the usual way (paragraph 6)

Critical thinking questions and answers

6 Work in pairs. What question does the author ask at the start of the blog? What is his answer?

7 Work in pairs. Look at these other questions that the blog raises. Is there an answer to them in the blog? What are the answers?

   1 Why do anthropologists seem to exaggerate cultural differences?
   2 Why do we need to be careful about making cultural comparisons?

Word focus *same* and *different*

8 The expression with *difference* below is from the blog. Complete the sentences (1–6) with the words *same*, *different*, or *difference*. Then compare answers with a partner. Which two **bold** phrases mean the same thing? Which two are complete opposites?

*In other words, the **difference** is minimal.*

   1 We didn't fight! We just **had a _____ of opinion**.
   2 I don't mind where we eat tonight. **It's all the _____ to me**.
   3 Being able to speak a language is one thing; being able to teach it is **a completely _____ matter**.
   4 You say money's not important, but if you were poor, you'd be **singing a _____ tune**.
   5 Really, **it makes no _____ to me** where we stay. A youth hostel is fine.
   6 A jail and a prison are **one and the _____ thing**.

Speaking myLife

9 Work in pairs. Discuss the customs in your own culture regarding personal space and turn-taking.

10 Look at this list of the most common first words in turn-taking in English conversation. Which of these words do *you* most use in conversation? Tell your partner.

Yeah	Umm	I	And	Oh	So
No	Yes	Well	But	You	Right

11 Work in pairs. Have short conversations using these opening questions and statements (a–c). Use words in Exercise 10 to give you time to respond.

   a Do all cultures smile to show they're happy?
   b Do you use gestures a lot when you speak?
   c You can tell a lot about people from their body language.

CULTURAL CONVENTIONS

▶ 64

1 Whenever I read about cultural differences in communication, I always find myself asking if these are real differences or something imagined or exaggerated. So recently, I decided I would investigate. I chose two areas—personal space and turn-taking—to try to find out the truth. Personal space means how close we stand or sit next to other people. Turn-taking refers to the rules of conversation—how long you speak for and how long the other person waits before responding.

2 The idea that different cultures perceive space differently was first investigated by an American anthropologist, Edward Hall. He put the range for "personal distance" (family or close friends) at 45 cm to 1.2 m, and for "social distance" (colleagues, neighbors, etc.) at 1.2 m to 3.5 m. Hall claimed that in "non-contact" cultures (the USA, northern Europe, parts of Asia), the distance is greater; in "contact" cultures (Latin America, the Middle East, southern Europe), it is smaller. He warned that not respecting the correct distance between people could lead to misunderstanding or, worse, offense. He gave an example of an American at an airport who finds a seat in an empty seating area. The man feels uncomfortable when a Mediterranean-looking man comes and sits right next to him.

3 There is a lot of anecdotal evidence to support claims of cultural differences, but little scientific evidence. While the ranges for the amount of space we need seem accurate, the actual amount depends on many more factors than just cultural background: the age of the people, gender, where they live, social position, and personality.

4 Anthropologists also give examples of big cultural differences in turn-taking. Nordic cultures (Denmark, Sweden, Norway, Finland) are reported to have long delays between one turn and the next. One anthropologist describes offering coffee to a Swedish guest in his house. After a minute's silence, the offer was accepted. Another gives an account of two men in Häme, Finland, walking to work one morning. The first man says, "I lost my knife here yesterday." As they return home from work that evening, the other man asks, "What kind of knife was it?" Cultures at the other end of the scale include Japanese, Korean, and Dutch. In Antigua, for example, studies have observed that speakers usually talk over one another, with no delay at all between turns.

5 However, scientific data shows that there is little cultural difference in the actual time delays in turn-taking. The typical pause across cultures is about 0.2 seconds. The maximum gap is 0.47 seconds (Danish), and the minimum only 0.07 seconds (Japanese). In other words, the difference is minimal.

6 How, then, do stories of exaggerated differences come about? One reason could be that when it comes to personal space and waiting for a response, we are sensitive to any variation from the norm. But I suspect the main reason is that we find contrasts entertaining. There is nothing wrong with that, but we must be cautious when we make comparisons and keep in mind that our similarities are, in fact, much greater than our differences.

Unit 7 **Customs and behavior** 87

7d Wedding customs

Vocabulary weddings

> **WORDBUILDING word pairs**
>
> Some words make a matching pair.
> *bride* and *groom*, *host* and *guest*
>
> For more practice, see Workbook page 59.

1 Look at these words and phrases related to weddings. Match them with their definitions (1–6).

| bride | groom | bachelorette party |
| reception | veil | bachelor party |

1 a pre-wedding party for the man
   _____
2 a pre-wedding party for the woman
   _____
3 a party after the wedding
   _____
4 a woman on her wedding day
   _____
5 a man on his wedding day
   _____
6 a piece of thin cloth that covers the woman's face _____

Real life describing traditions

2 ▶ 65 Work in pairs. Listen to the first part of a description of a traditional pre-wedding "henna night" in eastern Turkey. Who attends the event, and how is it celebrated?

3 ▶ 66 Listen to the second part of the description. Number the stages of the ceremony in the correct order (1–5).

____ A child presents the hennaed coin to the groom.
____ The bride's head is covered with a red veil.
____ The bride's hands and feet are decorated with henna.
____ A gold coin is put into the remaining henna, and the guests sing separation songs.
____ The henna is prepared by the daughter of another couple.

> ▶ **DESCRIBING TRADITIONS**
>
> It takes place a few nights before the wedding.
> It marks the last evening that a bride spends …
> It symbolizes the end of life as a single person …
> It's traditional/customary for this to be done by …
> Typically, / As a rule, / Usually, the women from …
>
> **Describing the sequence of events**
> The ceremony begins with the …
> Then, … / After that, … / Next, … / Finally, …
> After/Once the bride's head has been …
> While this is happening, the guests …
> On the morning of the wedding, …

4 ▶ 67 Work in pairs. Retell the stages of the ceremony (from Exercise 3) using the expressions for describing traditions. Then listen to the complete description again and compare your version.

5 **Pronunciation** the letter *s*

a ▶ 68 Work in pairs. Listen to these words. How is the underlined *s* pronounced in each word: /s/, /z/, or /ʒ/?

| cu<u>s</u>tom | dre<u>ss</u> | friend<u>s</u> | mu<u>s</u>ic | occa<u>s</u>ion |
| plea<u>s</u>ure | suppo<u>s</u>e | spend<u>s</u> | wedding<u>s</u> | |

b ▶ 69 Work in pairs. How do you think the underlined *s* is pronounced in these words? Listen and check.

| deci<u>s</u>ion | ea<u>s</u>tern | lo<u>s</u>e | plan<u>s</u> |
| ring<u>s</u> | <u>s</u>ingle | surpri<u>s</u>e | u<u>s</u>ual |

6 What special events or customs take place before, during, or after a wedding in your country? Choose one tradition and prepare a description. Think about:
- the timing of the event and its significance.
- the sequence of the events.

7 Work in small groups. Describe the event or custom you chose to your group members.

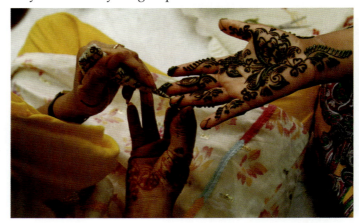

7e Fireworks festival

Writing a description

1 Work in pairs. Read the description below of a festival. What does the description say about each of these things?

   a the name and date of the festival
   b the reason for the festival
   c the main attraction at the festival
   d other activities that take place
   e the high point of the festival

2 Read the description again. Underline all the adjectives used to describe the festival. What overall impression do you think the writer wants to give? Discuss with a partner.

Las Fallas—or the "Festival of fire"—in Valencia, Spain, is one of the most unusual and exciting festivals in the world: a joyful mixture of parades, music, food, and fireworks. It takes place every year between March 15th and 19th, and marks the beginning of spring—a time when everything bad is burned to welcome in the new season.

The focus of the festival is extraordinary statues called *ninots*—many as tall as houses—made of cardboard, wood, and plaster. The *ninots* often poke fun at people from real life, like politicians and celebrities, and are placed at different points all around the city. Each *ninot* is judged for its creative design, and prizes are given to the winners.

During the festival, people celebrate in the streets, drinking, eating paella (the traditional local dish), and watching fireworks. Late in the evening on March 18th, young men cut holes in the *ninots* and stuff them with fireworks. Then at exactly midnight comes the climax of the festival, when all the *ninots* across the city are set on fire in one spectacular burning ceremony. It is a unique, and very noisy, display.

3 **Writing skill** adding detail

a When you write a description, it is important to add interesting details. Work in pairs and answer these questions.

   1 What details does the writer add about these things?

   | the beginning of spring | the *ninot* statues |
   | the people from real life | the celebrations |

   2 How are the details added: with adjectives, with an explanation, with a list, or with examples?

b Work in pairs. Add details to the description of a music festival, using the guide in parentheses.

   1 In the middle of the park, there is a … stage. (adjectives to describe the stage)
   2 People then make their way to the main square, … (list of activities while making their way, e.g., singing)
   3 There are all kinds of foods to eat, such as … (examples)
   4 The festival takes place in mid-July, a time when … (explanation)

4 Write a description of a festival you know well. Start with the basic facts (use the ideas in Exercise 1) and then add more interesting details.

5 Exchange descriptions with a partner. Use these questions to check your partner's description.

   • Does the description include the date of the festival, its significance, its high point, and the activities people do?
   • Does the description give you a strong overall impression of the festival?
   • Does it include interesting details?
   • After reading the description, would you like to go to the festival?

7f Eating insects

Unusual food for sale at a street market

Before you watch

1 Match the names of the insects with the photos (A–F). What do you know about each insect?

| caterpillar ___ | cockroach ___ | cricket ___ |
| mealworm ___ | mosquito ___ | fly ___ |

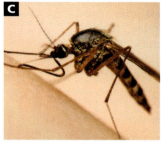

2 Key vocabulary

a Work in pairs. Read the sentences (1–4). The words in **bold** are used in the video. Guess the meaning of the words.

1. The chef Jamie Oliver is an **advocate** for healthy eating for kids.
2. She served the fish with a simple **garnish** of herbs.
3. There is a **niche** market for sugar-free chocolate.
4. Avocado ice cream? That sounds **revolting**.

b Write the words in **bold** in Exercise 2a next to their definitions (a–d).

a serving a small group _____
b someone who speaks in favor of something _____
c disgusting _____
d a small amount of food used for decoration _____

3 You are going to watch a video about eating insects. Work in pairs. Discuss the answers to these questions before you watch.

1. Which regions or continents include insects in their diets?
2. Is eating insects a new trend?
3. Why is producing insects better for the environment than producing meat?
4. Are insects nutritious?

While you watch

4 ▶ 7.1 Watch the video and check your answers from Exercise 3.

5 Work in pairs. Try to remember the insects that you saw in these foods.

1. apples covered with _____
2. a lollipop with a _____ in it
3. a cocktail made with _____, not shrimps
4. a banana and cream dessert with a _____ on top

6 ▶ 7.1 Look at these questions. Then watch the video again and take notes. Check your answers with a partner.

1. How long has Larry been trying to get Americans to eat insects?
2. According to Larry, why do most Americans not like eating insects?
3. How many species of insects are eaten around the world?
4. What does one of Larry's dinner guests want to know about the cockroach on his plate?

After you watch

7 Vocabulary in context

a ▶ 7.2 Watch the clips from the video. Choose the correct meaning of the words and phrases.

b Complete these sentences in your own words. Then share your sentences with a partner.

1. … is anything but new.
2. I can't stomach …
3. My friend disagreed with me about … , but I was able to win him/her over by saying …

8 Would you eat the meals shown in the video? Why or why not? Discuss with your partner.

UNIT 7 REVIEW AND MEMORY BOOSTER

Grammar

1 Circle the correct options to complete the description.

If you ¹ *used to eat / are used to eating* lunch in the middle of the day and dinner around 7:30 p.m., then you ² *get / will get* a shock if you go to Argentina. Lunch ³ *usually takes / is used to taking* place at around 2 p.m., and dinner after 9 p.m.

But it's not just eating times that are different. At home in England, I ⁴ *used to eat / didn't use to eat* a big breakfast, very little lunch, and then I ⁵ *will / would* have a reasonably big supper when I got home from work. Here, breakfast is just coffee and a piece of toast, and lunch is a big deal. And the meat! I don't think I'll ever ⁶ *be used to / get used to* eating so much meat. As you know, when you eat a big lunch, you generally ⁷ *feel / feels* pretty sleepy afterward. The answer to that is to take a short nap or "siesta" in the afternoon. Actually, in Buenos Aires, the traditional siesta is not as common as it ⁸ *was used to being / used to be*, but you still find people in the provinces taking them.

2 What are four things that the writer finds strange about eating habits in Argentina? Tell a partner.

3 Complete this sentence with the verb in parentheses. Use one of the grammatical forms from the description in Exercise 1.

My parents never wasted food. Often, we _____ (eat) leftovers from the day before.

4 >> MB Write two similar sentences with blanks about your own past or present eating habits. Then work in pairs. Ask your partner to complete the sentences.

I CAN	
use *usually, used to, would, be used to,* and *get used to*	☐
use the zero and first conditionals and time linking words	☐

Vocabulary

5 Complete these rules of good behavior. Reorder the letters of the words in parentheses.

1 Don't _____ others. (rupterint)
2 Try not to _____ at people. (estra)
3 Don't speak when you are _____ food. (whingec)
4 Show _____ to others. (isticonaroned)
5 Be aware of other people's _____ space. (nosapler)

6 >> MB Work in pairs. Cross out the word or phrase that doesn't belong in each group and explain why.

1 disobey   bring up   look after   raise
2 encourage   shame   praise   reward
3 beef   cheese   goat   lamb
4 tuna   raspberries   apple   banana
5 bride   guest   groom   veil

I CAN	
talk about parenting and behavior	☐
talk about food and eating habits	☐

Real life

7 Match the sentence beginnings (1–6) with the endings (a–f) to make sentences about a coming-of-age tradition.

1 It marks ____
2 It takes place ____
3 It's customary for ____
4 The ceremony begins ____
5 Typically, ____
6 Once the child ____

a people to give presents to the child.
b the moment when a child becomes an adult.
c the child stands up and gives a short speech.
d with the parent and child entering the hall.
e has given their speech, other people can also say a few words.
f on the child's sixteenth birthday.

8 >> MB Work in pairs. Take turns describing a special celebration in your country. Use the sentence beginnings (1–6) from Exercise 7.

I CAN	
describe a (traditional) celebration	☐

Unit 8 Hopes and ambitions

"Bucket list" wall: a public work of art on the wall of a local store

FEATURES

94 Rise of the rocket girls

The team that guided NASA's spacecraft

96 I wish I could …

Superpowers that people wish they had

98 Saving Madagascar

Hopes and fears for Madagascar's environment

102 What would you do if money didn't matter?

A video about people's true ambitions

1 Look at the photo and the caption. Find two wishes you like.

2 ▶70 Listen to someone speaking about this wall. Work in pairs. What are some examples of things that people write?

3 Complete the sentences (1–3) with these synonyms of the words in **bold**.

ambition	goal	hope

1 Our **aim** / _____ / **target** is to raise $10,000 for charity.
2 Her _____ / **dream** is to be a professional dancer.
3 My parents' **wish** / _____ / **expectation** was that I would study medicine in college.

4 ▶70 What verbs did the speaker use in these phrases? Listen again and complete the phrases with the verbs you hear.

1 the dreams they'd like to _____ true
2 goals that are easy to _____
3 people wanting to _____ up to other people's expectations of them
4 some people will _____ their ambitions and some won't

5 Work in pairs. What are your hopes, goals, and ambitions? How easy do you think they will be to achieve?

8a Rise of the rocket girls

Reading

1 Look at the title of the article and the photo. Discuss these questions with a partner. Then read the article and check your answers.

1 Who do you think the rocket girls were, and what did they do?
2 What do you think their ambition was?

2 Read the article again. Work in pairs. Correct the underlined words below using words from the article to make these sentences true.

1 The men who flew to the moon were more <u>experienced</u> than the women engineers and mathematicians who helped them get there.
2 In the 1950s, "computers" were <u>machines</u> who did mathematical calculations.
3 As time went on, the rocket girls started programming actual <u>scientists</u>.
4 The rocket girls worked <u>fixed</u> hours at the lab.
5 The author Nathalia Holt hopes that we will see more women <u>astronauts</u> in the future.

Word focus *make* and *do*

3 Look at the article again. Underline three expressions with the word *make* and two expressions with the word *do*. Then circle the correct options to complete the sentences below.

1 We usually use *make / do* to describe performing a repetitive task or an obligation.
2 We usually use *make / do* to describe producing or creating something.
3 We use *make / do* + an object pronoun (e.g., *something, it, that*).

4 Circle the correct verbs to complete these sentences.

1 Can I *do / make* a suggestion? Why don't we take turns *doing / making* the housework?
2 I want to *do / make* something to help them: something that will really *do / make* a difference.
3 I've *done / made* a note of all the things we need to set up and all the shopping we need to *do / make* before the party.
4 Their business is struggling. They're *doing / making* everything they can, but they're still not *doing / making* a profit.
5 I'm taking a very interesting evening class at the college, and I've *done / made* some good friends there.

▶ 71

Rise of the rocket girls

Everyone knows Buzz Aldrin, the famous astronaut. But how many of us have heard of Eleanor Francis Helin, an engineer behind numerous successful NASA space missions? Helin was part of a group of female
5 mathematicians working at NASA's Jet Propulsion Lab (JPL) in the 1960s. Nathalia Holt, the author of a book about these women—known as "rocket girls"—says, "If they hadn't worked on the lunar project, 'man' would not have reached the moon."

10 The rocket girls started out at JPL in the 1950s, having answered a job advertisement saying "Computers needed." They were called computers because, before today's digital devices, you needed humans to do mathematical calculations. And
15 the calculations had to be extremely accurate. If someone had made the smallest mistake, a spacecraft bound for the moon would still be traveling somewhere in outer space today, having missed its target entirely.

20 The rocket girls went from being "computers" to becoming the lab's first computer programmers and engineers. One of the group's early leaders, Macie Roberts, made the decision to hire only women, and this policy continued for the next thirty
25 years. They brought in many women who wanted to be engineers but didn't have the necessary qualifications. If anyone tried to employ only men or only women today, they wouldn't be allowed to. But Roberts made the work environment at the lab
30 special. The women formed close relationships and worked flexible hours to help each other balance home and professional lives. At the same time, they felt they were doing something really valuable. As a result, many women stayed on working at JPL for
35 thirty or forty years.

Holt says that if there were more women engineers today, she probably wouldn't have written the book. She hopes that the rocket girls will now get the recognition they deserve, and inspire a new
40 generation of female engineers.

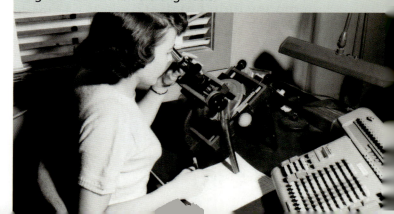

Grammar second, third, and mixed conditionals

▶ **SECOND, THIRD, and MIXED CONDITIONALS**

Second conditional
1 **If** anyone **tried** to employ only men or only women today, they **wouldn't be** allowed to.

Third conditional
2 **If** these women **hadn't worked** on the lunar project, "man" **would not have reached** the moon.

Mixed second + third conditional
3 **If** there **were** more women engineers today, she probably **wouldn't have written** the book.

Mixed third + second conditional
4 **If** someone **had made** a mistake, the spacecraft **would** still **be** somewhere in outer space today.

For more information and practice, see page 170.

5 Look at the grammar box. Circle the correct options to complete these explanations.

1 Sentence 1 describes a situation in the *present or future / past*. It refers to a(n) *real possibility / imagined situation*.
2 In sentence 2, the *if*-clause describes an imaginary situation in the *present / past*. The result it describes is in the *present / past*.
3 In sentence 3, the *if*-clause describes an imaginary situation in the *present / past*. The result it describes is in the *present / past*.
4 In sentence 4, the *if*-clause describes an imaginary situation in the *present / past*. The result it describes is in the *present / past*.

6 Work in pairs. Read the sentences (1–4). What type of conditional sentences are they? Complete the descriptions of the actual situations and the results.

1 If I were on a spaceship traveling to Mars, I would be worried that I might never come back.
   This is a second conditional sentence.
   I am not on a spaceship traveling to Mars, so I'm not worried that I might never come back.
2 If some of the engineers had been men, there wouldn't have been such a special working environment.
   None of the engineers _____ , so _____ a special working environment.
3 If I had read Nathalia Holt's book, I would know all the facts about the rocket girls.
   I _____ Nathalia Holt's book, so I _____ all the facts about the rocket girls.
4 If I were better at mathematics, I would have studied physics in college.
   I _____ at mathematics, so I _____ physics in college.

7 Work in pairs. Form conditional sentences using the information in these sentences (1–6). Notice the time of each action or situation and result.

1 We live a long way from the city, so we don't see our friends very often.
2 I really didn't understand the movie, so I walked out before the end.
3 I'm not used to the cold weather, so I had to put on an extra sweater.
4 Taking a vacation is expensive because we have three children.
5 She did well on her law exams. Now she's working for a top legal firm.
6 I didn't call you back because I was waiting for another call.

8 Pronunciation contracted or weak forms

a ▶ 72 Complete these conditional sentences. Then listen and check your answers. Notice how the missing words are pronounced: as contracted forms or as weak forms.

1 If the rent _____ cheaper, I _____ take the apartment.
2 What would you _____ done if you _____ me?
3 So sorry! If I _____ known you were here, I _____ asked Jo to get you a coffee.
4 If she _____ stayed in college, she _____ now be a fully qualified journalist.

b Work in pairs. Practice saying the sentences from Exercise 8a.

9 Complete these sentences in your own words. Then compare your sentences with a partner.

1 If I hadn't had a good English teacher, perhaps I …
2 If I were more ambitious, perhaps I …
3 If I had studied … instead of … , I …
4 If I hadn't met … , I wouldn't …

Speaking myLife

10 Work in pairs. Think of one friend or family member who has achieved their ambition and one who has changed their ambition. Describe what has happened to them using at least two *if*-sentences.

*If my mother **hadn't taken** evening classes when we were young, she **wouldn't be** a nurse now.*

8b I wish I could …

1 Albert Lin
Scientist and explorer

2 Laly Lichtenfeld
Big cat conservationist

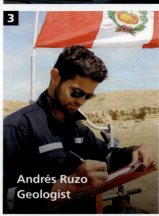
3 Andrés Ruzo
Geologist

4 Alizé Carrère
Geographer

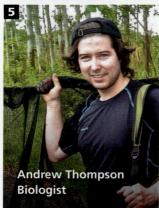
5 Andrew Thompson
Biologist

6 Catherine Workman
Conservation biologist

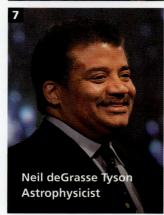
7 Neil deGrasse Tyson
Astrophysicist

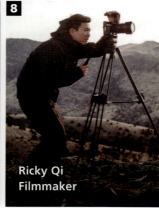
8 Ricky Qi
Filmmaker

Listening

1 Work in pairs. Look at the photos and captions of the National Geographic Explorers on the left. What do you think each job involves? Do any of the jobs interest you? Why or why not?

> **WORDBUILDING noun suffixes**
>
> We use certain suffixes when we talk about people who do particular jobs: -er, -or, -ian, -ist, -ant, e.g., *filmmaker, actor, politician, scientist, accountant*.
> Nowadays, we tend not to distinguish so much between male and female workers. For example, we say *police officer* rather than *policeman* or *policewoman*; or we use the male term for female roles, e.g., *actor* (not *actress*).
>
> For more practice, see Workbook page 67.

2 Look at the wordbuilding box. What are the job names from these verbs and nouns?

1 electricity _____
2 economics _____
3 to bake _____
4 to fight fires _____
5 law _____
6 to translate _____
7 history _____
8 reception _____
9 library _____
10 to consult about business _____

3 ▶ 73 The eight explorers in Exercise 1 were asked this question: "If you could have a superpower, what would it be?" Listen and take notes on which superpower each explorer wanted.

4 ▶ 73 Listen to the explorers again and complete these sentences (1–8).

If I had this power, …

1 I could see the world in the _____ way.
2 I could see the bigger _____ .
3 I could make people magically _____ me.
4 people couldn't _____ me.
5 it would have saved me a lot of _____ .
6 I'd go and listen to what people were saying in the _____ .
7 I would like to be able to turn [my power] _____ .
8 that would be an _____ superpower.

5 Work in pairs. What superpower would you like to have? What would you do if you had this power?

Grammar *wish* and *if only*

> ▶ **WISH and IF ONLY**
>
> **wish / if only + past tense**
> 1 *I wish I had* the ability to make people magically understand me.
>
> **wish / if only + could + base form of the verb**
> 2 *If only I could turn* anything into any kind of food I wanted.
>
> **wish / if only + past perfect tense**
> 3 *I wish I'd had* that power earlier in my career.
>
> **wish / if only + someone (or something) + would + base form of the verb**
> 4 Sometimes *you wish other people would get* what you're trying to say.
> 5 *I wish they'd stop* looking at me in that confused way!
>
> For more information and practice, see page 170.

6 Work in pairs. Look at the grammar box. Are these statements true (T) or false (F)? If the statement is false, correct it.

1	The speakers in sentences 1 and 2 are talking about a past situation.	T	F
2	*If only* in sentence 2 has a weaker meaning than *wish*.	T	F
3	The speaker in sentence 3 is talking about a present situation.	T	F
4	The speaker in sentences 4 and 5 is talking about a present situation.	T	F
5	The speaker in sentences 4 and 5 wants someone else to act to change the situation.	T	F

7 Circle the correct verb forms to complete this person's wishes.

"I wish I ¹ *had / would have* a superhuman memory. You could say that would be a bad thing because you'd remember all the things you wish you ² *didn't do / hadn't done* or all the missed opportunities you wish ³ *you took / you'd taken*. Your life would be full of regrets. But I don't mean that I wish I ⁴ *remember / remembered* everything; I just wish I ⁵ *could remember / would remember* the things I didn't want to forget, like names, dates, and interesting facts."

8 Complete the sentences (1–6) with the correct form of the verbs in parentheses.

1 I wish I _____ (learn) to play a musical instrument when I was younger.
2 Marta is very homesick. She wishes her mom _____ (be) here with her.
3 I wish the weather _____ (not / be) so cold. Then we could eat outside.
4 Jerry wishes he _____ (not / go) out last night. He's too tired to work today.
5 I wish the builders next door _____ (stop) making so much noise. I can't concentrate.
6 She has an amazing voice. If only I _____ (can / sing) like that!

9 Read the notes in the box below. Then complete the sentences (1–4) using the words in parentheses as a guide.

> Note that in affirmative sentences, we often use a comparative form.
> *I wish (something) were more …*
> In negative sentences, we often use *not so* + adjective.
> *I wish (something) weren't so …*

1 Marta is very homesick. She wishes her mom _____ (not / be / far away).
2 I wish the weather _____ (be / warm).
3 I love Tokyo. I just wish it _____ (be / cheap).
4 I wish the builders next door _____ (not / be / noisy).

10 Pronunciation /ʃ/ and /tʃ/

a ▶ **74** Listen to six words. Circle the word you hear.

1	wish	which	4	shin	chin
2	shop	chop	5	wash	watch
3	cash	catch	6	shoes	choose

b Work in pairs. Take turns saying one word from each word pair in Exercise 10a. Your partner should decide which word they hear.

Speaking *my Life*

11 Work in pairs. Choose one of these situations or your own idea.

- a new job you have just started
- a new hobby or class you have just started

1 Make a list of all the potential problems (e.g., the boss shouts at everyone all the time, the work is boring).
2 Make at least five wishes about the situation. Use each of the forms in the grammar box at least once.

I wish my boss would stop shouting at everyone.
If only the work were more interesting.

12 Work with a new partner. Compare your wishes from Exercise 11. Were any of your ideas the same?

Unit 8 Hopes and ambitions

8c Saving Madagascar

Reading

1 Work in pairs. What do you know about the island of Madagascar: its people, its landscape, its wildlife, its industry?

2 Work in pairs. Read the article and answer the questions.
1 Which of Madagascar's natural resources is the author most worried about?
2 How is this resource collected, and where does it go from there?
3 How is Olivier Behra saving Madagascar's natural resources and making money at the same time? Give a few examples.

3 Circle the correct option (a, b, or c) to complete each sentence.
1 Most people in Madagascar are ___ .
  a very poor
  b very sad about their situation
  c becoming more politically active
2 To grow crops, Madagascans had to ___ .
  a clear the forest carefully
  b set fire to the forest
  c get government permission
3 As president, Marc Ravalomanana was particularly concerned about ___ .
  a protecting the environment
  b promoting tourism
  c improving international relations
4 A change in the law allowed people to ___ .
  a cut down hardwood trees
  b camp near hardwood trees
  c sell wood from fallen hardwood trees
5 For many Madagascans, cutting down rosewood trees is ___ .
  a easy and quick work
  b necessary to make furniture
  c against their beliefs
6 Other lighter trees are cut down to ___ .
  a build big ships
  b make medicines
  c transport the rosewood
7 The forest offers locals other ways to make money, such as ___ .
  a developing new medicines
  b taking tourists on guided walks
  c exporting flowers

Critical thinking emotive language

4 When writers feel very strongly about an issue, they often use strong or emotive language. Work in pairs. Find the emotive words or phrases that describe the following things.
1 how special a place Madagascar is (paragraph 1)
2 what a bad state the island is in (paragraphs 2 and 6)
3 how strongly ecologists feel about the situation (paragraph 3)
4 how impressive the hardwood trees are (paragraph 4)
5 how tough the work of cutting trees is (paragraph 5)
6 how badly rosewood trees are being treated (paragraph 5)

5 Do you think the writer's argument is strengthened by using this kind of language? Or would it be better to give a more objective argument? How would you rewrite the first paragraph to make it more objective? Discuss with a partner.

Vocabulary and speaking
strong feelings myLife

6 Replace the words and phrases in **bold** below with these emotive words from the article.

| alarmed | back-breaking | bleak |
| majestic | unique | delight |

1 A lot of effort is being made to preserve this **individual** place.
2 You could see her **pleasure** when she was told she had gotten the job.
3 I was **worried** by the news that he was ill.
4 You get a beautiful view of the **tall and elegant** mountains.
5 Clearing the garden was really **physical and tiring** work.
6 With no prospect of a job, the future for many young people looks **hopeless**.

7 Think of a place that is very special and that you hope will be protected (e.g., a local green space or a traditional community). Write a short description of it (100–150 words) using emotive language. Then read your description to a partner.

▶ 75

Saving Madagascar

[1] At over 500,000 square kilometers, Madagascar is the world's fourth largest island. Although all islands have their own unique ecosystems, nature has given Madagascar incredible riches. Roughly ninety percent of its animal and plant life is found nowhere else on the planet. Its carrot-shaped baobab trees and strange-looking lemurs make even the most well-traveled visitor wide-eyed with amazement and delight.

[2] But the island's beauty hides its desperate situation. The average Madagascan lives on only a dollar a day, although you would not guess this from their cheerful optimism. Moreover, since the first humans arrived in Madagascar around 2,300 years ago, nearly ninety percent of the island's original forest has been lost—either cut down for use as timber, or burned to create room for crops or cattle.

[3] Alarmed ecologists identified Madagascar as a region in danger and demanded that the cutting and burning stop. In 2002, a new environmentally friendly president, Marc Ravalomanana, was elected. But seven years later, he was replaced.

[4] The new government made it legal to sell wood from hardwood[1] trees that had already been cut down or had fallen during storms. But it struggled to control the loggers[2] who continue to rob the forests of wood from living trees. The main targets of this environmental crime are the rosewood tree and the ebony tree. The wood from these majestic trees is in high demand: to make expensive furniture, or as a valued material in the manufacture of musical instruments.

[5] The locals are caught in a trap. Poverty and the high value of rosewood—$3,000 per cubic meter—have driven them to cut down trees they traditionally believed to be sacred.[3] It is dangerous and back-breaking work. In a few hours, they can bring down a tree that has stood tall for many centuries. Then they cut the trees into two-meter logs and drag them several kilometers to the nearest river. Rosewood trees are not the only victims.

In order to transport the heavy rosewood logs down the river, rafts[4] must be built from other wood. To make each raft, four or five lighter trees are cut down. All this disturbs the natural habitat of the islands' animals and puts their survival at risk.

[6] What can bring hope to this bleak landscape? One man's work may offer a possible route out of the darkness. Olivier Behra, who first came to Madagascar from France in 1987, believes that the only solution is to give local people economic alternatives. He has persuaded the locals to stop cutting down trees in the Vohimana forest, and instead, to collect medicinal plants to sell to foreign companies. Meanwhile, he has trained the village lemur hunter to act as a guide for tourists who wish to photograph lemurs. The same tourists also pay to visit the wild orchid conservatory that Behra has set up. Can small-scale actions like this compete with Madagascar's rosewood industry? Or will the government's promise to stop the illegal trade in rosewood come to anything? Only time will tell.

---

[1] **hardwood** (n) /ˈhɑːrdˌwʊd/ a type of strong, hard wood from certain slow-growing trees, e.g., rosewood, ebony, and mahogany
[2] **logger** (n) /ˈlɒɡər/ a person who cuts down trees (as a job)
[3] **sacred** (adj) /ˈseɪkrɪd/ having important religious significance
[4] **raft** (n) /rɑːft/ a platform, often with no sides, used as a boat

8d Choices

Real life discussing preferences

1 Work in pairs. Which of these things are you generally choosy or picky about (careful about choosing)? Which are you easygoing about?

- the food you eat
- the movies you watch
- the clothes you wear
- the people you spend time with

2 ▶ 76 Listen to four short conversations. Complete the choices given by the first speaker in each conversation. Write which is the second speaker's preference (1 or 2) and why.

	Choice	Preference	Reason
1	1 _drive_ 2 be driven	2	feels tired
2	1 pasta 2 _____	___	_____
3	1 walk in old town 2 _____	___	_____
4	1 Matt Damon movie 2 _____	___	more fun

3 ▶ 76 Work in pairs. Try to complete the expressions for discussing preferences. Then listen to the conversations again and check your answers.

> ▶ **DISCUSSING PREFERENCES**
>
> **In general**
> I prefer driving ¹_____ being a passenger.
> I like simple food ²_____ spicy food.
> **On a specific occasion**
> I'd rather ³_____ to a museum.
> I'd rather you ⁴_____ , if you don't mind.
> If it ⁵_____ up to me, I' ⁶_____ say let's go to the festival.
> I think that ⁷_____ probably be more fun.
> OK. I'd prefer ⁸_____ do that, too.

4 Pronunciation *do you, would you*

▶ 77 Listen to these sentences. Notice how the pronunciation of the words in **bold** becomes merged. Practice saying the sentences in the same way.

1 **Do you** prefer coffee or tea?
2 **Would you** rather eat out tonight?
3 **Would you** rather he stayed at home?

5 Complete these questions with the correct form of the verbs in parentheses.

1 Would you prefer _____ (have) noisy neighbors or nosy neighbors?
2 Would you rather people _____ (give) you an honest opinion about your work or _____ (say) something nice about it?
3 Do you prefer _____ (give) presents or _____ (receive) them?
4 Would you rather _____ (be) talented and _____ (not / be) famous, or _____ (have) fame without being talented?
5 Would you rather your parents _____ (give) you a lot of money, or would you prefer _____ (earn) it yourself?

6 Work in pairs. Take turns asking and answering the questions in Exercise 5. Give reasons for your answers.

7 Think of choices or possibilities for the following situations. Then work in pairs and have short conversations like the ones in Exercise 2. Take turns being the first speaker.

- something to do on the weekend
- something to eat tonight
- somewhere to go on vacation

8e A wish for change

Writing an online comment

1 Work in pairs. Do you read the comments after online articles or blogs? Why or why not? Have you ever written a comment on another person's article or blog?

2 Work in pairs. Read the online comment below. Answer the questions.

   1 Who wrote the comment, and what were they responding to?
   2 Why did they write the comment?
   3 Do you find the comment persuasive? Why or why not?

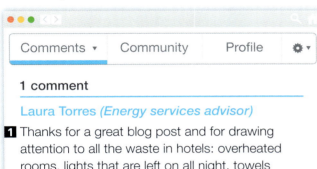

Laura Torres *(Energy services advisor)*

1 Thanks for a great blog post and for drawing attention to all the waste in hotels: overheated rooms, lights that are left on all night, towels that are used once and then sent to the laundry. But why stop with hotels? It would be better to mention all the other examples of unnecessary waste in modern life.

2 Every morning, I walk down the street past stores with doors wide open, blowing hot air into the street. At night, I walk home past fully-lit office buildings, after the workers have already left; and past enormous flashing screens where advertisers try to outdo their competitors. At the supermarket, I take my frozen vegetables from a freezer that is completely open. My children leave their computers on when they go out and their phone chargers plugged in with no phone on the other end (though of course they should know better).

3 What can we do about it? Just wishing that people would act more responsibly is not enough. We would be better off if we were forced to act. Increasing the price of energy would be one idea. Another would be to make laws—just as we have traffic laws to make us drive safely—against wasting energy.

3 Work in pairs. How is the online comment organized? In which paragraph(s) (1–3) can you find the following?

   a examples that illustrate the problem ____
   b a recommendation or request for action ____
   c a reference to the article it is commenting on ____
   d a summary of the problem ____

4 **Word focus** *better*

   Work in pairs. Underline the phrases in the online comment that use the word *better*. Match the phrases with their definitions (a–c).

   a (of a person) have enough sense not to do something _____
   b be in an improved situation (often financially) _____
   c be more useful or desirable _____

5 **Writing skill** giving vivid examples

   a Work in pairs. What does the writer say about lights and towels in the first paragraph to illustrate her argument?

   b Find five more examples of energy waste in the second paragraph.

6 Work in pairs. Look at this list of things that annoy some people about modern life. Complete the phrases to say what is annoying about each thing.

   • magazines that …
     magazines that are full of news about celebrities
   • trains that …
   • cell phones that …
   • TV shows about …
   • supermarket food that …
   • apps that …

7 Imagine you have read an article about one of the items in Exercise 6. Write a short online comment (120–150 words) on it.

8 Work in pairs. Exchange comments and compare what you have written. Use these questions to check your comments. Does your partner agree with the way you feel?

   • Is the online comment well-organized?
   • Does it give vivid examples?
   • Is it persuasive?

8f What would you do if money didn't matter?

A woman meditating near a waterfall

Before you watch

1 Look at the title of the video. Write down your answer to the question on a piece of paper. Don't show it to anyone else yet.

2 Key vocabulary

a Work in pairs. Read the sentences (1–5). The words and phrases in **bold** are used in the video. Guess the meaning of the words and phrases.

1. I didn't really know what I wanted to do when I left school, so I used the **vocational guidance** service.
2. How do directors of companies **justify** having salaries of a million dollars or more?
3. There is no better surfer in the world—she's a **master** of her sport.
4. Anyone can achieve their ambition—they just have to focus on it and **desire** it enough.
5. He hates his job. He feels completely **miserable** going to the office every day.

b Write the words and phrases in **bold** in Exercise 2a next to their definitions (a–e).

a someone who does something very well _____
b service to help someone to find the right career _____
c very unhappy _____
d show or prove to be right or reasonable _____
e want something a lot _____

While you watch

3 ▶ 8.1, 8.2 Watch Parts 1–2 of the video. Work in pairs and answer the questions.

1. What is the key question the narrator mentions at the beginning and end of the video that we must all ask ourselves?
2. If we don't ask this question, how does the narrator say we will spend our lives?

4 ▶ 8.1 Read the summary below. Then watch Part 1 of the video again. Circle the correct options to complete the summary. Sometimes there is more than one answer.

The narrator often gives career advice to
¹ *his own children / interns / college students*. They say that if money wasn't important, they would be ² *painters / writers / comedians*. The narrator keeps questioning them until he has found something they ³ *are really good at / really want to do / find really fun*, and then he says do that. He says that just going after money is ⁴ *a waste of time / selfish / stupid*.

5 ▶ 8.2 Watch Part 2 of the video again. What did the narrator say about these things (1–4)? Take notes as you watch the video. Then compare notes with a partner.

1. a short life and a long life
2. what happens when you keep doing something you enjoy
3. whether other people will share your interests
4. what we are teaching our children

After you watch

6 Vocabulary in context

a ▶ 8.3 Watch the clips from the video. Choose the correct meaning of the words and phrases.

b Complete these sentences in your own words. Then share your sentences with a partner.

1. I haven't the faintest idea how to …
2. If you keep trying out different jobs, eventually …
3. I don't know how long I will go on …

7 Work in groups. Look at these comments about the video. Discuss what you think of each comment. Then write your own comment.

> **Carla P**
> It's an inspirational speech. It's saying that money doesn't bring happiness. But more important than that, it's saying you can be whatever you want to be.

> **Shinji**
> This is a nice idea, but it's not very practical. If everyone is painting and writing poetry and riding horses, who will drive the trains and work in the banks and offices?

> **Stefan**
> I like this, but I think there is a contradiction. He says money doesn't matter, but then he says if you become a master of something, you will earn money from it.

8 Work in pairs. Read aloud your answer from Exercise 1 and ask each other for more details about this. Has your idea about what you would do changed in any way since watching the video?

Unit 8 **Hopes and ambitions**

UNIT 8 REVIEW AND MEMORY BOOSTER

Grammar

1 Read this post on a travel website. What two things does the writer suggest taking on the trip?

It has always been my dream to visit Antarctica, and I was not disappointed when I did. I spent ten amazing days sailing on a ship from South America to Antarctica. I want to share some tips about what to take and what to leave at home. ¹ **I regret not looking at this website before I left.** I would recommend packing light. ² **I took too many clothes. I didn't know they had a good laundry service on board.** But do make sure to bring lots of waterproof and windproof clothing. I brought a thick, waterproof jacket with me, and I was glad I did. I wore it every day. ³ **It stopped me from getting cold and wet.** It can get quite rough at sea, so take seasickness tablets, too. The trip is well organized, and I'm sure you'll have a wonderful time if you go. My only complaint is that ⁴ **there should be more hiking at the parks,** so check with your tour guide if that's possible.

2 Work in pairs. Form conditional or *wish* sentences to express the same idea as the sentences in **bold** in the text above.

1 I wish I'd …
2 If I'd …, I …
3 I would have … if …
4 It would be better if …

3 >> MB Work in pairs. Explain why the different grammatical forms are used in each pair of sentences below.

1 a I wish you lived closer.
  b I wish you would move back to the US.
2 a If I'd missed the plane, I would have been very upset.
  b If I'd missed the plane, I'd still be in Fiji.

I CAN	
make second, third, and mixed conditionals	
express wishes about the past and present	

Vocabulary

4 Circle the correct options to complete the sentences. Then discuss with a partner which of the sentences about the "rocket girls" are true.

1 They *did / made* tasks that computers now perform.
2 They *did / made* mathematical calculations.
3 If they *did / made* a small mistake in their calculations, it didn't usually matter.
4 They didn't *do / make* great friendships because they were focused on their work.
5 The head of NASA *did / made* the decision to hire only women.
6 They *did / made* a big difference to the NASA space program.

5 >> MB Complete the phrases (1–4) using these emotive words. Then make a sentence with each phrase to say to your partner.

alarmed	back-breaking	delight	majestic

1 _____ work
2 the _____ on her face
3 he was _____ by the news
4 a(n) _____ animal

I CAN	
use *make* and *do* correctly	
identify and use emotive language	

Real life

6 Complete these exchanges with one word in each blank.

A: Would you ¹_____ eat out tonight or stay in?
B: I think I'd ²_____ to stay in, if you don't ³_____ .

C: I don't know if it ⁴_____ be better ⁵_____ quit my job now or wait until I've found another one.
D: I think you'd be better ⁶_____ finding a new job first.

7 >> MB Work in pairs. Talk about your own preferences. Make sentences with *I prefer* + verb/noun + *to* … Use the *-ing* form of the verb.

I prefer driving to being driven.

I prefer Japanese food to Italian food.

I CAN	
ask and talk about preferences	

Unit 9 The news

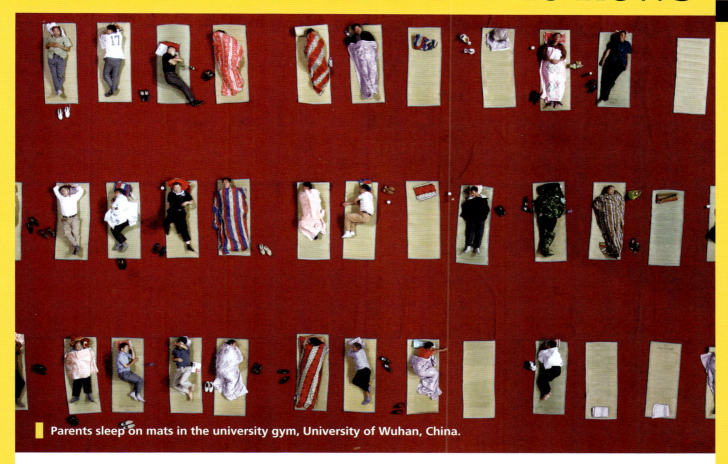

Parents sleep on mats in the university gym, University of Wuhan, China.

FEATURES

106 A life revealed
The power of the image

108 And finally …
Good-news stories

110 From hero to zero
The story of pilot Peter Burkill

114 News: the weird and the wonderful
A video about two good-news stories

1 Work in pairs. Look at the photo and the caption. Why do you think these parents are sleeping here?

2 ▶ 78 Listen to a radio news report. Work in pairs and answer the questions.

1 Why did these parents stay overnight at the university?
2 Why did they sleep on the gym floor?
3 What do you think of the dedication of these parents?

3 Look at the pie chart below showing how US university students get their news. Discuss the questions with a partner.

1 How do most students get their news? Are you surprised?
2 Which category in the chart would you put yourself in?
3 What kind of news do you follow mostly?

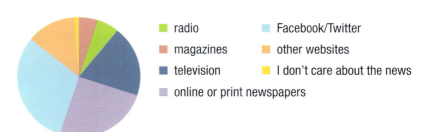

- radio
- magazines
- television
- online or print newspapers
- Facebook/Twitter
- other websites
- I don't care about the news

9a A life revealed

Vocabulary reporting verbs

1 Work in pairs. Look at the sentences. Cross out ONE word that doesn't fit in each sentence. Then discuss the difference in meaning between the other two words.

1 "It was a mistake," they ~~denied~~ / admitted / agreed.
2 "Be careful," he ~~offered~~ / advised / warned.
3 "Could you please help me?" he asked / ~~persuaded~~ / begged.
4 "It's the best restaurant in town," they claimed / ~~complained~~ / explained.
5 "It's a great opportunity. Take it," he recommended / urged / ~~convinced~~.
6 "I'll help you whatever happens," she ~~threatened~~ / promised / swore.

▶ 79

Reading

2 Work in pairs. Look at the photo and discuss these questions. Then read the article and check your answers.

1 Have you seen either of the photos that the photographer is standing between?
2 Where are these two women from, and how old do you think they are?
3 What do you think is the relationship between these two women?

3 Work in pairs. How do you think Sharbat Gula felt when she learned how famous her photo is?

A LIFE REVEALED

She remembers the moment the photographer took her picture. The man was a stranger, but he had asked if he could, and she agreed to let him. She had never been photographed before, and until they met a second time—
5 seventeen years later—she would not be photographed again. The photographer, Steve McCurry, remembers the moment too. It was 1984, and he was reporting on the lives of Afghan refugees in a camp in Pakistan. She was living in the camp, and he admits thinking at the time that his
10 picture was nothing special. Yet the "Afghan girl" (below, left) became one of the most famous images of our time. The girl's intense expression warned us not to ignore the victims of war. In 2002, *National Geographic* persuaded McCurry to return to Pakistan to look for the girl. After
15 showing her photo around the refugee camp, he found a man who knew where to find her. The man offered to fetch her from her home in the Tora Bora mountains.

After three days, the man returned with Sharbat Gula, who was now around 29 years old. McCurry knew
20 at once that this (below, right) was her. Time and hardship had erased her youth, but her eyes still had the same intensity. Her brother explained the story of their lives. He blamed the war for forcing them and many other Afghans out of their homeland. Sharbat
25 had escaped to the mountains when she was a child, where she hid in caves and begged people to give her food and blankets. She married when she was sixteen, and now her time was occupied with bringing up her three children: cooking, cleaning, and caring for them.
30 Yet she did not complain about having had a hard life. More amazingly, she was not aware of the impact that her photo and her sea-green eyes had had on the world.

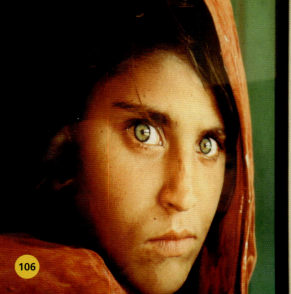
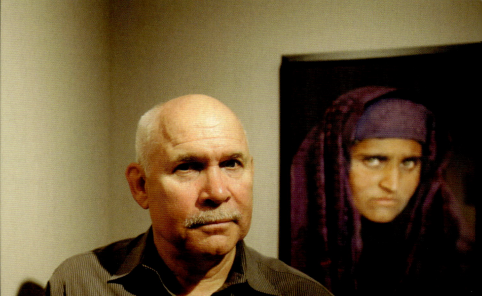

4 Work in pairs. Complete these sentences by finding the contrasting facts in the article.

1. In 1984, Sharbat Gula let McCurry take her picture, even though …
2. The picture became world famous, even though …
3. McCurry recognized 29-year-old Sharbat Gula immediately, even though …
4. Sharbat Gula did not complain about her life, even though …

Grammar verb patterns with reporting verbs

5 Find these verbs in the article. Underline them and the infinitive or *-ing* forms that follow them. How many different forms are there? Discuss with a partner.

agreed	admits	warned	persuaded
offered	blamed	begged	complain

> ▶ **VERB PATTERNS WITH REPORTING VERBS**
>
> 1 **verb + infinitive**
> e.g., *promise, refuse, swear, threaten*
> He **refused to help** me.
>
> 2 **verb + someone + infinitive**
> e.g., *advise, ask, convince, encourage, invite, recommend, urge*
> They **invited us to stay**.
>
> 3 **verb + -ing**
> e.g., *deny, recommend, suggest*
> I **suggest waiting**.
>
> 4 **verb + preposition + -ing**
> e.g., *apologize for, confess to, insist on, object to*
> He **apologized for missing** the meeting.
>
> 5 **verb + someone/something + preposition + -ing**
> e.g., *accuse … of, criticize … for, congratulate … on, praise … for, forgive … for, thank … for*
> She **thanked me for supporting** her.
>
> For more information and practice, see page 172.

6 Work in pairs. Look at the grammar box. In which category (1–5) would you place each verb from Exercise 5?

7 Work in pairs. Discuss what the person actually said (or thought) at the time for each verb you underlined in Exercise 5. Then compare your answers with another pair.

She agreed to let him take her picture.
"Yes, you can take my picture."

8 Complete this text with the correct form of the verbs in parentheses. Add a preposition where necessary.

People often accuse photographers
¹ _____ (be) unethical when they take pictures without people's permission. A photographer who photographs someone in their living room with a telephoto lens cannot deny ² _____ (act) unethically—they have invaded the person's privacy. We often criticize journalists ³ _____ (do) this kind of thing. But is this the same as taking a picture of a stranger without them knowing? The person hasn't invited you ⁴ _____ (take) their picture. Perhaps they would feel uncomfortable if you asked them ⁵ _____ (pose) for a shot; they might even refuse ⁶ _____ (let) you do it. A lot of photographers insist ⁷ _____ (be) "invisible" so that the photos are more natural. They object ⁸ _____ (ask) their subjects for permission first because this would spoil the moment. However, I always advise photographers ⁹ _____ (talk) to their subjects first. In fact, I strongly recommend ¹⁰ _____ (get) to know the subjects' own stories, because then the photographs will have more meaning.

9 Work in pairs. Report these statements using the reporting verbs in parentheses. You may need to change other words (e.g., pronouns). Begin each sentence with *She*.

1. "I think you've been very brave." (praise)
   She praised me for being very brave.
2. "You should consider a career in journalism." (encourage)
3. "He always puts his own interests first." (accuse)
4. "I'll look at your article when it's finished." (promise)
5. "I'm sorry I didn't introduce you to my boss." (apologize)
6. "I can lend you my camera, if you like." (offer)

Writing and speaking myLife

10 Choose one of these reporting verbs to write about something true that happened to you. Then read your brief story to a partner.

accuse	admit	apologize	complain
criticize	deny	encourage	warn
offer	thank	congratulate	

*I remember once at school, I was **accused of breaking** a window. I knew who had really done it, but I had promised not to say, so I was in a difficult situation!*

Unit 9 The news

9b And finally …

Vocabulary positive adjectives

▶ **WORDBUILDING forming adjectives from verbs**

We can add -ing to many verbs to form adjectives that describe something that causes a particular feeling.
entertain ➤ entertaining, move ➤ moving

For more practice, see Workbook page 75.

1 Look at the wordbuilding box. News programs often like to end with a good-news story. Complete the sentences (1–4) with the correct adjective form of the verbs below.

| amuse | astonish | charm |
| engage | inspire | |

1 A(n) _____ story makes you smile or laugh.
2 A(n) _____ story shows you how much people can achieve.
3 A(n) _____ story makes you feel amazed or very surprised.
4 A(n) _____ or _____ story interests and pleases you.

2 Think of an example of a good-news story you have heard recently. Then work in pairs and tell your partner about it. Use one of the adjectives in Exercise 1.

I saw a really inspiring local news story on TV about a five-year-old boy who raised money for his sick sister by …

Listening

3 ▶ 80 Work in pairs. Look at the photo. What good-news story do you think is illustrated here? Then listen to the three news stories and make notes on each.

4 ▶ 80 Listen again and answer these questions.

Story 1 How was the Syrian man rewarded for his honesty?

Story 2 What record did the pizza makers set? Who did they give the pizza to?

Story 3 Who has Dr. Zhavoronkov been testing his drugs on, and with what results?

5 Work in groups and retell the three news stories. Which did you find the most inspiring/charming/astonishing?

Grammar passive reporting verbs

▶ **PASSIVE REPORTING VERBS**

It + passive reporting verb + *that* + subject
1 *It is thought that the first Margherita pizza* was baked in Naples in 1889.

subject + passive reporting verb + infinitive
2 *The 25-year-old Syrian is believed to have been* in Germany for less than a year.
3 *Local police are now said to be looking* for the money's true owner.
4 *A Latvian scientist based in the UK is reported to be* close to finding …

For more information and practice, see page 172.

108

6 Work in pairs. Look at the grammar box on page 108. Do we know who is doing the thinking, believing, etc., in each sentence?

7 Look at sentences 2–4 in the grammar box. Which sentence contains:

a a simple infinitive? ____
b a continuous infinitive? ____
c a perfect infinitive? ____

8 Work in pairs. Rephrase sentences 2–4 in the grammar box using *It* + passive reporting verb + *that* + subject.

2 It is believed that the 25-year-old Syrian has …
3 It is said that the …
4 It is …

9 Rewrite these sentences using passive reporting verbs.

1 People think that the man is from the Homs area of Syria.
   The man is _thought to be_ _____.

2 People say that the man is taking language lessons and planning further studies.
   The man is _said to be_ _____.

3 The police confirmed that the man will receive a financial reward.
   It was _confirmed that_ _____.

4 Some people claim that the Margherita pizza originated in Naples, Italy.
   It is _claimed that_ _____.

5 People don't generally believe that drugs can prevent aging.
   It is _generally believed that_ _____ can't _____.

10 Rewrite these sentences. Change the passive reporting verbs from one structure to the other.

1 Costa Rica is said to be the happiest country in the world.
   It _is said that Costa Rica is the happiest country in the world_.

2 Frank was known to have been a gifted musician at school.
   It _is known that has_ _____.

3 It is known that laughing regularly increases life expectancy.
   Laughing regularly _is known to_ _____.

4 It was thought that he had given up hope of ever seeing his family again.
   He _____.

11 Complete the good-news story below using these passive reporting verbs and infinitives.

is known	it is now thought
it was demonstrated	to be
to be getting	to have stopped

And finally … Despite all the warnings about a growing hole in the world's ozone layer, ¹_____ that the hole may be shrinking. The ozone layer in the atmosphere ²_____ to protect us from the sun's radiation, since it absorbs ultraviolet rays. However, in the 1970s, ³_____ that this layer was becoming thinner and thinner, and that there was even a hole over the Antarctic. CFC gases in refrigerators and aerosol were said ⁴_____ the main reason for this. Consequently, many people urged governments to ban the use of these gases. Their efforts were successful, and the use of CFCs is believed ⁵_____ by the mid-1990s. Now, new research has shown that the ozone hole has shrunk by four million square kilometers. What's more, the ozone layer itself is thought ⁶_____ thicker again. This is good news for the planet, and for all of us who enjoy spending time in the sun.

Speaking *my* Life

12 Work in groups of three to prepare a good-news story. Choose one of the headlines below or your own idea. Write a good-news story, using at least one passive reporting verb. Then each person should share their story with a new group.

- Woman rescued from fire by pet
- Valuable painting found under bed
- Ten-year-old child compared to Shakespeare
- New clothing fabric invented
- Couple celebrate 80th wedding anniversary
- Dentist that people actually enjoy visiting

And finally, a woman was rescued from her burning house yesterday by her cat. **It is believed that the fire** *started shortly after midnight, on the first floor of the house. …*

Unit 9 **The news**

9c From hero to zero

Reading

1 The headlines below are about a British Airways (BA) pilot. Look at these headlines in the order they appeared in the newspapers over several months. Then work in pairs and discuss what you think happened.

HERO BA PILOT PETER BURKILL SPEAKS:
I THOUGHT WE'D DIE IN HEATHROW CRASH

"I AM NOT A HERO,"
SAYS BA CRASH PILOT CAPTAIN PETER BURKILL

REAL HERO OF BA FLIGHT 38
IS CO-PILOT JOHN COWARD

HERO PILOT "FORCED OUT OF BA"

FALLEN HERO: THAT DAY CHANGED MY LIFE FOREVER

OFFICIAL REPORT SAYS ICE FAULT CAUSED BA AIRPORT CRASH

2 Work in pairs. Read the story on page 111 quickly. Then discuss the sequence of key events with your partner. Does the story differ from your answer in Exercise 1? If so, how?

3 Read the article again. Are these statements true (T) or false (F)?

1 Some passengers were badly hurt during landing. T F
2 Burkill was unmarried at the time of the accident. T F
3 Burkill's crew read BA's internal report. T F
4 Burkill was praised in the AAIB report. T F
5 Other airlines refused to hire Burkill after he left BA. T F

4 Complete these sentences with appropriate words or phrases from the article.

1 Burkill went from being a hero to being a _____ (opposite of hero). (paragraph 1)
2 Perhaps Burkill's colleagues believed he wasn't _____ (good at his job). (paragraph 3)
3 The press claimed Burkill had _____ (failed) the people he was supposed to be responsible for. (paragraph 3)
4 After the official report was published, Burkill was _____ (given as a prize) a medal for his actions. (paragraph 6)

Critical thinking different perspectives

5 Work in pairs. Make notes to complete the chart about the event described on page 111. Which of these people would you have believed? Why?

People involved	Their initial view on the accident and Burkill's role in it	Motivation for taking this view
Peter Burkill	took a risk but it worked—the rest was luck	did what any captain would have done
BA staff		—
BA management		
the press		

Word focus *word*

6 Find these phrases in the article. What do you think they mean? Discuss with a partner.

1 **Word** went around (paragraph 3)
2 his **word** against that of the press (paragraph 3)
3 No **word** of it (paragraph 4)
4 had the last **word** (paragraph 7)

7 Work in pairs. What do these other expressions with *word* mean?

1 "When my husband handed me the keys to a new car for my birthday, I was **at a loss for words**."
2 "The hotel doesn't advertise at all. It just relies on **word of mouth** to get new customers."
3 "I can't believe the mayor is closing the library. He **gave his word** that he wouldn't."

Speaking myLife

8 Work in groups. Discuss these questions about the media in your country.

1 How respectful are journalists toward politicians?
2 How balanced is the reporting of public scandals?

FROM HERO TO ZERO

▶ 81

1 In January 2008, hours after saving his plane from crashing at Heathrow Airport, flight captain Peter Burkill was praised as a hero. Only days later, when reports appeared in the press accusing him of freezing at the controls, he became a villain. How did this extraordinary transformation come about?

2 Peter Burkill was the pilot on British Airways (BA) Flight 38 from Beijing, carrying 152 people on board. But 35 seconds before landing at Heathrow, two of the plane's engines failed. With the plane losing height fast, Burkill asked his co-pilot, John Coward, to take the controls while he himself adjusted the wing flaps to help the plane reach the runway. It was a risky decision, but it worked. The plane narrowly missed some houses and landed heavily on the grass just short of the runway. After a few hundred meters, the plane miraculously came to a stop without turning over. The passengers escaped without serious injury. As far as Burkill was concerned, he had done what any captain would have done—the rest was luck.

3 However, this was not the version of events that BA's staff heard in the following days. Word went around that rather than taking control of the plane, Burkill had panicked. The suggestion was that he was not competent to fly a plane. Some newspapers, seeing the chance to sell more copies, picked up the story, claiming that John Coward was the real hero. They published details of Burkill's past, painting a picture of a well-paid pilot who lived the life of a playboy. But—when it had mattered most, it was suggested—he had let down his crew and passengers. Worse still for Burkill, it wasn't even his word against that of the press. Afraid of bad publicity, BA banned him from speaking about the events until an independent investigation by the Air Accidents Investigation Branch (AAIB) was complete.

4 Overnight, Burkill's life changed. Before the accident, he had had everything: a great job, a beautiful home, a loving wife, and the respect of his colleagues. Now he felt betrayed and desperate. The stress put enormous pressure on his family, and Burkill became depressed. He begged the company to issue a statement to clear his name, but they refused, preferring to wait for the results of the official investigation. Even though BA's own internal report cleared him of any wrongdoing, it was only read by senior management. No word of it reached Burkill's colleagues, and rumors started going around that crew members were afraid to fly with him. He wrote to BA's chief executive asking for help, but got no reply.

5 When the official AAIB report was finally published in February 2009, it concluded that ice in the fuel system had been the cause of the problem, and that the actions of the crew had saved the lives of all on board. In particular, it praised Captain Burkill's decision to change the wing flap settings.

6 The pilots and the air crew were awarded the British Airways Safety Medal, and the story of Peter Burkill, the hero, once again made the headlines. But the damage had been done. In August 2009, Peter Burkill left the company that he had served for 25 years. He began applying for jobs with other airlines, but he was not invited to a single interview.

7 So did his critics win? No. Burkill himself had the last word. BA said that he was always welcome in the company, and in September 2009 they asked him to come back and fly for them. Burkill accepted.

Captain Peter Burkill (right), with John Coward

Unit 9 The news 111

9d Spreading the news

Real life reporting what you have heard

1 Work in pairs. Below are three common topics that people like to gossip about. Can you think of a recent piece of gossip that you have heard from any of these categories? Tell your partner.

- money and status
- celebrities' lives
- people's character and reputation

2 ▶ 82 Work in pairs. Listen to two conversations. Which category of gossip does each conversation fall into?

3 Work in pairs. Discuss the questions.

Conversation 1
1 What has happened to Liam, the man they are talking about?
2 Why are the speakers surprised about this news?

Conversation 2
3 What do they say has happened to Dr. Harris and why?
4 Do we know if the gossip about him is true?

4 ▶ 82 Look at the expressions for reporting what you have heard. Use the expressions to complete these sentences from the conversations. Then listen again and check your answers.

Conversation 1
1 **A:** By the way, _____ Liam? _____ , he's been promoted. … _____ Sarah, he's been given the job of area manager.
   B: Area manager? I _____ ! He's not even that good at his current job.
2 **A:** Sarah also reckons that he's going to get a huge pay raise.
   B: Well, I'd take that _____ . I don't think the company has that kind of money to throw around at the moment.

Conversation 2
3 **C:** Well, _____ that he was fired from his job yesterday. _____ that he's not even a real doctor.
   D: What? Who told you that?
   C: Tara.
   D: Hmm, I wouldn't take _____ of what Tara says. She _____ things.

5 Pronunciation the schwa

a ▶ 83 Unstressed syllables often produce the schwa sound /ə/. Listen to these examples and repeat. The stressed syllable (not a schwa) is underlined.

/ə/ /ə/   /ə/ /ə/
ap<u>par</u>ently   sup<u>pos</u>edly

b ▶ 84 Underline the stressed syllable in each of these words. Then listen and check. Notice how the schwa sound appears in the unstressed syllables.

| according | generally | happened |
| information | proportion | surprisingly |

c Work in pairs. Practice saying the words in Exercise 5b.

6 You are going to spread news around the class. Follow these steps:

- Work in pairs. Tell your partner two facts (one true, one false) about yourself or something you did, or two facts (one true, one false) about someone famous.
- Mingle with other students in the class and tell them the facts you heard from your partner. (Speak to at least three people.)
- Return to your partner and report the facts you heard from the other students.
- Discuss which ones you think are true. Use the expressions for reporting what you have heard.
- Tell the class what you thought and see if you were right.

▶ **REPORTING WHAT YOU HAVE HEARD**

Did you hear about …?
I heard/read the other day that …
Someone told me that …
According to (somebody), …
It seems that …
Apparently/Supposedly, …

Expressing belief and disbelief
That doesn't surprise me.
I can believe it.
I'd (I wouldn't) take his/her word for it.
They generally get their facts right.

I don't believe it.
He/She tends to exaggerate things.
I'd take that with a grain of salt.
I wouldn't take too much notice of what he/she says.

9e News story

Writing a news article

1 Read the newspaper article. Work in pairs and answer these questions.

1. What problem does the article describe?
2. What solution is being proposed?
3. Who might not be happy about this solution?

2 Read the newspaper article again. How is it structured? Complete the notes (1–5) using functions a–e below.

Headline: ¹_____
First short paragraph: ²_____
Second paragraph: ³_____
Third paragraph (optional):
⁴_____ or gives other relevant facts
Final paragraph:
states how the story ends, ⁵ _____ , or gives an alternative side to the story

a   gives the details of the story
b   what is likely to happen next
c   catches the reader's attention
d   introduces the key information (e.g., location, the people involved)
e   includes a comment or quotation about the events

3 Writing skill using quotations

a Look at the sentences (1–3). Then circle the correct options to complete the rules (a–d).

1. The head of the investigation said, "We haven't even started to write our report."
2. "Don't wait for me," she said with a smile.
3. "And what," he asked, "is the solution?"

a   If the quotation is a complete sentence, always begin it with a *small / capital* letter.
b   Always put the final punctuation of the quotation *inside / outside* the quotation marks.
c   If the quotation is followed by a phrase like "he said" or "she asked," put a comma *before / after* the final quotation mark.
d   If a phrase like "he said" or "she asked" comes before the quotation, put a comma *before / after* the opening quotation mark.

b Work in pairs. How would you rewrite these sentences with the correct punctuation?

1. Shall we eat Grandma he asked
2. I know exactly what he said she said
3. That's very kind she said but I can manage

A police officer on patrol in Bangkok

Bangkok bans illegal street racing

The military government in Thailand has issued new rules to stop street racing and to rein in teenage motorcycle racers.

Young motorcycle street racers—called *dek wan*—have drawn complaints over the years for their reckless riding in large groups. They often don't wear helmets, and many of them have been killed or involved in road accidents. Under the strict new laws, any person found guilty of possessing, selling, or modifying a motorcycle for street racing will face a six-month jail sentence and/or a US$600 fine. Their business licenses could also be revoked.

"Parents of teenage racers could face punishment as well," said the head of police. If their children violate the ban on street racing twice, the parents face three months in jail and/or a US$1,000 fine.

Authorities hope that these new laws will help control illegal street racing and lead to improved road safety in Thailand.

4 Write a short news article (150–170 words) for one of the following headlines. Use at least one quotation.

- Child's stroller given parking ticket
- Man takes wrong plane home
- Meeting to discuss shorter meetings runs out of time
- Burglar takes selfie with stolen phone

5 Exchange articles with a partner. Use these questions to check your partner's article.

- Does the article include a short first paragraph that gives the main idea or key information?
- Does the rest of the article use the structure described in Exercise 2?
- Do the quotations use the correct punctuation?

9f News: the weird and the wonderful

A humpback whale dives beneath the ocean, Tonga, South Pacific.

Before you watch

1 Work in pairs. You're going to watch two good-news stories. Look at the photo and the caption. What do you think the good-news story on humpback whales is about?

2 Key vocabulary

a Work in pairs. Read the sentences (1–6). The words and phrases in **bold** are used in the video. Guess the meaning of the words and phrases.

1. He has been **ruthless** in his career, pushing other people aside in his ambition to get to the top.
2. She **swiped at** the wasp with her hand.
3. Lions are not afraid to attack **prey**—like buffalo—that are larger than them.
4. I had chicken pox when I was a child, so I'm **immune to** it now.
5. I'm sorry. I dropped a spoon in my coffee and made it **splash** over the tablecloth.
6. I like to **dip** cookies in my tea and then eat them.

b Write the words and phrases in **bold** in Exercise 2a next to their definitions (a–f).

a. cause a liquid to fall or hit something in a noisy or messy way _____
b. made a swinging movement with the arm or hand _____
c. put something in liquid for a short time _____
d. not affected by something (e.g., an illness) _____
e. animals that are hunted and killed by other animals for food _____
f. not caring who you hurt as long as you get what you want _____

While you watch

3 ▶ 9.1, 9.2 Work in pairs. You are going to see two very different good-news stories. Watch and then:

1. say which story you think is "weird" and which is "wonderful."
2. write a headline for each story.

4 ▶ 9.1 Work in pairs. Read the questions below. Then watch the first news story again. Discuss the answers to the questions with your partner.

1. What adjectives are used to describe humpback whales?
2. What other species do they protect?
3. What adjectives are used to describe orcas?
4. How do the humpbacks fight off the orcas?
5. What benefit do humpbacks receive from protecting other species?

5 ▶ 9.2 Watch the second news story again. Circle the correct options to complete the statements.

1. Khan discovered his ability to handle hot oil when a *squirrel / monkey* dropped a *banana / mango* into his wok from a tree above, and the oil splashed all over his body.
2. The tourist describes Khan's ability as *inspiring / unbelievable*.
3. The tourist *thinks he knows / has no idea* how Khan can do this.
4. Khan's accident has actually helped his *sales / confidence*.

After you watch

6 Vocabulary in context

a ▶ 9.3 Watch the clips from the video. Choose the correct meaning of the words and phrases.

b Complete these sentences in your own words. Then share your sentences with a partner.

1. It has recently come to light that …
2. I am really put off when I see …
3. … is in a vulnerable situation because …

7 Work in groups. Discuss which news story interested you more and why. What else would you like to know about each news story?

8 ▶ 9.1 Work in pairs. Watch the first news story again and provide the narration for it. Follow these steps:

- Watch the video with the sound OFF. Discuss what you think the narrator was saying at each point.
- Decide how you will divide the narration between the two of you.
- Watch the video with the sound OFF again and provide the narration.

9 Work in groups of four and act out the second news story. Follow these steps:

- Decide on your roles: a) the narrator, b) Khan, c) the tourist visiting the stall, d) the director.
- Discuss what you are going to say and what the cues are for each speaker to speak.
- Try acting out the news story, with the director giving advice as necessary.
- Perform your version to another group.

Unit 9 **The news** 115

UNIT 9 REVIEW AND MEMORY BOOSTER

Grammar

1 Complete this good-news story with the correct verb pattern (passive, infinitive, preposition + *-ing*, etc.) of the verbs in parentheses.

A seven-year-old boy has been found alive and well in a forest in northern Japan, five kilometers from where he is said ¹ _____ (go) missing a week ago. Yamato Tanooka had been missing since Saturday. It ² _____ (believe) that he got out of the family car on a mountain road after arguing with his parents. Soon after getting lost, Yamato found a military shelter in the forest where he stayed until he was found. Police said that he was lucky because there ³ _____ (know) ⁴ _____ (be) bears in the forest. It is not clear if Yamato had food, but the shelter had beds and safe drinking water. "He did the right thing," said a police spokesperson. Soldiers who found the boy praised him ⁵ _____ (keep) calm and ⁶ _____ (not / panic).

2 Which of these things do we know to be true (T)? Which are false (F)? Which are possibly true (PT)?

1 Yamato was missing for two days. ____
2 Yamato came across a bear in the forest. ____
3 Yamato was able to get food at the shelter. ____
4 Yamato had access to safe drinking water at the shelter. ____

3 >> MB Work in pairs. Use a reporting verb or a passive reporting verb to make two sentences about what you think Yamato did after he was found.

I CAN	
use the correct verb patterns with reporting verbs	
use passive reporting verbs	

Vocabulary

4 Circle the correct options to complete these sentences.

1 Don't just *have / take* my word for it. I *persuade / suggest* trying it out for yourself.
2 She accused him *of / for* taking her car without permission, but he *denies / refuses* it. No one else was there, so it's her word *against / over* his.
3 It's such a terrible decision that I'm almost at a loss *for / without* words. I'm going to *threaten / urge* him to reconsider. I hope I can *warn / convince* him to change his mind.

5 >> MB Work in pairs. Answer the questions about these people from the news stories in Unit 9.

1 What did Sharbat Gula agree to let Steve McCurry do?
2 What was the pilot Peter Burkill accused of?

I CAN	
use a range of reporting verbs	
use expressions with *word*	

Real life

6 Decide if the speaker is expressing belief or disbelief. Write *B* for belief or *D* for disbelief.

1 I'd take that figure with a grain of salt. ____
2 I think newspapers often tend to exaggerate these things. ____
3 Well, they generally get their facts right. ____
4 I think we can take the organizer's word for it. ____
5 I wouldn't take much notice of what the promoters say. They just want publicity. ____

7 >> MB Write down a recent claim someone has made in the news (e.g., *Apparently, …*). Then work in small groups. Take turns reading aloud each claim and responding using expressions of belief or disbelief.

I CAN	
comment on stories and rumors, express belief and disbelief	

Unit 10 Talented people

A mahout leads his elephant, Havelock Island, India.

FEATURES

118 An ordinary man
The extraordinary career of an astronaut

120 The real-life Batman?
A man with an unusual talent

122 The king herself
The story of the pharaoh Hatshepsut

126 Queen of Egypt
A video about the life of Cleopatra

1 Match these words with their definitions (a–f).

| background | experience | qualifications |
| qualities | skills | talents |

a strong natural abilities _____
b abilities developed by practice _____
c (generally positive) characteristics _____
d certificates that show you have learned something _____
e what you've done in your life _____
f your past in general (where you come from, where you studied, etc.) _____

2 Work in pairs. Look at the photo and the caption. What qualities, skills, qualifications, and experience do you think mahouts need to do their job well?

3 ▶ 85 Listen to a description of a mahout's job. Compare the description with your answers in Exercise 2.

4 Make short notes about your own background, experience, talents, etc. Then work in pairs. Take turns asking and answering questions with your partner.

What qualifications do you have?

117

10a An ordinary man

Listening and reading

1 ▶86 Work in pairs. Look at the photo. Can you answer these questions? Then listen and check.

1 What does this photo show?
2 Who do you think the person in the photo is?
3 What quotation is associated with this event?

2 Work in pairs. Read the article. What were Neil Armstrong's qualities? Give reasons for your answers.

3 Read the article again. Work in pairs and answer the questions.

1 Why do you think Neil Armstrong was called "the ultimate professional"?
2 How did he gain his experience of flying?
3 What motivated Armstrong?
4 What is meant by "the rest … is history"?
5 What did Armstrong do to avoid publicity after the Apollo 11 mission?

▶87

Vocabulary careers

> **WORDBUILDING verb (+ preposition) + noun collocations**
>
> When you learn a new noun, try to note also the verb(s) that collocate with it and any prepositions that follow the verb.
> *pursue a career*
> *graduate from high school / college*
>
> For more practice, see Workbook page 83.

4 Work in pairs. Find verbs (+ prepositions) in the article that collocate with each of these nouns, and complete phrases 1–5.

1 to __start__ a career *build - change - pursue*
2 to __graduate__ from a school or college
3 to __start - finish__ a course *take - do*
4 to __become__ an astronaut
5 to __find__, __give up__, __look for__ a job *get - apply for*

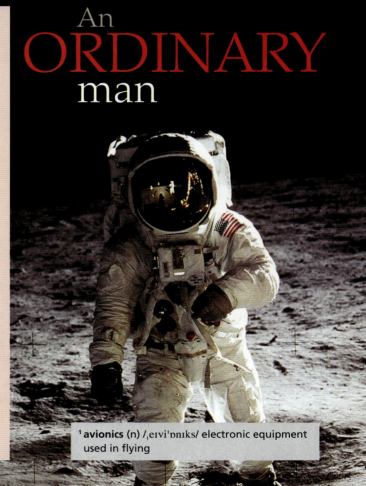

An ORDINARY man

Neil Armstrong, the most famous of the astronauts on the spacecraft Apollo 11, has been called the ultimate professional. He was hired to do a job. He did the job, and then he went home and kept quiet about it. In forty years, he only gave two interviews. But how could the man who first set foot on the moon remain such a mystery?

Armstrong pursued a career that came from a passion for flying that he developed as a child in the 1930s. He learned to fly before he had graduated from high school, and then took a course in aerospace engineering in the US. After that, he served for three years as a pilot in the US Navy, flying 78 missions in the war in Korea. He left the navy in 1952 and got a job with the Lewis Flight Propulsion Laboratory, where he flew experimental aircraft. He reached speeds of 6,600 kilometers an hour, and altitudes of over 60 kilometers.

It is not clear when Armstrong decided to become an astronaut, but it was never his ambition to be famous. His aim was simply to push the limits of flight. In 1962, news came that NASA was looking for astronauts for its Apollo program. Incredibly excited, he applied for the job and was accepted. The rest, as they say, is history.

When he and the other astronauts returned from the Apollo 11 moon landing in July 1969, Armstrong was a worldwide celebrity. He could have done anything he wanted. Instead, he became a teacher and also worked for an avionics[1] firm. On the weekends, he went flying to get away from all the attention.

Armstrong retired in 2002, ten years before his death. He had fulfilled his dream, but he did not feel any more special than the others who worked on the Apollo space program. He was just the pilot.

[1] **avionics** (n) /ˌeɪviˈɒnɪks/ electronic equipment used in flying

Grammar articles

> **ARTICLES: A/AN, THE, or ZERO ARTICLE?**
>
> **Indefinite article: *a/an*** (+ singular countable noun)
> *It is not clear when he decided to become **an astronaut**.*
>
> **Definite article: *the*** (+ singular/plural countable noun or uncountable noun)
> *He and **the other astronauts** returned from the Apollo 11 moon landing.*
>
> **Zero article** (+ plural countable noun or uncountable noun)
> *He learned to fly before he had graduated from **high school**.*
>
> For more information and practice, see page 174.

5 Look at the grammar box. Complete these statements (1–3) with the correct type of article (*a/an, the,* or write "zero article").

1 We use ___a or an___
 • to talk about one person or thing in general.
 • to say a person or thing is one of many.
 • when we first mention something.
2 We use ___zero article___
 • to talk about people or things in a general way.
 • before certain generally familiar places (school, work, hospital, college).
3 We use ___the___
 • to talk about a specific person/people or thing(s).
 • when we refer back to a person/people or thing(s) already mentioned.
 • before a superlative adjective.

6 Work in pairs. Read the first paragraph of the article again. Look at the articles and nouns (1–8) in **bold**. Which of the uses in Exercise 5 does each one match?

> Neil Armstrong, [1] **the most famous** of [2] **the astronauts** on the spacecraft Apollo 11, has been called the ultimate professional. He was hired to do [3] **a job**. He did [4] **the job**, and then he went [5] **home** and kept quiet about it. In forty years, he only gave two interviews. But how could [6] **the man** who first set foot on [7] **the moon** remain such [8] **a mystery**?

7 Find and underline an example in the article of each of the following:

1 zero article with:
 a a subject of study b a country
 c a month
2 *the* with:
 a a period of time b a country
 c a research lab

8 Complete the sentences. Use *the* or leave blank where no article is needed.

1 Where I live in _____ New Zealand, _____ weather is pretty nice.
2 He's thinking about joining _____ police force after he graduates from _____ college.
3 On _____ weekend, I often play _____ tennis or go for a run first thing in _____ morning. Then I come back and have _____ breakfast.
4 A survey showed that in _____ US, _____ most people go to _____ bed at around 11:00 in _____ evening and get up at _____ 7:30 in _____ morning.
5 I need to go to _____ store and get some food before I go _____ home tonight.

9 Complete the sentences. Use *a, an,* or *the*, or leave blank where no article is needed.

1 Armstrong could fly _a_ plane before he could drive _a_ car.
2 As _a_ boy, Armstrong played _the_ baritone horn, but he wasn't _a_ very good musician.
3 In _✗_ Korea, one of _the_ wings on Armstrong's plane broke off and he had to eject.
4 _The_ first meal that _✗_ they ate on _the_ moon was _✗_ bacon and _✗_ peaches.
5 Armstrong was _a_ member of _the_ team that investigated _the_ Challenger space shuttle disaster.

10 Pronunciation linking vowels

▶ **88** A /w/ or /j/ sound often links a word that ends with a vowel sound to the next word that begins with a vowel sound. Work in pairs. Listen and say which sound links the two words in 1–5 below. Then practice saying the phrases.

1 the‿ultimate professional
2 to do‿a job
3 she‿understood me perfectly
4 he‿only gave two interviews
5 a hero‿of our time

Speaking *my*Life

11 Work in pairs. Describe the path of your own career or the career of someone you know. Use these stages and try to use articles correctly.

> interests as a child → school subjects → early jobs → college or classes taken → other experiences → important events → future ambitions

As a child, I was very interested in drawing and painting. At school, I loved art and I had a fantastic art teacher.

10b The real-life Batman?

Listening

1 Work in pairs. Look at the photo and the caption. Discuss these questions.

1. What do you know about bats?
2. What is the man in the photo doing? Is it anything unusual?

2 ▶ 89 Listen to a description of Daniel Kish. How did he get his nickname? Discuss with a partner.

3 ▶ 89 Circle the correct options to complete the summary. Then listen again and check your answers.

Daniel Kish has been blind from ¹ *birth / a young age*. He taught himself to recognize how near objects are by clicking his ² *tongue / fingers* and then listening for an echo. Using this technique, he can ride a bicycle, go hiking in the countryside, and play ³ *ball games / board games*. He can "see" a house from a distance of about ⁴ *ten / fifty* meters. Using echolocation actively is a skill you can learn in just ⁵ *a couple of days / a month*. Kish ⁶ *likes / is offended by* his nickname.

4 Work in pairs. The speaker mentions an example of when echolocation could be useful for fully sighted people. What is it?

Vocabulary the senses

5 Complete the descriptions (1–4) with these five senses. Then compare your answers with a partner.

| sight | hearing | touch | smell | taste |

1. Eagles have an amazing sense of _____ and can spot small animals from high up. Rhinoceroses, on the other hand, are incredibly nearsighted.
2. Cats have sensitive noses, but, strangely, a poor sense of _____ . They can't recognize if something is sweet.
3. Dogs have a very keen sense of _____ . They can detect scents that would be impossible for humans to trace. They hear better than humans too, although some dogs go deaf or become hard of _____ when they are older.
4. People used to think crabs were basically numb—that they had no sense of _____ . But a recent experiment showed that crabs reacted negatively to small electric shocks.

6 Find words in Exercise 5 that mean the following:

a. unable to see far _____
b. unable to hear anything _____
c. unable to feel anything in the body _____

7 Work in pairs. What other animals can you think of that have one very strong or weak sense?

Daniel Kish, the real-life Batman

Grammar relative clauses

> **RELATIVE CLAUSES**
>
> **Defining relative clause**
> 1 Kish clicks his tongue and then listens for the echo **that comes back.**
> 2 He can do many things **that blind people cannot ordinarily do.**
> 3 "The real-life Batman" is a description **he welcomes.**
> 4 He is amused by the nickname **for which he is now famous.**
>
> **Non-defining relative clause**
> 5 Daniel Kish, **who has been blind since he was a year old**, taught himself to "see."
> 6 A wooden fence, **whose surface is softer than brick**, gives a "warmer" echo.
>
> **what …**
> 7 He just loves **what** he is doing.
>
> For more information and practice, see page 174.

8 Look at the grammar box. Work in pairs and answer these questions.

1 Which type of relative clause (defining or non-defining) contains essential information? Extra information?
2 If you put a relative pronoun in sentence 3, what and where would it be?
3 Can you leave out the relative pronoun in sentences 1 and 2? Why or why not?
4 Which relative pronoun means "the thing(s) that"?
5 In sentence 4, we can also say … *the nickname he is now famous for.* Which version sounds more formal?
6 Which relative pronoun is used for possession?

9 Work in pairs. Look at the relative pronouns in **bold** in track 89 of the audioscript on page 188. What does each **bold** word refer to?

1 *who = Daniel Kish*

10 Write definitions of these people and things (1–6) using defining relative clauses. Then compare your sentences with a partner.

1 Batman is a character …
  *Batman is a character **who** first appeared in a comic.*
2 Daniel Kish is a man …
3 A blind person is someone …
4 Echolocation is a technique …
5 A click is a sound …
6 Bats are animals …

11 Circle the correct relative pronoun to complete these sentences (1–6).

1 Ancient history is not a subject *that / whose / about which* I know much about.
2 The Queen, *which / who / that* will celebrate her ninetieth birthday this year, is a much-loved figure.
3 Modern smartphones, *whose / that's / who's* screens are made of glass, are easier to break than older cell phones *what / that / who* were made of plastic.
4 I don't understand *that / what / which* he means.
5 The house *where / whose / that* we stayed in belonged to a local teacher.
6 She shares an apartment for *what / which / that* she paid a lot of money with her cousin.

12 Rewrite the two sentences in each item below as one sentence using a relative clause. There is sometimes more than one possible answer.

1 That's the man. Maya was talking about him the other day.
  That's the man _____.
2 They wanted to achieve that. I think they did.
  I think they achieved _____.
3 The study looked at how well people can use maps. It had very interesting results.
  The study _____.
4 It's a small country. The country has had a big influence on the history of the region.
  It's a small country _____.
5 His brother is also a basketball player. His brother is six years younger than him.
  His brother _____.

13 Work in two pairs in a group of four.

Pair A: Look at the "Down" words in the crossword on page 153.

Pair B: Look at the "Across" words in the crossword on page 155.

Write clues for these words using relative clauses. Then take turns reading your clues to the other pair to complete the crossword.

1 *Down: an adjective that means "near" (can also be a verb)*
2 *Across: an adjective whose opposite is "quiet"*

Speaking myLife

14 Work in pairs. If you could choose to have one sense (sight, hearing, etc.) with superhuman ability, which one would it be and why?

Unit 10 Talented people

10c The king herself

Reading

1 Work in pairs. Look at the title of the article. What is strange about it?

2 Read the article. Number these events about Hatshepsut's (*Hat-shep-sut*) life in the correct chronological order (1–7).

___ Her mummy was discovered in a less important tomb.
___ The monuments she built were destroyed.
___ She became queen regent.
___ She ruled Egypt as king for 21 years.
___ Her mummy was identified and put in the Royal Mummy Rooms.
___ She married Thutmose II.
___ She was born the eldest daughter of Thutmose I and Queen Ahmose.

3 Circle the correct option (a or b) to complete each sentence.

1 Hatshepsut's mummy was not identified at first because it ___ .
   a was badly damaged
   b was not in a royal tomb
2 Hatshepsut was concerned that people would ___ .
   a not know she was royalty
   b not remember her achievements
3 Thutmose III did not want people to know that Hatshepsut had been ___ .
   a king
   b related to him
4 Thutmose II's children consisted of ___ .
   a one son and one daughter
   b two sons
5 According to tradition, the queen regent was supposed to ___ .
   a do nothing
   b help the king until he was old enough to rule
6 In later statues and images, Hatshepsut appears male because of ___ .
   a the items she is holding
   b her face and attitude

Critical thinking examining the evidence

4 Find evidence in the article to support each sentence (1–5). If there is clear evidence, write *100%*. If there is no evidence, write *0%*. If the evidence is not clear, write *NC*.

1 Hatshepsut was ambitious. ___
2 If Hatshepsut had had a male heir herself, she would have allowed him to be king. ___
3 Thutmose III thought his stepmother was wrong to act as king. ___
4 Hatshepsut knew that what she had done was wrong. ___
5 Hatshepsut's wish to be remembered has come true. ___

5 Work in pairs. Compare your answers and the evidence you found. Do you think overall this story has a happy or sad ending?

Word focus *self*

6 Work in pairs. Look at the expression below from the article. Then discuss what the other expressions with *self* (1–5) mean.

… standing in a **self-confident** manner …

1 If you want to know how to think more positively, you should read more **self-help** books.
2 My father is a **self-made** man. He started working in a shop at 16, and had a $2 million business by the time he was 30.
3 I saw my favorite actor in the street recently, but I looked a mess and I felt too **self-conscious** to go up to her.
4 Sticking to a diet is difficult. You need a lot of **self-control**.
5 Giving so much time to the college isn't just kindness; it's also **self-interest**—he hopes to become its president one day.

7 Choose two of the **bold** expressions from Exercise 6 and write your own sentences with them. Then read the sentences to a partner without the **bold** expression and see if they can guess which one it is.

Speaking myLife

8 Work in pairs. Look at these job descriptions. Which options do you think describe the job of a leader or manager?

- working regular hours (9 a.m. to 5 p.m.), or longer?
- working with people, or things?
- making decisions, or following instructions?
- traveling, or staying in one place?
- working indoors, or outdoors?
- working full-time, or part-time?
- working independently, or as part of a team?

9 Ask your partner questions about their work preferences using the list in Exercise 8. Then discuss what their dream job might be.

THE KING *herself*

1 Today her body lies in the Royal Mummy¹ Rooms at the Egyptian Museum in Cairo, alongside other pharaohs. Next to her is a sign that says "Hatshepsut, the king herself (1473–1458 BC)." But in 1903, when the archeologist Howard Carter found Hatshepsut's coffin² in the Valley of the Kings, it was empty. Had her mummy been stolen or destroyed? The truth only came out a century later, when Egyptian scientists identified a mummy from a less important tomb³ as that of Hatshepsut. None of the treasures normally found with pharaohs' mummies were with it. It was not even in a coffin.

2 Hatshepsut was one of the greatest builders of ancient Egypt. She built numerous monuments and temples. At Karnak, we can still see an inscription⁴ describing her hopes as to how she would be remembered: "Now my heart turns this way and that, as I think what the people will say. Those who see my monuments in years to come, and who shall speak of what I have done."

3 But following her death, her successor and stepson Thutmose III set about erasing her memory, ordering all images of her as the king to be removed from monuments and temples. Her statues were smashed and thrown into a pit. Yet, the images of her as queen were left undamaged. Why?

4 Hatshepsut was the eldest daughter of Thutmose I and Queen Ahmose. But Thutmose I also had a son by another queen, and this son, Thutmose II, became pharaoh when his father died. As was common among Egyptian royalty, Thutmose II married his sister, Hatshepsut. They produced one daughter. Another wife, Isis, gave Thutmose II the male heir⁵ that Hatshepsut was unable to provide.

5 When Thutmose II died from heart disease, Thutmose III was still a young boy. As was the custom, Hatshepsut took control as the young pharaoh's queen regent.⁶ At first, Hatshepsut respected convention and just handled political affairs while the young king was growing up. But before long, she began performing kingly duties. And after a few years she no longer acted as queen regent, but fully assumed the role of king of Egypt, the supreme power in the land.

6 No one really knows why Hatshepsut broke the conventional rules. Was it a key moment in Egypt's history when a strong leader was needed? Did she believe she had the same right to rule as a man? Did she feel a right as a direct descendant of the pharaoh, Thutmose I? Whatever the reason, her stepson was relegated to second-in-command, and "the king herself" went on to rule for an amazing 21 years.

7 At first, Hatshepsut made no secret of her sex—in images her body is unmistakably a woman's—but later, she is depicted as a male king, with headdress and beard, standing in a self-confident manner with legs apart. Many inscriptions still exist that have references to "my people." These suggest that she knew she had broken the rules and wanted her subjects' approval. Her stepson, Thutmose III, grew increasingly frustrated. After Hatshepsut's death, he took his revenge, doing his best to erase her memory as pharaoh from history. But, ironically, in the long term, it is Hatshepsut, the King Herself, who has achieved greater fame.

---

¹**mummy** (n) /ˈmʌmi/ a dead body wrapped in layers of cloth
²**coffin** (n) /ˈkɒfɪn/ a box in which a dead body is placed
³**tomb** (n) /tuːm/ a structure in which a dead person is placed
⁴**inscription** (n) /ɪnˈskrɪpʃən/ words cut into a hard surface
⁵**heir** (n) /eər/ someone who will receive a title when another person dies
⁶**regent** (n) /ˈriːdʒənt/ a person who governs a state because the real king or queen is too young or is absent

10d The right job

Real life describing skills, talents, and experience

Shelter BOX is a charity that sends boxes of essential items needed in an emergency (e.g., a tent, tools, cooking utensils, a water purification kit) to places where disasters—such as earthquakes and floods—have struck. Boxes are prepared in the US and delivered immediately by Shelterbox employees to anywhere in the world where they will help to save lives.

1 Read the description of Shelterbox. What kind of organization is it, and what service do they offer?

2 ▶91 Listen to someone being interviewed for a job at Shelterbox. Work in pairs and answer the questions.
  1 What aspect of their work is the candidate very interested in?
  2 What does the interviewer think might be a problem?

3 ▶91 Look at the expressions for describing skills, talents, and experience. Complete the sentences (1–10) with the correct prepositions. Then listen to the interview again and check your answers.

> ▶ DESCRIBING SKILLS, TALENTS, and EXPERIENCE
> 1 I'm familiar _____ your work
> 2 I have a friend who volunteered _____ you ...
> 3 I'm very interested _____ the idea of ...
> 4 I specialized _____ economics
> 5 I'm good at coping _____ difficult environments
> 6 I think I'd be suited _____ the work
> 7 I'm pretty good _____ computers
> 8 I'm comfortable _____ all the usual programs
> 9 I'm serious _____ wanting to help people
> 10 I need to become more knowledgeable _____ the world

4 Work in pairs. Do you think the candidate did a good job of selling himself to the interviewer?

5 Pronunciation difficult words

a ▶92 The spelling of a word in English does not always indicate how you should say the word. How confident are you that you can pronounce these words from the interview? For very confident, put a (✓); for quite confident, put a (?); and for not confident, put a (✗). Then listen and repeat.

☐ business	☐ comfortable	☐ environment
☐ though	☐ world	☐ months
☐ specialized	☐ suited	☐ knowledgeable

b ▶93 Listen to eight more words and try to spell them. Then compare your answers with a partner.

6 Work in pairs.

Student A: Choose one of the jobs below and think about why you should get the job. Convince Student B that this would be a good job for you.

Student B: You are the interviewer. Think of some appropriate questions. Interview Student A. Then swap roles and conduct a new interview.

- a salesperson in a children's bookstore
- a tester of new video games
- a fund-raiser for your old school or college
- a volunteer firefighter (part-time)
- a trainee chocolate maker

10e First impressions

Writing a personal profile

1 Work in pairs. Which of these contexts (a–e) have you written a personal profile for before? What kind of information did you give about yourself?

a a job application
b a social networking site
c a college application
d a vacation rental website (like Airbnb)
e a voluntary organization

2 Look at these three short personal profiles. Which of the contexts in Exercise 1 was each one written for? Match the profiles (1–3) with a context (a–e) from Exercise 1.

1 ____

I'm Rachel, 28 years old, from France. My husband Jack and I just moved to Montreal and are looking to make new friends in the area. We're both very easygoing, and are passionate about traveling and discovering new places. I love cooking for people. Send me a message if you want to join us for a home-cooked French meal!

2 ____

Bright and experienced retail manager with a background in men's and ladies' fashion both in large department stores and small boutiques. A creative and adaptable professional who has a great eye for design and detail. Willing to relocate and open to international opportunities.

3 ____

I am a self-reliant and curious learner whose ambition is to pursue a career in political journalism. My experience as the editor of my high school newspaper has inspired me to learn more about world affairs, and I hope very much to deepen my knowledge by studying politics at your institution.

3 Work in pairs. Look at the three profiles above and answer these questions.

1 Which profile(s) are written in the first person? And in the third person?
2 Which profile is written in a less formal style? How can you tell?
3 Which profile do you think is the most persuasive?

4 Vocabulary personal qualities

a Find adjectives in the profiles that mean the following:

1 intelligent ____
2 wanting to know more ____
3 very enthusiastic ____
4 imaginative ____
5 with a lot of practice ____
6 independent ____
7 relaxed ____
8 can change to fit the situation ____

b Which of the adjectives above would you use to describe yourself? Tell a partner.

5 Writing skill using *with*

a Work in pairs. How would you rephrase this sentence using a relative clause?

A retail manager with a background in men's and ladies' fashion

b Rewrite these phrases using *with*. Where you have to change an adjective or verb to a noun, you will need to add an appropriate preposition.

1 an IT expert who has experience in software design
2 a young couple who loves travel
3 a creative individual who is interested in fashion
4 a bright manager who is ambitious to succeed
5 an easygoing musician who is talented at cooking

6 Write your own short profile similar to one of the profiles in Exercise 2. Choose one of the contexts from Exercise 1.

7 Exchange profiles with a partner. Check your partner's profile using these questions.

- What was the main impression the profile gave?
- Is the profile written in an appropriate style?
- Does it include adjectives to describe personal qualities?
- Does it include at least one *with* + noun expression?
- Overall, was the profile effective?

Unit 10 Talented people

10f Queen of Egypt

A statue of Cleopatra

Before you watch

1 Work in pairs. Look at the photo and the caption. Make notes about what you know about Cleopatra.

- who she was
- when and where she ruled
- important events in her life

2 Key vocabulary

a Work in pairs. Read the sentences (1–4). The words and phrases in **bold** are used in the video. Guess the meaning of the words and phrases.

1 As the eldest son of the Queen of England, Prince Charles is her **successor**.
2 The company is well-equipped to compete with its international **rivals**.
3 The American **Civil War** was between the Northern and Southern states of the US.
4 His comment that he doesn't believe in global warming has caused a lot of **controversy** and has **infuriated** many people.

b Write the words and phrases in **bold** in Exercise 2a next to their definitions (a–e).

a a fight for control of a country between different groups within that country _____
b a person who takes over a job or position from someone else _____
c made someone very angry _____
d strong disagreement about something among a large group of people _____
e people or businesses you compete against for the same goal or for superiority in the same area _____

While you watch

3 ▶ 10.1 Watch the video. Match the people in the story (1–6) with their descriptions.

People	Descriptions
1 Cleopatra ○	○ Cleopatra's younger brother and co-ruler
2 Ptolemy 13th ○	○ a rival to Mark Antony in Rome
3 Julius Caesar ○	○ Cleopatra and Julius Caesar's son
4 Caesarion ○	○ winner in Rome's civil war
5 Mark Antony ○	○ Queen of Egypt
6 Octavian ○	○ a potential successor to Caesar and, later, Cleopatra's husband

4 ▶ 10.1 Look at these events in Cleopatra's life. Then watch the video again and complete the sentences.

1 Cleopatra was born in _____ BC into the Ptolemaic dynasty of Egypt.
2 She became Queen at the age of _____ and ruled Egypt with her brother, but he soon forced her from power.
3 When Julius Caesar arrived in Egypt, Cleopatra managed to get to see him by hiding in a _____ .
4 Julius Caesar was charmed by Cleopatra. He defeated her _____ and helped her take back the throne.
5 Soon after that, Cleopatra had a baby that she claimed was _____ son.
6 After Caesar was murdered, Cleopatra looked for someone else in Rome to help her. She met _____ , who was also hungry for power.
7 Together, Cleopatra and Mark Antony ruled Alexandria, and eventually they _____ .
8 Mark Antony said that _____ was the true successor to Caesar. This infuriated Mark Antony's rival, Octavian.
9 Octavian defeated Antony and Cleopatra in battle in _____ BC.
10 Legend says that Cleopatra spread rumors that she was _____ , and when Mark Antony heard this, he killed himself.
11 Cleopatra tried to make peace with Octavian, but when she couldn't, she too killed herself with a _____ bite.

After you watch

5 Vocabulary in context

a ▶ 10.2 Watch the clips from the video. Choose the correct meaning of the words and phrases.

b Complete these sentences in your own words. Then share your sentences with a partner.

1 I was overjoyed when I heard that …
2 I think that … is in decline.
3 Although he is dead, Michael Jackson's … lives on.

6 What three adjectives would you use to describe Cleopatra? Discuss with a partner.

7 Work in groups and discuss these questions.

1 Who are the most famous people in the history of your country?
2 What qualities are these people known for? Are they all good qualities?

Unit 10 Talented people

UNIT 10 REVIEW AND MEMORY BOOSTER

Grammar

1 Complete the first part of the article (1–10) with *a*, *an*, *the*, or no article (–). Then complete the second part (11–15) using relative pronouns.

Constance Adams has had ¹_____ interesting career. She studied ²_____ architecture at ³_____ Yale University before working as ⁴_____ architect in Berlin and ⁵_____ Japan. She then joined the Johnson Space Center in ⁶_____ US, where she helped design TransHab, a module for ⁷_____ International Space Station. ⁸_____ module was designed to provide ⁹_____ living accommodations for astronauts during their stay in ¹⁰_____ space.

In order to accommodate a crew of astronauts ¹¹_____ mission was to reach Mars, the designers of the TransHab module had to achieve two things. They had to design a module ¹²_____ would be only 4.3 meters in diameter when it was launched. But once it was in space, it needed to become three times that size to be big enough for the six astronauts ¹³_____ would live there. So they made a structure ¹⁴_____ could inflate and unfold in space to become a three-level "house" ¹⁵_____ astronauts could eat, sleep, and work.

2 Work in pairs. What two important design features of the TransHab module does the text describe?

3 Work in pairs. Make sentences defining two of these things. Use articles and relative pronouns in your definitions.

| blind | echo | flood | heir |

> **I CAN**
> use *a/an*, *the*, and zero article accurately ☐
> use relative pronouns in different relative clauses ☐

Vocabulary

4 Complete these sentences about jobs and careers. The first letter of each missing word is provided.

1. I s_____ in the army for four years, so I understand the importance of discipline.
2. I'm very a_____ and e_____ . I can work in whatever environment you need me to.
3. I a_____ for the job because I'm good at selling and I want to p_____ a career in sales.
4. Both my parents are doctors, so it was a natural choice for me to b_____ a doctor, too.

5 ▶▶ **MB** Work in pairs. Discuss which of these areas is being described in each sentence in Exercise 4. Then make sentences describing yourself in each of these areas.

| background | experience | qualifications |
| qualities | skills | talents |

> **I CAN**
> describe my experience, skills, and qualifications ☐

Real life

6 Complete these sentences with the correct prepositions.

1. I'm familiar _____ all the usual computer programs.
2. I specialized _____ mechanical engineering in college.
3. I think I'd be well-suited _____ working abroad.
4. I'm good _____ coping _____ difficult people.
5. I'm serious _____ pursuing a career _____ the fashion industry.
6. I'm very interested _____ the idea of creating new designs.

7 ▶▶ **MB** Rewrite the sentences in Exercise 6 so that they are true for you. Make two of the sentences false. Then read all your sentences to a partner and ask your partner to guess which two are false.

> **I CAN**
> use expressions to present myself at a job interview ☐

Unit 11 Knowledge and learning

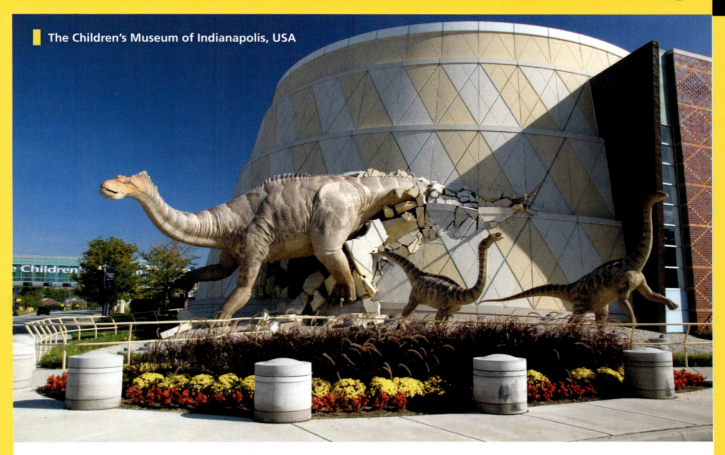

The Children's Museum of Indianapolis, USA

FEATURES

130 Innovation in learning
An innovative school in Brazil

132 Memory
What is it like to have an amazing memory?

134 Who's a clever bird?
What goes on in the mind of an animal?

138 Paraguay shaman
A video about the uses of medicinal plants

1 Work in pairs. Look at the photo and the caption. Answer these questions.

1 What kinds of things might you find in this museum?
2 What's your favorite museum? Why?

2 Look at the verbs (1–5) to do with learning. Match them with the verbs on the right with a similar meaning.

1 acquire (e.g., a new skill)   ○   ○ motivate
2 be unaware of (e.g., a fact)   ○   ○ not know about
3 get (e.g., the meaning of something) ○   ○ pick up or learn
4 inspire (e.g., a person to learn)   ○   ○ understand
5 take in (e.g., a lot of information) ○   ○ understand and remember

3 ▶ 94 Work in pairs. Listen to someone talking about taking her children to the Children's Museum and answer the questions.

1 What did the speaker's kids engage with?
2 Which section at the museum really inspired the speaker?

4 Work in pairs. Discuss these questions.

1 Which classes inspired you most at school? Why?
2 What knowledge or skill that you acquired at school or in college has been most useful (to you)?

129

11a Innovation in learning

Vocabulary education

1 Circle the correct options to complete these sentences about education.

1. Learning *by heart / from experience* is the best way to learn your multiplication tables.
2. *Studying / Cramming* for your exams is not a good idea—trying to remember lots of information at the last moment doesn't help you remember things in the long term.
3. He *turned up for / dropped out of* high school when he was sixteen and started working full-time instead.
4. At school, I acquired a lot of *academic knowledge / practical experience*, but not many life skills.
5. I always got good *notes / grades* in English because I read a lot of English books.

▶ 95

2 Work in pairs. Discuss these questions about education in your country.

1. Does education in your country focus more on practical skills or on academic knowledge? Is there a lot of learning by heart?
2. How much emphasis is put on grades and exams? Do you think this is a good or bad thing?
3. Is there a big problem of absenteeism at school? What about people dropping out completely?

Reading

3 Read the article about the Lumiar School in Brazil. What are the main ways in which it is different from a traditional school? Discuss with a partner.

INNOVATION in LEARNING

Ricardo Semler with some of his students at Lumiar School

It is a question that has troubled educators for centuries. How do they ensure that students don't just turn up to school to pass exams, but that they are truly engaged in their learning?

The Lumiar International School in São Paulo, Brazil, may have
5 found the answer. The founder of the school is Ricardo Semler, a businessman who developed a management style in which employees were trusted to do their jobs and make their own decisions. They were even able to set their own working hours and salaries. Semler managed to make this approach work in his own company, increasing
10 sales from $4 million to $212 million in twenty years.

Lumiar is a school unlike any other. Pupils occupy "spaces" rather than rooms, and learning takes place everywhere: in play areas, the hall, the dining room. If pupils do not feel engaged in a lesson, they can go to another one or to the library to read. Most learning is done through
15 projects that pupils design with their fellow students and teachers. Teachers are more like subject experts than traditional teachers.

On the day I visited, I attended a weekly meeting where all pupils could discuss issues affecting school life. The meeting was an opportunity for students to raise concerns, but also an occasion when they were
20 able to practice important life skills like debating and collaboration. The problem they succeeded in solving that day concerned some plates that two of the pupils had broken while running in the kitchen. Punishment was not the issue. The question was how to prevent this from happening again. Someone suggested a "No running in school"
25 rule. Then another boy spoke up: What if the school pays, but the boys themselves have to go and find the same china in the shops? I was amazed. This boy was only six years old, but he had managed to come up with an excellent solution to a difficult problem.

4 Complete these sentences using words from the article. The first letter of each missing word is provided.

1. Ricardo Semler based the Lumiar School's approach to education on that of his own c_____ .
2. Pupils learn by participating in p_____ with other students.
3. The weekly meetings provide an opportunity for the pupils to practice important l_____ s_____ .
4. The six-year-old boy's suggestion was accepted as a very reasonable form of p_____ .

Grammar *could, was able to, managed to,* and *succeeded in*

> ▶ **COULD, WAS ABLE TO, MANAGED TO,** and **SUCCEEDED IN**
>
> **could + base form of the verb**
> 1 *I attended a weekly meeting where all pupils* **could discuss** *issues affecting school life.*
> 2 *He was six years old, and he* **could speak** *confidently in front of a large group of people.*
>
> **was/were able + to + base form of the verb**
> 3 *They* **were** *even* **able to set** *their own working hours.*
>
> **managed + to + base form of the verb**
> 4 *Semler* **managed to make** *this approach work in his own company.*
>
> **succeeded in + -ing**
> 5 *The problem they* **succeeded in solving** *that day concerned some plates …*
>
> For more information and practice, see page 176.

5 Look at the grammar box. Complete these rules (1–3) with *could*, *was/were able to*, *managed to*, or *succeeded in*.

1. We use _____ and *was/were able to* to describe a general ability to do something in the past.
2. We use _____ and _____ to say we had a possibility or opportunity to do something in the past.
3. We use _____ , _____ , and *was/were able to* to describe success in a specific (difficult) task in the past.

6 Work in pairs. Look at these two sentences from the article. Which of the other forms in the grammar box could you use in each sentence?

1. The meeting was … an occasion when they **were able to practice** important life skills.
2. … he had **managed to come up** with an excellent solution to a difficult problem.

7 Circle the correct options to complete these sentences.

1. He had such a strong accent that I *couldn't / didn't manage* understand him.
2. He failed his exams the first time, but he *succeeded in / was able to* take them again.
3. She *could / managed to* read and write from the age of three.
4. Did she *succeed / manage* to pass her driving test last week?
5. When we got to the top of the mountain, we *could / succeeded* see for miles.
6. After trying the key for several minutes, they *managed / succeeded* in getting the door open.

8 Complete this text with the correct form of the verbs in parentheses. Add a preposition if necessary.

> Ricardo Semler's philosophy is the same in education and in business: to be democratic and to let people manage their own work. For example, if a salesperson managed ¹_____ (reach) their weekly sales target by Wednesday, they could take the rest of the week off. At Semler's weekly board meetings, two seats were open for anyone in the company—including the cleaners and lower-level staff—who could ²_____ (get) there on time. The important thing for Semler was to have people around him who were able ³_____ (think) for themselves. That's why he set up a school: to teach people to be independent. With the Lumiar School, he succeeded ⁴_____ (achieve) this.

Speaking *myLife*

9 Work in pairs. Describe your learning experience of TWO of the following. Use the correct forms of *could*, *was/were able to*, *managed to*, or *succeeded in* in your answers.

- riding a bike
- driving
- speaking English
- cooking
- playing a sport or musical instrument
- mastering a job or a work skill

I remember my dad teaching me to ride a bike when I was six. At first, I **couldn't keep** *my balance. Every time he let go, I* **managed to ride** *for about ten meters before …*

Unit 11 Knowledge and learning

11b Memory

Competitors memorize names and faces at the World Memory Championships, London.

Listening

1 Work in pairs. What kinds of things do you often forget? Do you find this annoying?

2 ▶ 96 Listen to the first part of a talk on memory by a psychologist. He mentions some common failures of memory. Were any of them the same as the ones you talked about in Exercise 1?

3 ▶ 97 Work in groups. Listen to the rest of the talk and answer the questions.

1 What does the woman (AJ) remember?
2 How does AJ feel about her good memory?
3 Why are people's memories now perhaps not as good as they used to be?

4 ▶ 98 Circle the correct options to complete the psychologist's statements. Then listen to the whole talk again and check your answers.

1 AJ's memory is stimulated by *events / dates* in the same way that our memories can be stimulated by certain *images / smells*.
2 Our memories are selective: We remember mostly *urgent / important* things and *good / bad* things.
3 We should be *grateful for / conscious of* all the things that our memories hide.
4 Psychologists call the technology we use to store information our "*extra / external* memory."
5 Now medical science is trying to address the problem of *poor / selective* memory.

Wordbuilding homonyms

▶ **WORDBUILDING homonyms**

Homonyms are words that are spelled and pronounced in the same way but have a different meaning.
cross (adj) = angry; *cross* (v) = to go across, e.g., a bridge or road; *cross* (n) = a symbol made of two intersecting lines

For more practice, see Workbook page 91.

5 Look at the wordbuilding box. Then read the sentences below (1–4) and look at the words in **bold** from the talk. Circle the correct meaning of these homonyms (a or b).

1 AJ's memory is stimulated in the most intense way by **dates**.
 a fruit that grows on a palm tree
 b days of the year specified by a number
2 When you **found** a pen and paper, the idea was gone.
 a established
 b located
3 I'm sure everyone recognizes these **common** failures of memory.
 a shared
 b usual, normal
4 It's a bit like it is for the **rest** of us when certain smells bring back strong memories.
 a remainder
 b period of relaxing

Grammar future in the past

> **▶ FUTURE IN THE PAST**
>
> **was/were going to** and **was/were about to** (+ base verb)
> 1 You **were going to write** down a great idea you had, but when you found a pen and paper, …
> 2 You **were about to make** a comment in a meeting, and then …
>
> **would** (+ base verb) and **would have** (+ past participle)
> 3 You recognized someone in the street and **would have spoken** to them, but you didn't because …
>
> **was/were supposed to** (+ base verb)
> 4 You **were supposed to send** a friend a birthday card, but then …
>
> For more information and practice, see page 176.

6 ▶96 Work in pairs. Look at the grammar box. Try to remember what the speaker said in Exercises 2 and 4 to complete each sentence in the grammar box (1–4). Then listen again and check.

7 Work in pairs. Look again at sentences 1–4 in the grammar box. Do the verbs in **bold** describe actions that were completed?

8 Circle the correct verb forms to complete this description of another memory patient.

> There was another interesting patient who couldn't form new memories. He could only remember events before 1960. I ¹ *was going to ask / would ask* his doctor how someone with no memory managed to cope with daily life, but she suggested I speak to the patient directly. So I went to interview him. Our appointment ² *was supposed to be / would be* at 2 p.m., but the time made no difference to him since he lived only in the present. I ³ *would tell / would have told* him my name and why I was there, but I realized there was no point: ⁴ *it was supposed to mean / it would have meant* nothing to him. So I began by asking him about his past, and he talked about his childhood during the Second World War. But then the telephone rang. When he came back, I ⁵ *was about to ask / would ask* him to continue, but it was clear he had completely forgotten our earlier conversation. I thought he ⁶ *was about to be / would be* frustrated by this, but not at all. If anything, he seemed glad not to be burdened by memory.

9 ▶99 Rewrite these original plans (1–5) using future in the past forms. Then listen and check your answers.

1 I'm going to invite Sarah.
 I *was going to invite* Sarah, but I asked Kate instead.
2 Her calendar says she should be in Cairo this week.
 She _____ in Cairo this week, but she's sick, so she couldn't go.
3 I'll send you the original, if I can find it.
 He _____ me the original, but he couldn't find it, so he sent me a copy.
4 We are supposed to arrive there by ten o'clock.
 We _____ there by ten o'clock, but the train didn't get in until eleven.
5 He's about to announce his retirement.
 He _____ his retirement, but now he thinks he'll stay until next year.

10 Pronunciation contrastive sentence stress

a ▶99 Work in pairs. Underline the words in the rewritten sentences in Exercise 9 that give the contrasting facts. Listen again. Then practice saying each sentence using contrastive stress.

b Complete these sentences with a contrasting idea. Underline the words in the sentence that make the contrast. Then say your sentences to your partner. Your partner should say which words you stressed and why.

1 He was going to take the <u>day off</u>, but …
 they needed him at work after all.
2 We were supposed to be going to Chile, but …
3 I would have driven, but …
4 They were about to buy a new TV, but …
5 I was going to order the fish, but …

Speaking myLife

11 Work in pairs. Look at these three situations. Think of a good excuse to explain why each one happened. Then tell your excuses to the class. At the end, vote on which excuses were best.

- You were thirty minutes late for an important business meeting and didn't call to inform them.
- You borrowed someone's car and were supposed to return it the next day, but they had to call you to find out where it was.
- It was a close friend's birthday two days ago. You didn't send a card or get them a present.

*"Sorry I'm late. My train was delayed. I **was going to call** you, but …"*

11c Who's a clever bird?

Reading

1 Work in pairs. What kinds of things can animals learn to do? Which animals seem the most intelligent?

2 Work in pairs. Read the article and say how Alex the parrot demonstrated his intelligence.

3 Read the article again. Do these statements agree with the information given in the article? Circle true (T), false (F), or not given (NG) if there is no information.

1. Pepperberg's idea was to let Alex communicate to her how he saw the world.   T   F   NG
2. Pepperberg didn't want people to think she had chosen Alex for his intelligence.   T   F   NG
3. Alex showed that he could distinguish between colors and shapes, but not numbers.   T   F   NG
4. Pepperberg concluded that cognitive skills are necessary for survival in the wild.   T   F   NG
5. Alex felt very proud of his ability to communicate in English.   T   F   NG
6. Alex was capable of expressing his thoughts and emotions.   T   F   NG

Critical thinking explaining ideas

4 When writers express an idea, they often explain it to make sure the reader understands. Read the article again and underline the sentences or phrases used to explain each idea below.

1. that a good way to find out what an animal is thinking is to teach it to speak
2. that researchers had no confidence in her idea
3. that Alex made up words for new things
4. that birds need to be able to adapt to their environment
5. that Alex showed an understanding of feelings

5 Work in pairs. Which of these ways (a–c) does the writer use to explain each idea (1–5) in Exercise 4?

a   by rephrasing or saying the same thing in other words
b   by giving examples
c   by quoting someone who made the same point

Word focus *learn*

6 Work in pairs. Find these two expressions with the word *learn* in the article. Discuss what each expression means.

1. learn (something) by heart (lines 23–24)
2. learn (something) the hard way (line 69)

7 Work in pairs. Look at the expressions in **bold** in the sentences below. Can you figure out what these expressions mean? Which expression means the same thing as "learn the hard way"?

1. Tom's a professional photographer—ask him for advice if you're interested in **learning some tricks of the trade**.
2. Jessica wants to design the new brochure, but she's only been here a month. I told her that you have to **learn to walk before you can run**.
3. It**'s never too late to learn**. My grandfather took up the piano when he was 73 years old.
4. I've **learned my lesson**. I'm never going to try to put together a piece of furniture again without reading the instructions first.
5. There's no point complaining about the changes in the organization. We're just going to have to **learn to live with it**.
6. You'd think that the company would **learn from its mistakes**, but it never does.

8 Choose two of the **bold** expressions from Exercise 7 and write your own sentences with them. Then read your sentences to a partner, omitting the **bold** expressions with *learn*. Can your partner figure out the missing expressions?

Speaking *myLife*

9 Take the quiz on page 154 to find out what type of learner you are. The answers are on page 155. Then work in pairs and discuss if you agree with this.

10 Work in small groups. Discuss how your learning style affects your language learning. What things can you do to learn more effectively? Look at the ideas below and add any others you can think of.

- watching English language movies with the subtitles on
- reading stories (in English newspapers, books, magazines) and retelling them
- keeping a vocabulary book and drawing illustrations of each new word

▶ 100

How do you find out what an animal is thinking? How do you know if it is thinking at all? One good way, thought Harvard graduate Irene Pepperberg, might be to ask it.

In 1977, she decided she would teach a one-year-old African grey parrot named Alex to speak English. "I thought if he learned to communicate, I could ask him questions about how he sees the world."

Pepperberg bought Alex in a Chicago pet store. She let the store assistant choose him because she didn't want other scientists to say that she had deliberately chosen a clever bird. Given that Alex's brain was the size of a walnut, most researchers thought Pepperberg was certain to fail. "Some people actually called me crazy for trying this," she said.

But with Pepperberg's patient teaching, Alex learned how to imitate almost one hundred English words, including the names of food. He could count to six and had learned the sounds for seven and eight. But the point was not just to see if Alex could learn words by heart and then repeat them. Pepperberg wanted to get inside his mind and learn more about a bird's understanding of the world.

In one demonstration, Pepperberg placed Alex on a wooden perch[1] in the middle of the room. She then held up a green key and a small green cup for him to look at. "What's the same?" she asked. Without hesitation, Alex's beak opened: "Co-lor." "What's different?" Pepperberg asked. "Shape," Alex said. She demonstrated that Alex could tell what a key was, whatever its size or color. He also made up words for new things: he called an apple a "banerry" (a combination of banana and cherry, his favorite fruits). Many of Alex's cognitive[2] skills, such as his ability to understand the concepts of same and different, are rare in the animal world. But parrots, like humans, live a long time in complex societies. And like humans, these birds must adapt to changing relationships and environments.

"They need to be able to distinguish colors to know when a fruit is ripe or unripe," Pepperberg explained.

"They need to categorize things—what's edible, what isn't—and to know the shapes of predators. And it helps to have a concept of numbers if you need to keep track of your flock.[3] For a long-lived bird, you can't do all of this with instinct; thinking must be involved."

Alex also expressed feelings and awareness of other people's feelings. If Pepperberg grew frustrated, Alex could notice this and offer an "I'm sorry" to her. "Wanna go back" he would say when he had had enough of the tests and wanted to go back to his cage. "Talk clearly!" he commanded, when one of the other birds that Pepperberg was teaching mispronounced the word *green*. "He's moody," said Pepperberg, "so he interrupts the others, or he gives the wrong answer just to be difficult." Through her experiments, Pepperberg certainly learned more about the mind of a parrot, but like the parent of a teenager, she learned the hard way.

[1] **perch** (n) /pɜːrtʃ/ a wooden bar that a bird stands on
[2] **cognitive** (adj) /ˈkɒɡnətɪv/ related to thinking and thought processes
[3] **flock** (n) /flɒk/ a large group of birds

Who's a clever *bird?*

11d Keep learning

Real life getting clarification

1 Work in pairs. Look at the list of short courses offered by a local college. Which of these courses interest you and why?

ROUSHAM
ADULT EDUCATION COLLEGE

COURSE TITLE	FREQUENCY	EXAM COURSE
Basic Car Repair *Apr. 5, 10 wks.*	1 × 2 hrs.	✗
Introduction to Psychology *Jan. 22, 18 wks.*	1 × 2 hrs.	✓
Vlogging* *Apr. 11, 8 wks.*	1 × 1.5 hrs.	✗
First Aid *Apr. 12, 4 wks.*	2 × 1.5 hrs.	✓
Fitness Instruction *Mar. 1, 12 wks.*	1 × 2 hrs.	✓
Flower Arranging *Jan. 22, 18 wks.*	1 × 2 hrs.	✗
Art Appreciation *Apr. 5, 10 wks.*	1 × 2 hrs.	✗
Screenwriting *Jan. 21, 18 wks.*	1 × 2 hrs.	✗
Web Design *Apr. 12, 6 wks.*	1 × 1.5 hrs.	✗
Starting Your Own Business *Apr. 11, 8 wks.*	1 × 1.5 hrs.	✗

* A vlog (or video blog) is a blog that features mostly videos rather than text or images. Vlogging is the act of keeping a video blog.

2 ▶ 101 Listen to a telephone conversation with someone inquiring about a class. Work in pairs and answer the questions.

1. What kind of class does Ahmad initially ask about?
2. What class does Liz suggest for him instead? Why?
3. What does Ahmad decide to do?

3 Work in pairs. Look at the expressions for getting clarification that Ahmad used. Which expressions does he use to ask for repetition, and which does he use to ask for explanation?

▶ GETTING CLARIFICATION

What do you mean by ^{1}_____?
Can you speak up a little?
Can you explain what ^{2}_____?
Sorry, I don't understand.
Are you saying that ^{3}_____ the history of art?
Could you give me an example of ^{4}_____ in the class?
What was ^{5}_____ called again?
Sorry, I didn't catch ^{6}_____ .
Did you say ^{7}_____?

4 ▶ 101 Listen to the conversation again. Complete the expressions for getting clarification in Exercise 3 with the words you hear.

5 Pronunciation linking in question forms

a ▶ 102 In certain commonly used combinations (*did you, could you, what do you,* etc.), the words are strongly linked together. Listen to these examples. Notice how the speaker links the words together.

1. Are you saying the class is full?
2. Did you say Tuesday?
3. What do you mean?
4. Could you give me an example?

b Work in pairs. Practice saying these questions.

- What are you trying to say?
- Could you repeat that?
- Did you mean September?
- What do you think?

6 Work in pairs.

Student A: You are a potential student. Choose one of the courses from the list in Exercise 1 or another class you are interested in. Tell Student B your choice. Prepare questions about the class (e.g., how long it is, what is covered exactly).

Student B: You are a college administrator. Prepare what you are going to say about Student A's chosen class (e.g., what it covers, if it offers a degree or a certificate).

Act out a conversation inquiring about the class. Then change roles and have a new conversation.

11e The wrong course

Writing an email about a misunderstanding

1 Read the email from a student to an adult education college. Answer the questions below.

> Dear Sir/Madam,
>
> I enrolled in your course Car Repair 1 in August and have attended three classes. When I originally inquired about the course, I was told that it was suitable for people with no previous knowledge of car repair. But, in fact, everyone else in the class seems to know a lot already. So despite the fact that the lessons generally start with a basic concept, they move very quickly on to more complicated ideas.
>
> I don't blame the teacher. On the contrary, he does his best to explain concepts to me. But I feel that I am just holding everyone else back. They know how an engine works already, whereas I have no background at all in mechanics.
>
> I was going to wait a couple of weeks before saying anything, but the last class was so difficult that I have decided to write now and ask for a refund. While I appreciate it's not really anyone's fault that this has happened, I hope you will understand how unsatisfactory the situation is for me.
>
> I look forward to hearing from you.
>
> Sincerely yours,
>
> Silvia Redman

1 What is the misunderstanding about the course?
  a the level
  b the timing
2 How would you describe the student's feelings about the situation?
  a offended
  b frustrated
3 How would you describe the tone of the email?
  a aggressive
  b reasonable

2 Work in pairs. What do you think the college should do in response to the email? Give reasons for your answer.

3 **Writing skill** linking contrasting ideas

a Work in pairs. Look at the contrasting ideas in each item below. Find the sentences in the email that express these ideas. Then underline the words or phrases that are used to link them.

1 The course should be for beginners. No one else is a beginner.
2 Each lesson starts with a simple idea. It progresses quickly to difficult ideas.
3 The teacher is not at fault. He helps me as much as he can.
4 The other students know a lot. I know nothing.
5 No one is to blame for this. I still feel it is unfair.

b Look again at the sentences in the email with *despite* and *whereas*. How would you rewrite them using *although* and *on the other hand*? Tell your partner.

c Complete these sentences (1–4) with appropriate linking words and phrases from the box.

| on the other hand | but |
| despite the fact that | on the contrary |

1 _____ the brochure says the start date is September 12th, the first real class is a week later, on the 19th.
2 The course is advertised as "practical," _____ you learn a lot of theory as well.
3 The art history course is a two-year program. The art appreciation course, _____ , is only ten weeks long.
4 Training as a fitness instructor is not easy. _____ , it's one of the toughest classes I've ever taken.

4 Imagine you enrolled in one of the other courses listed on page 136. Think of a misunderstanding that occurred with the course. Write an email to the college explaining the misunderstanding and asking for a refund.

5 Exchange emails with a partner. Compare what you have written. Use these questions to check your emails.

- Does the email make clear what the misunderstanding was?
- Is the tone of the email reasonable?
- Has the writer used linking words and phrases correctly?
- Do you think the email will get the response or action the writer wants?

11f Paraguay shaman

A shaman (or tribal healer) from the Amazon, Paraguay

Before you watch

1 Work in pairs. Look at the photo and the caption. What do you know about shamans? How do you think they treat sick people?

2 Key vocabulary

a Work in pairs. Read the sentences (1–5). The words in **bold** are used in the video. Guess the meaning of the words.

1 We have a nature **reserve** near our house. A lot of people go there to watch birds.
2 At the moment, there is no **cure** for cancer. However, scientists say they are getting close to finding one.
3 They live in an **isolated** part of Scotland two hours from the nearest town.
4 After I broke my arm, it took three months for it to **heal** properly.
5 The yoga class always begins with the teacher leading a **chant**.

b Write the words in **bold** in Exercise 2a next to their definitions (a–e).

a remote and on its own _____
b a word or phrase that is repeated in a rhythmic way, usually by a group of people _____
c become healthy again _____
d an area of land where plants or animals are officially protected _____
e a medicine or treatment that makes an illness or disease go away _____

While you watch

3 ▶ **11.1** Watch the video about medicinal plants. Work in pairs and answer the questions.

1 Where do the medicinal plants come from?
2 Why are these plants now at risk?
3 What are the scientists visiting Paraguay hoping to find?

4 ▶ **11.1** Read these statements (1–7). Then watch the video again and circle the correct options to complete the statements.

1 The plants in the forest could contain cures for diabetes, malaria, and *heart disease / common fevers and colds.*
2 As the plants disappear, the *shamans / potential cures* disappear with them.
3 Paraguay has one of the highest *deforestation / infant mortality* rates in the world.
4 At the village, Gervasio is *using chants / dancing*, perhaps to make a spiritual connection with the forest.
5 Together, they look for a specific type of plant that the scientists want to use in *fever / cancer* research.
6 Gervasio's wife then makes a local *dish / tea* with the plant.
7 The scientists have published *a book / online articles* about Paraguay's medicinal plants.

After you watch

5 Vocabulary in context

a ▶ **11.2** Watch the clips from the video. Choose the correct meaning of the words and phrases.

b Complete these sentences in your own words. Then share your sentences with a partner.

1 I have extensive knowledge of …
2 … is a good source of …
3 A potential disadvantage of drinking too much coffee is …

6 Work in small groups. Make a list of herbs, spices, vitamins, or other remedies commonly used in your country to help treat these medical problems. Add another problem and cure. Then tell each other if you have tried any of these cures and with what success.

Problem	Cure
1 Cold	*vitamin C (orange juice)*
2 Sore throat	
3 Toothache	
4 Stomachache	
5	

7 Work in pairs. Read the statements below. Which do you think are true? Do you have any similar beliefs in your country?

1 Eating fish is good for your brain.
2 Spicy food causes stomach ulcers.
3 Chicken soup helps cure a cold.
4 If you go outside with wet hair, you'll catch a cold.
5 Eating cheese before bed can give you bad dreams.
6 Drinking lemon tea with honey soothes a sore throat.

UNIT 11 REVIEW AND MEMORY BOOSTER

Grammar

1 Circle the correct options to complete this story about a linguist.

When police in Brazil interviewed an immigrant who spoke an unrecognizable language, they called Ziad Fazah, hoping that he ¹ *will / would* be able to help them. Fazah, originally from Lebanon, claimed that he ² *could / managed to* speak 54 different languages. He quickly realized that the man was speaking a dialect used in Afghanistan. With Fazah's help, the man ³ *could / was able to* explain that he had escaped from Afghanistan and was seeking asylum in Brazil.

Fazah's talents were first noticed by the Lebanese government when he was seventeen. They ⁴ *would / were going to* use him as an interpreter, but soon afterward he moved to Brazil with his parents. There, he married a Brazilian and began giving private language lessons. Fazah ⁵ *would remain / would have remained* unknown, but in 2006 his language abilities were tested on a Spanish television show, and he received international attention. Some people questioned his abilities. ⁶ *Was he really able / Did he really manage* to speak fluently in over 50 languages? The evidence was not completely convincing, but even if it is half that number, it is still impressive.

2 Work in pairs. Answer these questions about the story in Exercise 1.

1 Why were the police interviewing the man from Afghanistan?
2 What does the writer conclude about Ziad Fazah's language-speaking abilities?

3 >> MB Work in pairs. Tell your partner something:

1 you could do when you were younger, but can't do now.
2 you were going to do yesterday, but forgot.
3 you couldn't do at first, but managed to do in the end.

I CAN	
talk about past ability	
express the future in the past	

Vocabulary

4 Complete each expression about learning with a verb, a preposition, or an adjective.

1 Learning _____ your mistakes is learning the _____ way, but it works!
2 Don't worry if you don't understand the system at first; you'll soon pick it _____ .
3 There's just too much information to _____ in all at once. Do they expect us to learn it all _____ heart?

5 >> MB Work in pairs. Look at the photos.

1 How are children encouraged to learn in these places?
2 How is this similar to or different from the way you learned at school?

I CAN	
use expressions related to learning	
talk about knowledge and education	

Real life

6 Match sentences 1–4 with sentences a–d that have the same meaning.

1 What do you mean by that?
2 Could you give me an example?
3 Can you speak up a little?
4 I don't really get what you're saying.

a I don't really understand. ___
b For instance? ___
c Can you explain that? ___
d I can't hear you very clearly. ___

7 Think of two things you learned in Unit 11 about learning and memory. Then work in pairs and tell your partner about them. For each statement, your partner should respond with a different expression from Exercise 6.

I CAN	
ask for and get clarification	

Unit 12 Money

Costing US$3 million, the Lamborghini Sesto Elemento brings new meaning to luxury driving.

FEATURES

142 Saving for a rainy day
Norway, the richest country in the world

144 Get someone else to do it
The growing service economy

146 Start-up
How one take-out food van launched an $800 million industry

150 The Farmery
A video about one man's mission to sell food locally

1 Work in pairs. Look at the photo and the caption. Would you buy this car if money were no issue? What luxuries would or wouldn't you spend money on?

2 ▶ 103 Look at the statement below. Do you agree with it? Listen to two people's responses to it. Work in pairs. Which speaker do you agree with more?

"It doesn't matter if the gap between rich and poor is getting wider as long as everyone's standard of living is rising anyway."

3 ▶ 103 Listen to the speakers again. Complete these phrases about the economy that the speakers use. Then tell your partner what you think each expression means.

1 the standard of ___*living*___
2 the haves and the have _____
3 the _____ gap
4 people's buying _____
5 the cost of _____
6 quality of _____

4 Work in pairs. Are these statements true or false for your country? What evidence is there of this?

1 The cost of living is higher now than a few years ago.
2 People have a better quality of life now than in the past.

141

12a Saving for a rainy day

Vocabulary money

1 Complete the sentences (1–6) with the correct form of these verbs. One verb is extra.

borrow	earn	invest	lend
owe	save	spend	

1 According to a recent study, the best-paying jobs in the US are in the medical field. Most surgeons, for example, __earn__ six-figure salaries.
2 The best thing you can __invest__ in is a good education.
3 It's OK to ask people to __lend__ you money if you know you can pay it back.
4 Why do some people __save__ money all their lives and never use it?
5 We're told to manage our money carefully, but our government always __spend__ more money than it has.
6 It is very stressful to always __owe__ money—to the bank, the credit card company, etc.

2 Complete these sentences with nouns that express the same ideas as in Exercise 1. The first letter is provided.

1 Most surgeons have a very high i__ncome__.
2 The best i__nvestment__ you can make is …
3 Asking for a l__oan__ is OK if …
4 What's the point of having s__avings__ if you don't use them?
5 Why does government s__pending__ always exceed its income?
6 It is very stressful to always have d__ebts__.

Reading

3 Work in pairs. What do you know about Norway: its landscape, its people, its industry?

4 Read the article. Work in pairs. In what ways is Norway a rich country?

5 Work in pairs. Read the article again. Complete these summaries of the four paragraphs.

1 For a long time, Norway has had a better … than other countries.
2 The two reasons for Norway's success are … and …
3 For Norwegians, being rich means …
4 Norway is saving money for …

6 Work in pairs. Do you think that the Norwegians are right to save their money? Why or why not?

SAVING FOR A RAINY DAY

▶ 104

Come on, Norway; this doesn't even feel like a competition anymore! Consistently listed among the top five happiest countries in the world, Norway offers a quality of life that other countries can only dream of.
5 It is one of the wealthiest countries in the world; only Luxembourg and a couple of others are richer. As well as earning a good salary, Norwegians also get a good education, usually find a job they want—unemployment is just 2.5 percent—and enjoy good health. People say
10 even the prisons are quite comfortable!

Norway hasn't always been a rich country. Just last century, Norwegians were emigrating to the USA in the thousands in search of a better life. The rise in oil prices in the 1970s changed all that (Norway has a lot of oil). But it isn't only
15 Norway's huge oil reserves that account for its success—other less successful economies have even greater resources. It is also due to the Norwegians' strong work ethic. Norwegians are always near the top in global surveys of worker productivity rates.

20 In Oslo, don't expect to see Dubai-style skyscrapers and rows of Ferraris and Porsches. Norway may be rich, but it is modest. In fact, the people of Norway are trying to redefine wealth to mean "having a balanced life." The government has passed laws that emphasize the
25 importance of family and time off, offering subsidized childcare, long vacations, and generous maternity and paternity leave.[1] It has even said that fathers must—by law—take time off to be with their children. It is one of the only countries to do so.

30 At the same time, the country is saving for the future. Every dollar earned from oil is put straight into what is now the world's biggest pension fund—worth over $200 billion. None of this money is spent on infrastructure projects—not even new schools and
35 hospitals. At a time when most other countries just borrow money to finance the pensions of their growing retired population, Norway is sitting pretty.[2]

[1] **leave** (n) /liːv/ time off from work
[2] **sitting pretty** (v) /ˌsɪtɪŋ ˈprɪti/ in a good situation

Grammar focus adverbs: *only, just, even*

▶ **FOCUS ADVERBS: *ONLY, JUST, EVEN***

only
1 **Only** Luxembourg and a couple of other countries are richer.

just
2 **Just** last century, Norwegians were emigrating to the USA.
3 Most other countries **just** borrow money to finance the pensions of their growing retired population.

even
4 People say **even** the prisons are quite comfortable!
5 This does**n't even** feel like a competition anymore!

For more information and practice, see page 178.

7 Look at the grammar box. Which of these statements (a, b, or c) is true of each of the three focus adverbs: *only, just,* and *even*?

  a The focus adverb comes directly after the word or phrase it is emphasizing.
  b The focus adverb comes directly before the word or phrase it is emphasizing.
  c When emphasizing a verb, the focus adverb comes directly after the main verb.

8 Work in pairs. Find and underline other examples of *only, just,* and *even* in the article. What word or phrase does each adverb focus on?

9 Work in pairs. Discuss the meaning of each sentence (1–6). Then match each one with the sentence that follows it (a–f).

  1 Only visitors think Norway is expensive. _e_
  2 Visitors think only Norway is expensive. _c_
  3 Among Scandinavian countries, I have visited Norway just once. _b_
  4 Among Scandinavian countries, I have visited just Norway. _d_
  5 Even fathers are given time off to be with their children. _a_
  6 Fathers are given time off to be with their children, even when the children are older. _f_

  a Of course, mothers are given a lot of time off, too.
  b I have visited the other countries several times.
  c However, all Scandinavian countries are expensive.
  d I haven't visited the other countries at all.
  e The locals themselves find it reasonable.
  f This is in addition to the time they are given off when the children are babies.

10 Put the focus adverbs in parentheses in the correct place in these sentences.

  1 No, thanks. I'm looking. (just)
  2 The most difficult problems have a solution. (even)
  3 I'm going to brush my teeth, then we can leave. (just)
  4 Don't worry. It's money. (only)
  5 He's always losing things. He lost his own wedding ring once. (even)
  6 It's a suggestion—you don't have to follow it. (only)
  7 It's the second time we've met. (only)

11 Pronunciation focus adverbs

a ▶ 105 Listen and check your answers to Exercise 10. Are the focus adverbs stressed?

b Work in pairs. Practice saying the sentences in Exercise 10 in the same way.

Speaking *myLife*

12 Work in pairs. Place a focus adverb (*only, just, even*) in the correct place in each sentence below. There is sometimes more than one possible answer. Discuss whether these facts are true of your country.

  1 Many people work long hours during the week, so they see their children on weekends.
  2 People with college degrees are finding it difficult to get jobs these days.
  3 For many people, a job is a way to make money, not something they particularly enjoy.
  4 The rich are a very small part of the population.
  5 The state's welfare program gives financial aid to the poor, but it meets their basic needs.

13 Work in pairs. Write two sentences about your country using focus adverbs. Choose from these topics:

  • the cost of living
  • work-life balance
  • retirement and pensions
  • transportation
  • employment

*The cost of living is high in our capital city. **Even** basic things like bread and milk are expensive.*

14 Work with another pair. Read your sentences from Exercise 13 to each other. Were your descriptions similar?

12b Get someone else to do it

Vocabulary services

1 Work in pairs. Match the words in box A with the words in box B to make as many services as you can.

A		B	
car	carpet	alterations	
child	clothing	cleaning	cutting
computer	dog	installation	care
furniture	hair	painting	planning
house	party	repair	restoration
shoe	window	walking	washing

2 Work in pairs. Discuss these questions about the services in Exercise 1.

1 Which of these things do people generally do themselves?
2 Which of these services might people pay someone else to do?
3 Which services do you think involve the greatest skill?

Listening

3 ▶ 106 Work in pairs. Listen to an interview with an economics professor. Discuss the questions.

1 Which services from Exercise 1 do the speakers mention?
2 Does the professor think people paying for these services is a good thing or a bad thing? Why?

4 ▶ 106 Work in pairs. Listen to the interview again. Discuss the following things.

1 why more people are paying for these services
2 the reaction of the interviewer to the story of the person who hired some help at Christmas
3 what the professor says about the people who provide these services

Wordbuilding *the* + adjective

> ▶ **WORDBUILDING** *the* + adjective
>
> We can use *the* + adjective to refer to a group of people.
> *the rich, the poor, the powerless*
>
> For more practice, see Workbook page 99.

5 Look at the wordbuilding box. Match the groups of people (a–c) with the expressions on the right.

a people who are over 70   ○   ○ the homeless
b people with no jobs   ○   ○ the elderly
c people without housing   ○   ○ the unemployed

Grammar causative *have* and *get*

> ▶ **CAUSATIVE HAVE and GET**
>
> **have/get + something + past participle**
> 1 *Nowadays, you can **have your car washed** inside and out by professional car washers for as little as $8.*
> 2 *I've even heard of people who **get their Christmas tree put up**.*
>
> **have + someone + base form of the verb**
> 3 *You don't have to be rich to **have a house cleaner clean** your home once a week.*
>
> **get + someone + infinitive**
> 4 *The idea of **getting someone to wash** your car was unthinkable.*
>
> For more information and practice, see page 178.

6 Look at the grammar box. In which sentence(s) (1–4) is:

a someone doing a job for you? _____
b the person doing the job not mentioned? _____
c the person who does the job always mentioned? _____

7 Look at track 106 of the audioscript on page 190. Underline other examples of each type of causative verb.

8 Complete the summary of a survey about paying for services. Use the correct form of the verbs in parentheses.

> We all have tasks that need to get ¹_____ (do) that we would rather not do ourselves. These days, an increasing number of Americans are outsourcing their chores. Nearly half of those surveyed have other people ²_____ (do) their gardening, and a third get someone ³_____ (help) with house cleaning. People are happy to pay for having the house ⁴_____ (clean) regularly, getting the lawn ⁵_____ (mow), and having a handyman ⁶_____ (fix) things that are broken. With online sites, almost any odd job can be outsourced for the right price. It costs around $25 per hour to have a personal assistant ⁷_____ (organize) your affairs, and up to $50 per hour to have children or pets ⁸_____ (look) after. It seems that more households have decided that it is worth spending some money to save time.

9 Look at these things (1–3) that an affluent couple gets other people to do for them. Complete the sentences with causative forms. Use the correct form of the verbs in parentheses.

1 When they had a party last month, someone organized everything for them.
They _____ everything for them. (get)
2 A personal trainer takes their children to the park to play soccer.
They _____ their children to the park to play soccer. (have)
3 A driver picks their children up from school every day.
They _____ from school every day. (have)

10 Look at the services in Exercise 1 again. Using the causative verbs *have* or *get*, write down:

• one thing that you usually get someone else to do.
• one thing that you would never get someone else to do.

Compare your sentences with a partner.

11 Pronunciation /ʃ/, /tʃ/, /ʒ/, and /dʒ/

a ▶ 107 Listen carefully to how the underlined letters are pronounced in the following words. Then practice saying them with a partner.

/ʃ/	/tʃ/	/ʒ/	/dʒ/
carwa<u>sh</u>	<u>ch</u>ores	deci<u>s</u>ion	chan<u>ge</u>
<u>sh</u>elves	ri<u>ch</u>er	gara<u>ge</u>	colle<u>ge</u>
<u>sh</u>opper	wat<u>ch</u>	plea<u>s</u>ure	fri<u>dge</u>

b ▶ 108 Work in pairs. Listen to these words. Discuss which of the four sounds /ʃ/, /tʃ/, /ʒ/, or /dʒ/ is in each word. Then practice saying them.

agent	arrange	cheese	choice
fashion	general	January	machine
sugar	television	usual	

Speaking *my* Life

12 The letters DIY stand for "do it yourself." Work in pairs. Match the verbs in box A with the nouns in box B to make as many jobs as you can. How many of these are DIY jobs?

A
assemble	clean
decorate	hang
install	fix
put up	tile

B
the roof	some shelves
a carpet	the kitchen
a picture	a bed frame
a faucet	

13 Work in pairs. Look at the apartment in the photo below. Make a list of all the things that you would need to get done before you could live in it. Then decide which things you would do yourself and which things you would get professional help to do. Explain your plans to another pair.

Unit 12 Money 145

12c Start-up

Reading

1 Work in pairs. Look at the photo on page 147 and answer these questions.

1. What kind of food do you think is sold from this truck?
2. Do you think businesses like this make a lot of money? Why or why not?
3. Do you go to these kinds of take-out food trucks? Why or why not?

2 Read the article and make brief notes on the following. Then compare your notes with a partner.

1. the basic business idea
2. the gap or opportunity in the market
3. advertising
4. why the business is popular

3 Look at the subheadings (A–F) below. Match each subheading with one of the paragraphs (1–6) in the article.

A Spreading the word ____
B Hard times can be good times ____
C Big business ____
D Making yourself attractive ____
E Small beginnings ____
F A social event ____

Vocabulary business words

4 Work in pairs. Find these words or phrases (a–g) related to business in the article. What do you think they mean? Check your answers on page 155.

a trend (paragraph 1)
b recession (paragraph 2)
c set up (paragraph 2)
d upscale (paragraph 3)
e passing fad (paragraph 3)
f buzz (paragraph 4)
g catchy (paragraph 5)

Critical thinking opinion words

5 Writers often use adjectives, adverbs, and adverbial phrases to give their opinion. Find these words or phrases in the article and discuss in pairs what the writer is saying about each situation.

1. Even more significantly (line 6)
   The writer thinks this is very important.
2. Strangely (line 12)
3. even (line 25)
4. impressive (line 43)
5. definitely (line 57)
6. And after all, (lines 59–60)

6 Work in pairs. Overall, how would you sum up the author's opinion of this business idea? Do you agree with him? Why or why not?

Speaking myLife

7 Work in small groups. Imagine that you have bought the old railway carriage in the photo below. Discussing each of these points, come up with a business idea for it.

- the service you will offer (e.g., restaurant, vacation accommodations, take-out food and drink, something else?)
- the location (e.g., in a town, the countryside, a beach, a sports venue?)
- the customers (a particular group or the general public?)
- the promotion of the idea (how will you attract customers?)

8 As a group, present your ideas to the class. At the end, vote on which you think is the best business plan.

146

START-UP

▶ 109

1 It started as a simple business idea. Two friends in Los Angeles thought it might be fun to mix Korean barbecue recipes with Mexican tacos and sell the take-out food from a van. That was in 2008, and the resulting tacos—what founder Roy Choi calls "Los Angeles on a plate"—became an instant success. Even more significantly, their Kogi BBQ food truck started a whole new trend in mobile cuisine.[1]

2 Food trucks and vans have been around for a long time. There are hot dog and hamburger vans selling cheap eats along roadsides and next to construction sites all over California. What Kogi BBQ food did was to bring higher quality food to consumers at a reasonable price. Strangely, the economic recession of 2008 was an excellent opportunity for this kind of business. Choi could set up a business at a fraction[2] of the cost of opening a new restaurant. He could also easily find staff from among the increased number of unemployed workers that had become available. At the same time, consumers—now less willing to spend their money in traditional restaurants—were happy to find that they could still go out and find good food at an affordable price.

3 Today, thousands of upscale food trucks are parked on city streets from San Francisco to Washington, D.C., selling everything from luxurious lobster rolls to handmade ice cream. What seemed at the time to be a passing fad is now a growing, $800-million annual industry. There has even been a Hollywood movie, *Chef*, about the phenomenon.

4 Choi is modest about his part in this revolution. "I picked up on the feeling that food was important," he writes, "not just a meal to fuel yourself to do something else." But it wasn't simply the idea to fuse[3] Korean and Mexican cuisine that brought in the customers. What really put Kogi on the map was its early use of social media. Initially, Kogi's small team didn't have much luck selling their food outside nightclubs on Sunset Boulevard. Then they started exploiting the growing power of social media. Kogi used Twitter to constantly update customers on its changing location. Little by little, a loyal group of plugged-in[4] young followers appeared, tracking Kogi, and they started to create a buzz around the brand. Within a few months, Kogi was attracting hundreds of customers—and serving up to 200 kilos of meat—at several stops every day. *Newsweek* called it "America's first viral eatery." Kogi BBQ now has an impressive 152,000 Twitter followers, four trucks, and a full catering operation.

5 Branding and a catchy name are very important: *Banh in the USA* (Vietnamese sandwiches), *Ragin' Cajun* (Creole food), and *Waff 'n' Roll* (waffles) are some good examples. The trucks themselves are brightly painted and covered with colorful stickers.

6 At 10 p.m. on a cold Saturday night, I join the line outside the Kogi BBQ truck. It's a long line, mostly of young people. Customers take photos of their tacos as they buy them and send the photos to their friends. One couple has driven two hours to be here, and they joke and chat with a local couple who are regulars. There is definitely an important social aspect to this. It may be take-out food, but it's a shared experience, and—from what I can see—a very happy one. And after all, isn't that what eating should be about?

[1] **cuisine** (n) /kwɪˈziːn/ a style of cooking
[2] **fraction** (n) /ˈfrækʃ(ə)n/ a small amount (of something)
[3] **fuse** (v) /fjuːz/ combine (often to make something new)
[4] **plugged-in** (adj) /ˈplʌɡd ɪn/ technologically connected

12d The bottom line

Real life negotiating

1 Work in pairs. Which of these things have you negotiated for? Are there any other things that you have negotiated for recently? Did you get the deal you hoped for?

- your salary
- a car or other expensive item
- who does the chores at home
- more time to finish a piece of work

2 Read this advice about negotiating. Do you agree with it? How does it relate to your own experience? Discuss with a partner.

"Never get emotionally involved in the thing you are negotiating for. If the other person sees how much you want something, you will be at a disadvantage."

3 ▶ 110 Listen to a woman who is trying to negotiate with a real estate agent for a lease (or contract) on a building. Work in pairs. Answer the questions.

1 What point do they have trouble agreeing on?
2 What does the woman suggest to get around this problem?
3 How does the negotiation end?
4 How important is it to each person to agree on this lease?

4 ▶ 110 Look at the expressions for negotiating. Listen again and complete these expressions with the words you hear.

> ▶ **NEGOTIATING**
>
> A key thing for us is ¹_____ the lease.
> I was hoping we could ² _____ down.
> If you look at it from our point of view, we're a ³_____ and …
> Let's face it, five years is a ⁴_____.
> Do you think your client would be willing to ⁵_____ a bit on that?
> I'm sure you'll appreciate that my client's ⁶_____ is …
> To tell you the truth, that's why the rent is ⁷_____.
> Isn't there some way around that?
> Not that I can think of.
> What did you have in mind?
> If I were in your shoes, I think I'd just ⁸_____.
> At the end of the day, it has to ⁹_____ for you.

5 Work in pairs. Look at the expressions for negotiating again. Which expressions are used for the following?

- to say what the important thing is
- to be direct and clear
- to talk about an obstacle to the agreement
- to ask the other person to see your side

6 Could each person have done better in the negotiation? If so, how? Discuss with your partner.

7 **Pronunciation** long vowel sounds

a ▶ 111 Listen to the long vowel sounds and repeat the words.

/eɪ/ del<u>ay</u>   t<u>a</u>ke   /əʊ/ l<u>ow</u>   neg<u>o</u>tiate
/iː/ m<u>e</u>dium   d<u>e</u>tailed   /uː/ incl<u>u</u>de   sh<u>oe</u>s
/aɪ/ f<u>i</u>nal   l<u>i</u>ne

b ▶ 112 Work in pairs. Listen to these phrases and underline the long vowel sound in each phrase. Then practice saying the phrases.

1 A key thing for us is …
2 I was hoping we could …
3 Let's face it, …
4 At the end of the day, …
5 What did you have in mind?
6 To tell you the truth, …

8 Work in pairs.

Student A: You are living in a foreign country for eight months and want to buy a car to use while you are there. You see a secondhand car advertised in the newspaper. It seems to be exactly what you are looking for. Look at the information on page 153.

Student B: You have a secondhand car that you want to sell. Look at the information on page 155.

Have a conversation to negotiate the sale of the car.

A: The car is great. It's exactly what I'm looking for.
B: That's good. You'd like to buy it then?
A: Well, ideally, yes, I would. But …

12e Get to the point

Writing a short report

1 Read this brief report about a training course that someone attended. Work in pairs and answer the questions.

1 What was the aim of the course? Was it successful?
2 What was unusual about the course?

> As requested, here is my feedback on the one-day public speaking course at the LeGard School in Paris.
>
> Overall, it was a great experience, although not at all what I had expected. The teachers all have a background in theater and acting. So rather than learning about how to structure a talk or use PowerPoint slides, we concentrated on various drama techniques: specifically, voice control, breathing, posture, and movement. Initially, I was very skeptical about this. However, as the day progressed, the value became clearer. We were asked to use the techniques in short role plays—a family argument, or a friend's dinner party. Normally, I would feel very embarrassed about acting or performing in front of other people, but I didn't; the techniques improved my confidence enormously. Consequently, I now feel much more ready to take on the challenge of public speaking.
>
> To sum up, I would strongly recommend this innovative course as an introduction to public speaking, although a follow-up course on how to write a speech might be necessary.

2 Read the report again and make brief notes about the following. Then compare your notes with a partner.

1 type of course
2 location
3 general impression
4 details of the course
5 positive points
6 what the course lacked
7 recommendation

3 Writing skill key phrases in report writing

a Underline words or phrases in the report with these meanings. (They are listed in the order that they appear in the report.)

1 Because I was asked to do this
2 When you look at the whole thing
3 To give precise details
4 At the beginning
5 As a result of this
6 My conclusion is that

b Complete these sentences. Use four of the words or phrases you underlined in the report.

1 _____ , I am sending you a price list for our courses, _____ the courses in report and letter writing.
2 The course is very expensive. _____ , I would not recommend it.
3 _____ , I thought it would be too difficult, but the teacher explained everything very carefully during the lesson.

4 Write a short report (150–180 words) giving feedback on a course you have taken. Include these points:

- the name and length of the course
- the number of participants
- the methods used
- the effectiveness of the course
- your recommendation

5 Exchange reports with a partner. Use these questions to check your partner's report.

- Does the report include all the points listed in Exercise 4?
- Does it use some of the key phrases for report writing?
- What is your overall impression of the course?

Unit 12 **Money** 149

12f The Farmery

Plants growing in an urban farm market in North Carolina, USA

Before you watch

1 Work in pairs. Look at the photo and the title of the video. What new business idea do you think is shown here?

2 Key vocabulary

a Work in pairs. Read the sentences (1–5). The words and phrases in **bold** are used in the video. Guess the meaning of the words and phrases.

1. We have a small **greenhouse** in the backyard where we grow tomatoes.
2. Supermarkets generally experience between five and ten percent **inventory loss** in fruit and vegetables.
3. The company is planning to **consolidate** its business activities at a new site in Arizona.
4. The grape **harvest** takes place every September and needs a lot of extra workers to complete.
5. We walked along the beach, collecting seashells and interesting colored **pebbles**.

b Write the words and phrases in **bold** in Exercise 2a next to their definitions (a–e).

a. the cutting and collecting of crops when they are fully grown or ripe _____
b. losing items of stock because they are damaged, wasted, or stolen _____
c. small round stones _____
d. a glass building in which plants or vegetables are grown _____
e. combine things in order to make them more effective or easier to deal with _____

While you watch

3 ▶ 12.1, 12.2 Watch Parts 1–2 of the video and check (✓) the things you see. Then work in pairs and compare your answers. Tell your partner what you think Ben Greene's business idea is and what makes it original.

- ☐ fields
- ☐ farm animals
- ☐ crops
- ☐ farm buildings
- ☐ a restaurant
- ☐ a greenhouse
- ☐ shipping containers
- ☐ mushrooms
- ☐ vegetable greens
- ☐ frogs

4 ▶ 12.1 Watch Part 1 of the video again. Complete the summary with the correct form of these verbs.

| consolidate | grow | hang | lose |
| transport | sell | use | |

Most food grown on farms has to be harvested, packed, and then ¹_____ to the shops. At every stage, you ²_____ some of the harvest. So Ben Greene's idea was to ³_____ this whole process into one site. At The Farmery, a structure made from shipping containers and greenhouse parts, Greene ⁴_____ the food within the building and then ⁵_____ it in an area at the bottom of the building. The plants grow on living walls that ⁶_____ off the outside of shipping containers. It's a very different method—Greene ⁷_____ systems where the plants grow in water. The Farmery focuses on mushrooms, herbs, and salad greens.

5 ▶ 12.2 Read the questions below. Watch Part 2 of the video again and make notes. Then discuss the questions with a partner.

1. What does Ben Greene say he is giving customers with this new way of buying food?
2. How would he like to expand his business?
3. What are the two markets he has identified for food grown in this way?
4. How does Ben Greene hope people will look at food after experiencing The Farmery?
5. Above all, how does he want people to feel when they have visited The Farmery?

After you watch

6 Vocabulary in context

a ▶ 12.3 Watch the clips from the video. Choose the correct meaning of the words and phrases.

b Complete these sentences in your own words. Then share your sentences with a partner.

1. I want to pursue a career in … because …
2. … is a very complex subject.
3. I'm on a mission to …

7 Work in pairs. What do you think of The Farmery? Do you think it would be a good idea in your area? Why or why not?

8 Work in small groups. Below is a list of products that could be made and sold at the same site. Choose one and decide how to make buying it an interesting experience for customers. Present your ideas to the class. Which was the best idea?

- clothes or shoes
- chocolate
- bread or cakes
- furniture

Unit 12 **Money** 151

UNIT 12 REVIEW AND MEMORY BOOSTER

Grammar

1 Put the words in parentheses in the correct order to complete the text.

The internet has changed the economy in more ways ¹_____ (how / just / than) we shop. It has also encouraged us to share more, such as by giving free online advice on how to do things. Whereas before we might have gone straight to a garage ²_____ (to / repaired / our car / have), now we look online first to see if someone can tell us how to fix it. ³_____ (set up / some communities / have / even) internet groups where neighbors lend each other things. If you have a hole in your roof, in the past you would ⁴_____ (paid / to / fix / someone / have) it. But now, you might ask a neighbor if you could borrow a ladder, or you ⁵_____ (even / ask / might / for) their help. We are all winners in this sharing economy because ⁶_____ (help / to / other people / getting) us saves money and builds social connections.

2 Read the text above again. According to the author, what are the benefits of the sharing economy brought about by the internet?

3 Work in pairs. Tell your partner about a) two jobs you would only get someone else to do, and b) something you have just had done.

I CAN
use focus adverbs to add emphasis
use causative *have* and *get*

Vocabulary

4 Match each verb (1–3) with a suitable noun to make phrases. Which of these jobs could you do yourself? Which would you have someone do for you? Tell a partner.

1 assemble   ○   ○ a leaky faucet
2 put up   ○   ○ a bed frame
3 fix   ○   ○ some shelves

5 Complete the definitions (1–4) with four of these words.

| earnings | invest | lend | life |
| living | loan | owe | salary |

1 If you have an obligation to pay someone, you _____ them money.
2 Your _____ is the money that you receive from your work or investments.
3 Your quality of _____ refers to your level of health, well-being, and happiness.
4 A(n) _____ is money you borrow to buy something.

6 **>> MB** Work in pairs. Write definitions for these words and phrases: *debt, the income gap, standard of living*.

I CAN
talk about money and the economy

Real life

7 Complete the conversation by matching each of the travel agent's statements (1–4) with the customer's responses (a–d).

1 **TA:** So, how does our proposal look? We've suggested four different hotels in different cities. ___
2 **TA:** Well, you asked for top hotels, and I'm sure you'll appreciate that they aren't cheap. ___
3 **TA:** Exactly. This is a once-in-a-lifetime trip. ___
4 **TA:** I'm not sure about that, but I can check if you like. ___

a **C:** I understand that. Nice hotels are a key thing for us, because it is our honeymoon, at the end of the day.
b **C:** If you could, that would be great. I'm sure there must be a way around this.
c **C:** It looks amazing, but to tell you the truth, it's more money than we were hoping to spend.
d **C:** Would it be cheaper if we stayed in just one hotel for the whole two weeks?

8 **>> MB** Work in pairs. Act out the conversation in Exercise 7. Add one more exchange between the travel agent and the customer to finish the negotiation.

I CAN
negotiate a proposal

UNIT 10b Exercise 13, page 121
Pair A

		¹c					
	²l			³d		⁴	⁵a
⁶a		o		o			c
⁷v		s		n			t
e		e		⁸t			i
r							v
a		⁹b		¹⁰s			e
¹¹g	¹²o		r		u			l
¹³m	e	n		i		n		¹⁴e	y
a		c		c		n		a	
n		e		¹⁵k		y		r	

UNIT 12d Exercise 8, page 148
Student A

You want to buy this car. It is a seven-year-old VW Golf, and the advertised price is $3,000. It is in good condition but has done a lot of miles (100,000). You would like to get it for less, if you can. The problem is you have been looking for a long time and want to get a car quickly so that you can drive to work every day.

UNIT 11c Exercise 9, page 134

Quiz

Circle A, B, or C to complete each sentence below so that it is true for you. Then look at the key on page 155 to find out what type of learner you are. Work in pairs and discuss if you agree with this.

1 WHEN I STUDY GRAMMAR, I LEARN BEST BY …
   A reading clear rules   B writing down examples
   C putting it into practice in conversation

2 IN LESSONS, I PREFER …
   A discussing   B looking at pictures, maps, diagrams, or videos
   C doing something practical

3 I REMEMBER NEW VOCABULARY BEST WHEN IT IS ACCOMPANIED BY …
   A a clear definition   B an image   C a demonstration

4 IF I AM DISTRACTED IN CLASS, I USUALLY …
   A hum or sing to myself   B make little drawings in my book
   C play with a pen or pencil

5 WHEN LEARNING A NEW SKILL, I PREFER …
   A someone to explain it to me   B someone to demonstrate it
   C just to get on with it myself

6 WHEN I'M NOT SURE HOW TO SPELL A WORD, I …
   A say the word aloud to myself   B try to visualize it in my mind
   C write down different versions

7 I PREFER TO READ STORIES WITH LOTS OF …
   A dialog   B descriptive passages   C action or adventure

8 I PROBABLY LEARN MOST WHEN I'M …
   A listening to other people speak English
   B watching an English movie or documentary
   C trying to use English myself

UNIT 11c Exercise 9, page 134

Answers to quiz

Mostly A's—This means you have an auditory learning style. In other words, you remember best when you hear things.

Mostly B's—This means you have a visual learning style. In other words, you remember best when you see things.

Mostly C's—This means you have a kinesthetic learning style. In other words, you remember best when you do things or when things are acted out.

UNIT 12c Exercise 4, page 146

Vocabulary—business words

a trend (n) = a fashion or direction
b recession (n) = a period of economic decline
c set up (v) = establish
d upscale (adj) = high quality and more expensive
e passing (adj) fad (n) = something that is popular for only a short time
f buzz (n) = excitement and activity
g catchy (adj) = easy to remember

UNIT 12d Exercise 8, page 148

Student B

You want to sell this car. It is a seven-year-old VW Golf, and the advertised price is $3,000. It is in good condition but has done a lot of miles (100,000). You would like to get as close to the asking price as possible. However, it has been advertised for two months, and you would like to sell it soon.

UNIT 10b Exercise 13, page 121

Pair B

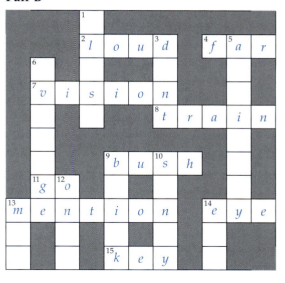

Across/Down entries filled in:
2. loud
4. far
7. vision
8. train
9. bush
13. mention
14. eye
15. key
11. g
12. o

GRAMMAR SUMMARY UNIT 7

Zero and first conditionals

Zero conditional

We use the zero conditional to talk about facts or things that are generally true. The form is:
If + simple present + simple present
If you **punish** a child, you **need** to tell them why.

We can also use *when* instead of *if*. The meaning is the same.
When children **misbehave**, it's often because they **want** attention. (= ***If*** children **misbehave**, …)

First conditional

We use the first conditional to talk about a particular possible future event or situation. The form is:
If + simple present + *will/won't* + base verb
If he **does** well in high school, he**'ll get** into a good college.

We can put the clause with *if* first, or we can put the main clause first. When the *if*-clause comes first, we add a comma before the main clause. When the *if*-clause comes second, we don't need a comma.
They**'ll cancel** the concert ***if*** it **rains**.

Unless, as long as

We can use *unless* or *as long as* in place of *if* in conditional sentences. We use *unless* to say *if not*.
You **won't pass** your exam **unless** you **work** hard.
(= If you don't work hard, you won't pass your exam.)

We use *as long as* to say "if and only if."
You can play in the park **as long as** you don't get your clothes dirty.

We never use a future form after *if*, *unless*, or *as long as*.
~~If the weather will be nice this weekend, we'll go to the beach.~~
If the weather **is** nice this weekend, we'll go to the beach.

▶ **Exercises 1 and 2**

Time linkers

Like *if*, *unless*, and *as long as*, we don't use a future form after the time linkers **when**, **as soon as**, **before**, **after**, **while**, or **until**. We use a present tense, even when we're referring to the future.
I'll call you **when** I**'m getting** ready to leave.
I'll pick you up **as soon as** I **finish** work.
We can eat **before** we **go** out.
School starts a day **after** we **get** back from vacation.
You can make dinner **while** I**'m taking** a shower.
You can't go out **until** you **finish** your homework.

▶ **Exercise 3**

usually, used to, would, be used to, and *get used to*

usually + simple present

We use *usually* + simple present to talk about a habit or action that happens regularly or is generally true.
I **usually eat** a sandwich for lunch.

used to and would + base form of the verb

We use *used to* + base verb to talk about a repeated past action, habit, or situation. It is sometimes used in contrast with a present situation.
I **used to eat** unhealthily, but I'm more careful now. (= repeated past action/habit)
My parents **used to own** a restaurant. (= past situation)

The negative is *didn't use to*. We ask questions with *Did you use to …?*
I **didn't use to like** vegetables when I was a child.
Did you **use to walk** to school or **catch** the bus?

We use *would* + base verb to talk about a repeated action or habit in the past. We normally say when the action/habit happened.
I remember when I was little, my dad **would make** pizza every Saturday night.

We don't use *would* to talk about a state or situation in the past. We use *used to* or simple past.

▶ **Exercise 4**

be/get used to + noun or -ing

We use *be used to* + noun or *-ing* to say that something isn't strange or difficult.
I start work at 7 a.m. every morning, so I**'m used to getting up** early.
I've lived in Minnesota for a long time, so I**'m used to the cold winters.**

We can also use this form in the past or the negative.
It was hard to go on a diet because I **wasn't used to eating** healthily. (= It was difficult/strange for me.)

We use *get used to* + noun or *-ing* when we are learning to adapt to something difficult or unfamiliar, and it is becoming normal.
I'm **getting used to cooking** for myself now that I live on my own.
Driving a car was scary at first, but I soon **got used to it**.

Note that we always use the *-ing* form or a noun after *be/get used to*, not the base verb.

▶ **Exercises 5 and 6**

Exercises

1 Correct the mistake in each conditional sentence.
1. If you won't buy a ticket before you go, you won't get a seat at the concert.
2. If I was late to my lesson, the teacher gets angry.
3. It's dangerous to drive when it will snow hard.
4. You'll do better in your exams, if you study hard.
5. The soccer match will being canceled if the weather is bad.

2 Rewrite the sentences with *unless* or *as long as.*
1. You won't get the job if you don't practice for your interview. (unless)
   _____
2. You can borrow my car, but only if you promise to be careful. (as long as)
   _____
3. You can borrow my umbrella only if you remember to return it. (as long as)
   _____
4. If you don't practice every day, you won't get better at playing the piano. (unless)
   _____

3 Match the sentence beginnings (1–5) with the endings (a–e). Then complete the sentences with the correct form of the verbs in parentheses.
1. Please call me
2. I'll wait with you at the station
3. While you're cleaning the house,
4. You'll never be able to run the marathon
5. I always get a headache

a. until your train _____ (arrive). ____
b. when I _____ (not drink) enough water. ____
c. I _____ (take) the dog out for a walk. ____
d. unless you _____ (start) training. ____
e. as soon as you ___get___ (get) this message. _1_

4 Rewrite the sentences (1–5) with *used to* or *would*.
1. When I was living with my parents, I cooked with my mom a lot. (would)
   _____
2. We lived downtown until two years ago. (used to)
   _____
3. When they were little, their grandma took them to the movies once a month. (would)
   _____
4. Did you have a best friend at school? (used to)
   _____
5. For years, I visited my aunt in Vancouver every summer. (would)
   _____

5 Rewrite the sentences (1–4) with the correct form of *be/get used to + -ing*.
1. It's normal for me to make speeches in front of a lot of people.
   I _____ in front of a lot of people.
2. It's starting to feel normal for me to commute to work every day.
   I _____ to work every day.
3. It wasn't normal for him to eat out so often.
   He _____ out so often.
4. It was hard, but I learned to live on my own.
   It was hard, but I _____ on my own

6 Complete the text with these verbs. Use the correct form of *used to* + base verb or *be/get used to + -ing*. Note they can be affirmative or negative.

| do | dream | live | see | take |

When I was a kid, I always ¹_____ of living abroad. So I was really happy when I moved to Hong Kong three years ago for work. When I first arrived, it was a bit of a culture shock for me. I'm from a small town, so I ²_____ so many tall buildings and skyscrapers. I also had to ³_____ in a very small apartment and paying a lot of rent. In my own country, I lived a five-minute walk from my office. But I ⁴_____ the train to work here—the trains are very punctual and frequent. Living abroad can be difficult, but I think everyone can do it—you soon ⁵_____ things in a different way.

Grammar Summary 169

GRAMMAR SUMMARY UNIT 8

Second, third, and mixed conditionals

Second and third conditionals

We use the second conditional to describe a situation in the present or future. It suggests that the situation and result are unreal or imagined. The form is: *if* + simple past, *would* + base verb.

    If I **had** a lot of money, I'**d travel** around the world. (+)
    If the traffic **weren't** so bad, I **wouldn't mind driving**. (–)
    Would you **be** able to come to the wedding **if we changed** the date? (?)

We use the third conditional to describe an unreal or imagined situation and result in the past. The form is: *if* + past perfect, *would have* + past participle.

    If I'**d worked** harder at school, I **would have become** a doctor. (+)
    If I **hadn't had** such an inspiring teacher, I **wouldn't have gone** to college. (–)
    If you **had been** able to travel more, where **would** you **have visited**? (?)

As with first conditionals, we can put the clause with *if* first, or we can put the main clause first. When the *if*-clause comes first, we add a comma before the main clause. When the *if*-clause comes second, we don't need a comma.

    I **would have applied** for the job if the pay **had been** better.

▶ Exercise 1

Mixed conditionals

We can also use a combination of second and third conditionals. We use a mixed second and third conditional to describe an unreal situation in the present with an imagined result in the past.

    If I **had** more money, I'**d have booked** a better hotel.

We use a mixed third and second conditional to describe an unreal situation in the past with an imagined result in the present.

    If you'**d gone** to bed earlier, you **wouldn't be** so tired now.

We can use *were* instead of *was* after *if* to talk about an unreal/imagined present or future situation. When we do this, it sounds more formal.

    If I **were** wealthy, I **would have bought** the house.

The phrase "if I were you" is fixed. We don't normally say "if I was you," even in informal situations.

▶ Exercises 2 and 3

wish and *if only*

Form and use

We use *wish* and *if only* to talk about unreal or imagined situations that we would like to be true or to come true. The basic meaning of *wish* and *if only* is the same, but *if only* is stronger.

We use *wish* / *if only* + past tense to talk about a situation in the present.

    I **wish** it **was** summer. I'm tired of this cold weather!

We use *wish* / *if only* + *could* + base verb to talk about an ability or possibility we would like to have in the present.

    If only I **could play** a musical instrument. It would be a lot of fun.
    I **wish** we **could stay** for lunch. But we've got other plans.

As with conditionals, we can also use *were* instead of *was*. It sounds more formal.

    I **wish** Martin **weren't** always so busy.

▶ Exercise 4

We use *wish* / *if only* + past perfect to talk about a situation in the past that we want to be different.

    If only our plane **had arrived** on time. Now we're stuck here in the airport!

We use *wish* / *if only* + someone + *would* + base verb to talk about a situation in the present that we want somebody else to act to change. We often use this structure when we are dissatisfied with the situation or when we are complaining.

    I **wish** you **wouldn't complain** so much.
    I **wish** Sarah **would listen** to other people more.

We sometimes use *wish* / *if only* + *would* + base verb with things, as well as people.

    I **wish** it **would stop** raining.
    I **wish** my phone **wouldn't** always **stop** working just when I need it!

We don't normally use *wish* to talk about the future. We use *hope* instead.

    We **hope** that we'll see you again soon.
    (not ~~We **wish** that we'll see you again soon.~~)

▶ Exercises 5 and 6

Exercises

1 Complete the sentences with the verbs in parentheses to make second or third conditionals. Use the context to help you decide which form to use.

1 I'm so busy at the moment. If I _____ (have) more time, I _____ (take) up a new hobby.
2 She felt cold when she left the house that morning. She _____ (wear) a warmer coat if she _____ (know) how cold it was.
3 He can't afford to go on vacation this summer. He _____ (go) to Thailand if he _____ (have) enough money.
4 You look very pale these days. If you _____ (spend) more time outside, you _____ (not be) so pale.
5 He failed his driving test. He _____ (do) better if he _____ (practice) more.

2 Match the sentence beginnings (1–6) with the endings (a–f) to make mixed conditionals. Then decide whether each sentence describes:

i an unreal situation in the past with an imagined result in the present.
ii an unreal situation in the present with an imagined result in the past.

1 If public transportation was more efficient,
2 If you hadn't decided to become a doctor,
3 They would have bought a bigger house
4 He wouldn't feel so hungry now
5 We'd be able to get into our car
6 If she liked playing soccer,

a what job would you do instead? _____
b if they had more money. _____
c if you hadn't lost the keys! _____
d I would have come here by bus. _____
e she would have joined our team. _____
f if he'd eaten more in the morning. _____

3 Complete the sentences (1–5) to make mixed conditionals, using the verbs in parentheses.

1 If I _____ (not leave) so late, I _____ (not be) in such a rush now.
2 He _____ (come) to the theater with us tomorrow if he _____ already _____ (not / see) the play.
3 If they _____ (live) closer to me, I _____ (go) to their party.
4 My life _____ (be) very different now if I _____ (not meet) my husband all those years ago.
5 If she _____ (not be) so busy at the moment, she _____ (help) us move last weekend.

4 Complete the sentences with the correct form of the verbs in parentheses.

1 It's cold today. I wish it _____ (be) warmer!
2 I wish I _____ (not have to) work on the weekend.
3 If only he _____ (live) closer to me.
4 I wish I _____ (can) play the guitar.
5 The bus is so crowded. If only there _____ (not be) so many people!

5 Circle the correct options to complete the conversation.

A: How did your exams go?
B: OK, I hope. I just wish ¹ *I'd had / I had* more time to study before the exams! But it's difficult to study and work at the same time.
A: Yes, that must be tiring! What do you do?
B: I work in a restaurant. I enjoy it, but I just wish I ² *wouldn't have to / didn't have to* work on the weekends. I sometimes wish that I ³ *had taken / took* a year off before coming to college to work and save some money.
A: But do you like your major? You're studying biology, aren't you?
B: Yes, that's right. It's good, but there are very few women in my year. I often wish there ⁴ *were / had been* more of us.
A: Yes, I'm sure. So, where are you going now?
B: I'm going home. I need to clean the house. I love my roommates, but I wish they ⁵ *hadn't made / wouldn't make* so much mess all the time!

6 Complete each sentence (1–4) with the correct form of one of these verbs. Note they can be affirmative or negative.

learn	leave	stop	shout

1 If only that dog _____ barking at night. He keeps waking me up!
2 I wish I _____ how to drive a car when I was younger.
3 He wishes his boss _____ at him so often.
4 Someone stole my bag from my car last night. If only I _____ it there overnight.

Grammar Summary

GRAMMAR SUMMARY UNIT 9

Verb patterns with reporting verbs

Form and use
We can use different verbs to report speech and thoughts. The patterns we use change, depending on the verb.

Verb + infinitive
We use the infinitive after *agree, offer, promise, refuse, swear,* and *threaten.*
> Jack **offered to take** a photograph of me.
> I **refused to leave** the building.
> He **swore to tell** the truth.

Verb + object + infinitive
We use object + infinitive after *advise, ask, beg, convince, encourage, invite, persuade, recommend, urge,* and *warn.*
> Julia **asked me to drive** her to the airport.
> I don't like concerts, but Max **convinced me to come**.

Verb + -ing
We use *-ing* after *admit, deny, recommend,* and *suggest.*
> They **denied taking** the money.
> Luke **suggested going** to the park.

Verb + preposition + -ing
We use *-ing* after verb + preposition combinations, e.g., *apologize for, complain about, confess to, insist on,* and *object to.*
> You should **apologize for being** so rude.
> Sara **insisted on eating** at home.

Verb + object + preposition + -ing
With some other verb + preposition combinations, we place an object between the verb and preposition, e.g., *accuse … of, blame … for, criticize … for, congratulate … on, praise … for, thank … for.*
> Anna always **accuses me of being** lazy.
> Lars **praised his son for winning** the competition.

Note that when we use reporting verbs, we often have to make changes to pronouns, time expressions, etc.
> "**You**'ve broken **my** phone!" → She blamed **me** for breaking **her** phone.
> "I'll be back **tomorrow**." → She promised to be back **the next day**.

Some reporting verbs can also be followed by *that* + clause. When we use a reporting verb + *that*, we often make a change to the tense.
> "We'**ll** be late." → I warned you **that** we **would** be late.

▶ Exercises 1, 2, and 3

Passive reporting verbs

Form and use
We sometimes use passive verbs to report feelings, beliefs, opinions, and rumors, especially in journalism or other formal contexts. We often do this when we don't know or don't want to say who made the statement.

There are two patterns:

- *it* + passive verb + *that* + subject
> **It is thought that** the prime minister will make an important announcement later today.

- subject + passive verb + infinitive
> A man aged 95 **is reported to be** a lottery winner for the third time.

To report a past action in the present perfect or simple past with the second pattern, we use a perfect infinitive (an infinitive form with *have* + past participle).
> Three people are said **to have been rescued** from a house fire.

To report an action in the future or in progress now with the second pattern, we use a continuous infinitive (an infinitive form with *be* + *-ing*).
> The company is said **to be looking** for a new manager.

We commonly use the following verbs with both patterns: *believe, confirm, expect, know, report, say, think,* and *understand.*
> A 22-year-old man **is known to have stopped** the global spread of the computer virus.
> **It is known that** a 22-year-old man stopped the global spread of the computer virus.

▶ Exercises 4, 5, and 6

Exercises

1 Match the sentence beginnings (1–5) with the endings (a–e).

1. He asked me
2. She admitted
3. They complained about
4. Do you promise
5. I congratulated her on

a. having to work on the weekend. 3 ✓
b. to help him, but I'm too busy. 1 ✓
c. passing her driving test. 5 ✓
d. not to be late to the meeting? 4 ✓
e. taking the money from my wallet. 2 ✓

2 Complete the second sentence in each item (1–4) so it has the same meaning as the first sentence. Use the verb in **bold**.

1. She said it was a good idea to visit the museum.
   recommend
   She _recommended me to visit_ the museum. ✓

2. "I'm going to leave without you if you don't hurry up."
   threaten
   He _threatened me to leave_ without me if I didn't hurry up. ✓

3. She said sorry because she was late.
   apologize
   She _apologized for being_ late. ✓

4. I told her that she should see a doctor.
   advise
   I _advised her to see_ a doctor. ✓

3 Complete the text with the correct form of these verbs.

do	recycle	introduce
start	stop	watch

The town of Modbury in Devon, England, was the first town in Europe to stop using plastic bags. The story started in 2007 after Rebecca Hosking, a wildlife camerawoman, invited local shop owners ¹ _to watch_ ✓ a documentary about the damage plastic bags cause to the environment. The owners were so shocked that they promised ² _to stop_ ✓ giving plastic bags to customers. They agreed ³ _to recycle_ all their bags and encouraged their customers ⁴ _to do_ ✓ the same. Soon, Modbury became plastic bag-free, and not long after, the UK government decided to ⁵ _introduce_ a charge for all plastic bags in supermarkets. The residents have praised Rebecca Hosking for ⁶ _starting_ ✓ this revolution, which has generated interest around the world.

4 Correct the mistake in each sentence.

1. It is believe that two prisoners have escaped.
2. The director is expected resign.
3. The photos are thought to been taken in 1990.
4. She is said to write a book at the moment.

5 Circle the correct options to complete the sentences.

1. The team is expected *to arrive / to have arrived* later today.
2. The man is said *to be finding / to have found* a priceless painting in his attic.
3. More people than ever are believed *to have lived / to be living* with their parents because they cannot afford to buy a home.
4. Eating more vegetables and fruit is known *to be / to being* good for your health.
5. The accident is thought *to have been caused / to be causing* by bad weather.

6 Rewrite the underlined phrases with passive reporting structures. Use the prompts and verbs below (1–4).

A: Have you seen that Main Street is closed? I wonder what's happening.
B: It's for the carnival. It's going to be a big event this year. Apparently, ¹the local council has spent a lot of money on it.
A: Oh, of course. Did you go last year?
B: No, I didn't. But I heard that ²it was really crowded and badly organized. But someone told me that this year, ³the organizers have made some improvements. And there are going to be more police on the streets.
A: That's good.
B: Should we go and take a look? I'm sure I heard somewhere that ⁴some stalls are offering free food on the first day.
A: Free food? Let's go!

1. The local council _____ (believe).
2. Last year's carnival _____ (say).
3. It _____ (think).
4. Some stalls _____ (expect).

Grammar Summary 173

GRAMMAR SUMMARY UNIT 10

Articles: *a/an*, *the*, or zero article?

We use the **indefinite article** (*a/an*) with a singular countable noun. We use it:

- to talk about a non-specific person or thing.
  *I need to buy **a** new car.*

- to say a person or thing is one of many.
  *I think Tereshkova is **a** very interesting astronaut.*

- when we first mention something.
  *One evening, **a** man and **a** woman rang my doorbell.*

- in the structure *as + a(n) + noun*.
  *As **a** child, she loved basketball.*

We also use the indefinite article: to say what somebody does (e.g., *He's a student*); or to talk about frequency (e.g., *twice a month*).

We use the **definite article** (*the*) with a singular or plural countable noun or an uncountable noun. We use it:

- to talk about a specific person/people or thing(s).
  ***The** prime minister gave a speech in Paris today.*

- when we refer back to a person/people or thing(s) already mentioned.
  *One evening, a man and a woman rang my doorbell. **The** man introduced himself.*

- before a superlative adjective.
  *That's **the** best movie I've seen this year.*

We also use the definite article: when there is only one of something (e.g., *the moon*); with some countries (e.g., *the US*); with an organization (e.g., *the navy*); with some time periods (e.g., *the 1930s*); with inventions (e.g., *the saxophone*); to talk about parts of a country/area (e.g., *the north of Germany*); with places in a town/city (e.g., *the stores*); with the names of oceans and rivers (e.g., *the Nile*).

We use the **zero article (no article)** with a plural countable noun or an uncountable noun. We use it:

- with uncountable or plural nouns to talk about people or things in a general way.
  *I think **nurses** should be paid more.*

- before certain generally familiar places (school, work, hospital, college).
  *My older brother is studying medicine at **college**.*

We also use the zero article: with the names of most countries; with subjects of study (e.g., *math*); with days and months; with meals (e.g., *breakfast*); in phrases like *this month, last week, next year*; with the names of sports; with the names of lakes; in many phrases with "home" (e.g., *go home*).

▶ Exercises 1, 2, and 3

Relative clauses

We use **defining relative clauses** to give essential information in order to identify someone or something. The choice of relative pronoun depends on the type of noun.

- For things, we use *that*.
  *Is this the book **that** you told me about?*

- For people, we use *who*.
  *I know three people **who** study at this college.*

- For possession, we use *whose*.
  *I know someone **whose** mother was a famous actor.*

Note that *whose* can also be used for things.

We can use *what* before a subject and verb to say "the thing(s) that."
  *That's exactly **what** I wanted.*

We can leave out *that* and *who* when they are the object of the verb in the relative clause, but not when they are the subject.
  *I enjoyed the movie (**that**) you recommended.*
  *That's the scientist **who** won the Nobel Prize.*

When we form relative clauses with a preposition, we normally put the preposition at the end of the clause, except in very formal usage. Note that *who* becomes *whom* after a preposition.
  *I'm the person (**who**) you wrote **to**.*
  *I am the person **to whom** you wrote.* (formal)

We also make relative clauses with the relative adverbs *where* and *when*. *Where* means the same as (the more formal) *in which*.
  *This is the restaurant **where** I had my birthday dinner.*

▶ Exercises 4 and 5

Non-defining relative clauses contain extra, non-essential information. We can understand which thing, person, place, etc., is being mentioned without the relative clause.
  *My brother, **who lives in New York**, is coming to visit next month.* (It's clear as I only have one brother.)

We use *who* for people and *which* for things. We never use *that* in non-defining clauses. Note that we can use *whose* in both defining and non-defining clauses.

In non-defining relative clauses, we use a comma before the relative clause. If the clause is in the middle of the sentence, we also put a comma at the end of it.

Some non-defining clauses refer to the whole of the main clause. We often use clauses like this to give opinions or to make a comment.
  *They've canceled the concert, **which is disappointing**.*

▶ Exercise 6

Exercises

1 Correct the mistake in each sentence.

1. She hasn't found the job yet.
2. I'd like to live in the Paris.
3. As an doctor, she really understands how important your diet is.
4. That's probably worst movie I've ever seen.

2 Read the conversation. Add seven missing articles in the correct places.

A: Thanks for inviting me to your party. Your friends are all so nice!
B: Thanks for coming! Did you manage to speak to everyone?
A: Yes, I think so. I had a long conversation about gardening with a man … I can't remember his name … Oh, it's the man over there.
B: That's Thomas—he's my neighbor. And he does have an amazing garden.
A: Yes, he showed me a picture of it on his phone.
B: And did he tell you about the Everest?
A: Everest? No, what about it?
B: Well, Thomas is actually a famous mountaineer! He's climbed mountains all over the world, including the Everest!
A: Wow! That's amazing! Does he still go climbing?
B: Yes, he does. And he takes tour groups up mountains three or four times a year. He also gives talks about it all around the world.

3 Complete the text with *the*, *a*, or zero article (–).

It seemed like another normal flight for Captain Chesley Sullenberger and Jeffrey Skiles, flying from New York City to North Carolina in ¹ **the** USA, on ² _____ January 15, 2009. But three minutes after take-off, ³ **the** plane hit a flock of geese. The geese damaged both engines, which stopped working. ⁴ **The** pilots had to make a quick decision about where to make the emergency landing. Sullenberger realized they didn't have time to go back to the airport, so he decided to land the plane on ⁵ **the** Hudson River. Incredibly, Captain Sullenberger landed the aircraft safely. Within minutes, boats came to help, and all the passengers and crew were rescued. Sullenberger became ⁶ **a** hero, famous all over the world. He was later hired as ⁷ **a** safety expert, and thanks to him, ⁸ _____ new measures for airline safety have been introduced. In 2016, ⁹ **a** movie about his life was made, starring Tom Hanks.

4a Complete the sentences with appropriate relative pronouns or adverbs.

1. ✓ This is the laptop ~~that / which~~ I bought last week.
2. ✓ Isn't this the restaurant **where** we had a really bad meal a few years ago?
3. ✓ They thanked the police officers **who** caught the criminal.
4. The students weren't told ~~that~~ **what** would be on the exam.
5. We stayed in a hotel ~~whose~~ **which/that** has a huge swimming pool.
6. ✓ Is that your friend **whose** party we went to last month?

4b Work in pairs. In which of the sentences in Exercise 4a can the relative pronoun be omitted?

1, 2

5 Rewrite the sentences so they are more informal. Leave out the relative pronoun when possible.

1. That's the woman with whom I played tennis last week.
   That's the woman ~~who~~ I played ~~with~~ tennis last week?
2. Are you the person to whom I spoke when I called earlier?
   Are you the person ~~who~~ I spoke ~~to~~ when I called earlier?
3. This is the kind of music to which I always listen when I'm driving.
   This is the kind of music that I always listen ~~to~~ when I'm driving.

6 Combine the sentences in each item (1–4) to make non-defining relative clauses.

1. We live in Salto. It's in the northwest of Uruguay.
   _____
   _____

2. My friend Louis has just started a new job. He lives in Vermont.
   _____
   _____

3. The museum was closed when we went there. That was disappointing.
   _____
   _____

4. DDT Bank has serious financial problems. It employs over 20,000 people.
   _____
   _____

Grammar Summary 175

GRAMMAR SUMMARY UNIT 11

could, was able to, managed to, and *succeeded in*

We use *could, was able to, managed to,* and *succeeded in* to talk about ability and possibility in the past.

General ability

We use *could* and *couldn't* + base verb to describe a general ability to do something in the past.
> Jacky **could run** really fast when she was a teenager.
> I **couldn't speak** French until I went to study in Paris.

We also use *was/were able to* for the same meaning. It is more formal than *could/couldn't*.
> Jacky **was able to run** really fast when she was a teenager.
> I **wasn't able to speak** French until I went to study in Paris.

Success/failure in a specific task

We cannot use *could* to talk about success in a specific task in the past. We use *was/were able + to* + base verb, *managed + to* + base verb, or *succeeded in + -ing* instead.
> I **was able to get / managed to get / succeeded in getting** tickets for the concert! I bought the last three tickets available.

We normally use *managed to* + base verb and *succeeded in + -ing* when the task was difficult. We tend to use *succeeded in* (and *was/were able to*) in more formal contexts.

In informal contexts, we often use the simple past to talk about success in a specific task in the past, especially if we don't want to suggest it was difficult.
> I **got** tickets for the concert. There were plenty left.

Note that we DO use *couldn't* to describe failure in a specific task in the past.
> We **couldn't find** a karate class, so we decided to take judo instead.

Possibility/opportunity in the past

We also use *could* and *was/were able to* to say we had a possibility or opportunity to do something in the past.
> I really loved the class because we **could / were able to practice** all the theory we had studied.

▶ Exercises 1, 2, and 3

Future in the past

was/were going to and *was/were about to* (+ base verb)

We use *was/were going to* and *was/were about to* (+ base verb) to say that we intended to do something but didn't.
> I **was going to watch** the baseball game, but I had too much work to do.
> Tania **was about to sit down** when she heard her baby cry.

We also use *was/were going to* and *was/were about to* after verbs like *say, know, promise,* and *think*. When used like this, it is not clear whether the described action happened or not.
> We thought **they were going to finish** the work by the end of the month. (It could mean they finished the work or that they're still doing it.)
> He said **he was going to arrive** at 7 p.m. (It could mean he did arrive at 7 p.m. as expected or that he actually arrived at 9 p.m.)

would (+ base verb) and *would have* (+ past participle)

We use *would* + base verb to talk about the future in the past when we report thoughts, ideas, expectations, etc., after verbs like *say, know, promise,* and *think*. We use this structure to describe both events that happened and those that didn't.
> He promised he **would help** me, but then he disappeared!
> I knew we **would be** late. (= and we were)

We use *would have* + past participle to talk about something that didn't happen in the past.
> I **would have called** you, but I thought you were busy.

was/were supposed to (+ base verb)

We use *was/were supposed to* + base verb to describe something that we expected to happen but didn't.
> Where have you been? You **were supposed to be** here at noon!

▶ Exercises 4, 5, and 6

Exercises

1 Work in pairs. In which of these sentences can the underlined phrase be replaced with *could* or *couldn't*?

1. She <u>was able to</u> pass her exam last week, even though she didn't study for it.
2. Sorry, but I <u>didn't manage to</u> go to the supermarket.
3. He <u>was able to</u> sing beautifully when he was a child.
4. We <u>weren't able to</u> visit the museum because it was closed.
5. I <u>managed to</u> book a flight to Los Angeles for just $48.

2 Read the sentences. Cross out the incorrect option(s).

1. She *was able to / managed to / succeeded in* get the job that she really wanted.
2. I *couldn't / didn't manage / wasn't able* find the way to the castle.
3. We *succeeded in / managed to / were able to* finishing the project on time.
4. Anna *managed to / could / was able to* get a discount on her new car.
5. They *didn't succeed in / couldn't / weren't able to* come to the meeting.
6. I *managed to / was able to / could* eat chocolate whenever I wanted when I was little.

3 Match the sentence beginnings (1–4) with the endings (a–d). Then complete the sentences with the correct form of the verbs in parentheses.

1. My leg was hurting, but I still managed
2. Our hotel was great because we could
3. The company succeeded in
4. Our house is big, but we managed

a. _____ (eat) at the restaurant for free. ___
b. _____ (paint) it in just two days. ___
c. _____ (increase) its profits considerably. ___
d. _____ (run) ten kilometers. ___

4 Circle the correct options to complete the conversation.

A: Here you are, finally! I ¹ *was about to go / would go* home.
B: Sorry I'm late. I ² *would have called / would call* you, but … well, to be honest, I just forgot!
A: I thought so. You're so forgetful! And yesterday you promised you ³ *wouldn't have been / wouldn't be* late this time!
B: I know, I know. I'm so sorry!
A: Maybe you should do something to improve your memory.
B: I actually downloaded an app on my phone last week that said it ⁴ *would have improved / would improve* my memory within five days.
A: And what happened?
B: Well, I used it on the first day, and it seemed quite good. Then I ⁵ *was / were* supposed to use it every day for ten minutes. But then …
A: Let me guess—you forgot?
B: Of course!

5 Complete the sentences (1–4) with these phrases.

were going to	was supposed to
would have	wouldn't

1. We _____ make an offer on the house, but then we saw another house that we liked even more.
2. You promised you _____ lie to me ever again!
3. The package _____ arrive an hour ago, but it's still not here.
4. A: I'm soaking! It's pouring rain out there.
   B: Why didn't you call me? I _____ picked you up!

6 Complete the second sentence in each item (1–4) so it has the same meaning as the first sentence. Use the word in bold.

1. Just moments before Jaime went to bed, his doorbell rang.
   about
   Jaime _____ to bed when his doorbell rang.

2. He expected it to be a nice day today, but it was cloudy.
   supposed
   It _____ a nice day today, but it was cloudy.

3. You said these words to me: "I'll never borrow your car again without asking."
   would
   You promised you _____ my car again without asking.

4. I didn't buy you a present because I didn't know it was your birthday.
   would
   I _____ you a present, but I didn't know it was your birthday.

Grammar Summary

GRAMMAR SUMMARY UNIT 12

Focus adverbs: *only*, *just*, *even*

Use

We use the focus adverbs *only*, *just*, and *even* to focus on or draw attention to particular information in a clause. The focus adverb comes directly before the word or phrase it is emphasizing.

We use *only*:

- to emphasize that a number, size, age, etc., is small or smaller than we expected.
  Our flights cost **only** $90.

- to emphasize that something is true only for a single person/thing or a limited number of people/things.
  Only customers can park here.

- to say that something is unimportant.
  Don't be offended—I was **only** joking.

- with *not* to say that more than one thing is true.
  I'm **not only** interested in money; I also want to find a job that is interesting.

We use *just*:

- to emphasize that a number, size, age, etc., is small or smaller than we expected.
  She left the job after **just** six weeks.

- to emphasize that something happened recently or will be finished soon.
  They've **just** arrived home.

- to mean "simply."
  There's a good bus service in my town, but I normally **just** walk wherever I want to go.

- with *not* to say that more than one thing is true.
  They're **not just** friends—they're married!

Note that we can sometimes use both *only* and *just* without any change of meaning.

We use *even*:

- to introduce something surprising.
  Even I enjoyed the concert, and I don't like rock music!

- with *not* to emphasize that something isn't true or doesn't happen.
  The city was so busy that we couldn't **even** find a room in the worst hotels.

- in a comparison, to say that although something is good, bad, big, etc., another thing is better, worse, bigger, etc.
  Her latest movie is **even** better than her last one.

Form

Position of focus adverbs

We can put *only*, *even*, and *just* in different places in a sentence. If the focus of the adverb is on the subject, we put it at the beginning of the sentence.
  Even summer is quite cool in this part of the world.

If the focus of the adverb is on another part of the sentence, we normally put it in the middle of the sentence, before the main verb or after auxiliary verbs (*have*, *do*, *be*) and modal verbs.
  My phone can't make long-distance calls. It can **only** make local calls.
  I'm **just** getting ready. I won't be long.

▶ Exercises 1, 2, and 3

Causative *have* and *get*

Form and use

We use *have* and *get* in different ways to say that we cause something to happen or cause somebody to do something.

have/get + something + past participle

We use *have/get* + something + past participle when we pay somebody to do something for us. We don't say who does the job. *Get something done* is more informal than *have something done*.
  She **got her hair cut** yesterday.
  I'm **having my computer fixed** this morning.

We also use *have/get* + something + past participle to say that we experienced something bad.
  Maria **had/got her phone stolen** last night. (She didn't want this to happen.)

have + someone + base form of the verb

We use *have* + someone + base verb when we ask or tell somebody to do something for us. We normally use this structure when we have some kind of power over the other person, because he or she is our employee, child, etc. It is quite formal.
  José **had his lawyer write** a new contract.

We always say who did the action with this structure.

get + someone + infinitive

We also use *get* + someone + infinitive when we ask or tell somebody to do something for us. We use this structure in any context (not just with people we have power over). It is informal.
  We **got our teacher to explain** the grammar again.

We always say who did the action with this structure.

▶ Exercises 4 and 5

Exercises

1 Read the sentences. Circle the best options to complete the explanations below.

1. He stayed at the party for only twenty minutes.
   I *think* / *don't think* this is a long time.
2. Even Martino came to the exhibition.
   I'm *surprised* / *not surprised* he came.
3. The drive to the airport took just half an hour.
   This is *more* / *less* than I expected.
4. Miki's not only a musician.
   Miki does *other things, too* / *just this*.
5. You look even more tired than yesterday.
   You *looked* / *didn't look* tired yesterday.

2 Circle the correct options to complete the conversation.

A: What are you reading?
B: An article about a man who retired when he was ¹*only* / *even* 35 years old.
A: Wow! He must be really rich. Did he work for a big bank or something?
B: That's the interesting thing. He had a regular job, and he didn't earn a lot. He was ² *even* / *just* very careful about spending money, and so he saved 75% of his salary every year. Once he had saved enough money, he retired.
A: How did he save that much money?
B: Well, he made lots of small changes. For example, he sold his car and bought a bike. If you ride your bike everywhere, you don't ³*even* / *just* get around more cheaply, you also get free exercise!
A: That's true. Anything else?
B: Another thing was that he never ate out. He had dinner parties at home instead. Often, he told his friends to bring a dish each, so that made it ⁴*only* / *even* cheaper.
A: That's smart. So what's he doing now?
B: Well, he ⁵*just* / *only* moved to Brazil last month.

3 Complete the sentences with *even*, *just*, or *only*. Sometimes more than one focus adverb is possible.

1. Tickets for the concert are available for a very low price—$5.
   Tickets for the concert are available for ___only/just___ $5.
2. It's going to rain tomorrow and for several days after that.
   It's not ___only___ going to rain tomorrow, but also in the following days.
3. I'm going to leave in thirty seconds.
   I'm ___just___ about to leave.
4. I passed all my exams. I'm surprised I passed my math exam.
   I ___even___ passed my math exam.
5. The pizza I had last week was good. This pizza is better than that last one.
   This pizza is ___even___ better than the one I had last week.
6. I find it strange you're wearing your sunglasses. It isn't sunny.
   Why are you wearing sunglasses? It isn't ___even___ sunny.

4 Circle the correct options to complete the sentences.

1. We had our house *repainted* / *to repaint* / *repaint* last week.
2. The teacher had the students *stayed* / *to stay* / *stay* after class because of their bad behavior.
3. I'll get them *brought* / *to bring* / *bring* us the check.
4. They had a mechanic *checked* / *to check* / *check* their car because it was making strange noises.
5. I had a dress *made* / *to make* / *make* in Milan for the wedding.
6. We got a company *installed* / *to install* / *install* our new carpet.

5 Complete the text with the correct forms of these phrases.

clean your house	deliver the ingredients
do the cooking	send an information pack
find the perfect gift	

Life Solutions is here to make your life easier by doing the little jobs that you don't have time for. No time to clean? We'll find a cleaning company and have ¹_____ for you. Need to buy a present for a friend or relative? Just give us the details, and we'll get one of our highly trained advisors ²_____ . Friends coming for dinner? We'll plan the menu and get ³_____ to you. You can even have one of our chefs ⁴_____ for you—before your friends arrive, of course! For further details, just call or email and we'll have ⁵_____ to you immediately!

Unit 7

▶ 58

I'm from New York, so I'm used to the subway, but there are some things about the Tokyo subway that were definitely new to me. First, don't use your phone. If someone calls, it's OK to answer quickly—you know, say "I'm sorry, I'm on the train," and then hang up. But in general, people are really quiet and private, so don't ever talk loudly. Some rules of behavior are the same as in New York, like giving up your seat to an old person and not eating hot food. And if you have a large backpack, you should put it on a shelf so it's not in people's way. But some other customs seem pretty odd. The one that got me the first time was when someone next to me fell asleep and put their head on my shoulder. It seems there's nothing wrong with that—I've seen it happen to a few people now. You'll also often see people wearing face masks when they have a cold. That's because coughing, sneezing, or using a tissue in public is considered rude. What else? Oh yeah, when you get on a train during rush hour, you'll find there are people—they're called *Oshiya*—who are employed to push you, like, physically, into the crowded car.

▶ 60

On the whole, most of us eat a pretty balanced diet—a mixture of fruits, vegetables, grains, meat, fish, eggs, and dairy. Diet fashions come and go—the protein diet, the grapefruit diet, the starving-two-days-a-week diet, and so on—but, for the most part, we are used to eating a range of foods. It's true that in poorer regions of the world, people eat less meat and more grains and vegetables, and in richer parts more meat and sugary foods … and more fatty food. But everyone at least aims to have some kind of balance. And that's why I was so intrigued to read recently about the traditional diet of the indigenous people of northern Alaska, who are collectively known as Alaska Natives.

Historically, Alaska Natives didn't use to have a so-called balanced diet at all. Because of sub-zero temperatures and a lack of plant life, they had to survive on what they could hunt and fish close to home. They would hunt seal and walrus and reindeer, and then they'd cook the meat in seal oil. Sometimes they'd eat frozen fish, and when times were really hard in winter, they used to eat whale skin and blubber, which, I'm told, is like chewing car tires.

But how could a diet of just meat and fat possibly be healthy? Well, according to Harold Draper, an expert in nutrition, there's no such thing as essential foods—only essential nutrients. And there's not only one way to get those nutrients. In the West, we have gotten used to eating certain foods in order to get each nutrient. For example, we usually eat fruit to get more vitamin C, and dairy products for calcium and vitamin D. But during the long winters, the Alaska Natives found the nutrients and vitamins they needed from their diet of fish and wild animal meat. As for the large amount of fat they consumed, it was a healthier kind of fat, not the saturated fats that cause people in the West so many health problems these days. In fact, heart conditions among people on a traditional Alaska Native diet used to be about half the number in the wider population of North America. I say "used to" because nowadays, a lot of the indigenous population live close to towns and eat more processed food—pizza, fries, and soda—and unfortunately with this has come a rise in obesity, diabetes, and heart conditions.

▶ 63

1 Fruit and vegetables: apple, raspberries, cucumber, lettuce
2 Dairy products: cheese, butter
3 Breakfast cereals: muesli
4 Sauces: mustard, ketchup
5 Meat and seafood: beef, lamb, tuna

▶ 65

M = Marie, E = Esther
M: I know of henna painting as a custom at Indian weddings, but you came across it in Turkey, didn't you?
E: Yes, in eastern Turkey when I was traveling there. It takes place a few nights before the wedding.
M: Was it kind of like a bachelorette party?
E: Well, in the sense that it marks the last evening that a bride spends as a single woman—with her female family and friends—I suppose it is kind of like that. What happens is, typically, the women from both families get together with the bride, to celebrate with music, song, and dance. But it's not just a party. It's an occasion for sadness too, because it symbolizes the end of life as a single person and the start of another stage.

▶ 66

M = Marie, E = Esther
M: So what happens exactly?
E: Well, the ceremony begins with the preparation of the henna. It's traditional for this to be done by the daughter of a couple who have had a successful marriage themselves. Then, after the bride's head has been covered with a red veil, her hands and feet are decorated with henna. After that, a gold coin is put into the remaining henna. While this is happening, the guests start to sing, umm, separation songs—these are kind of sad, as you can imagine. The party continues well into the night. Then, on the morning of the wedding, a child presents the hennaed coin to the groom as a symbol of future prosperity and good fortune.

▶ 67

M = Marie, E = Esther
M: I know of henna painting as a custom at Indian weddings, but you came across it in Turkey, didn't you?
E: Yes, in eastern Turkey when I was traveling there. It takes place a few nights before the wedding.
M: Was it kind of like a bachelorette party?
E: Well, in the sense that it marks the last evening that a bride spends as a single woman—with her female family and friends—I suppose it is kind of like that. What happens is, typically, the women from both families get together with the bride, to celebrate with music, song, and dance. But it's not just a party. It's an occasion for sadness too, because it symbolizes the end of life as a single person and the start of another stage.
M: So what happens exactly?
E: Well, the ceremony begins with the preparation of the henna. It's traditional for this to be done by the daughter of a couple who have had a successful marriage themselves. Then, after the bride's head has been covered with a red veil, her hands and feet are decorated with henna. After that, a gold coin is put into the remaining henna. While this is happening, the guests start to sing, umm, separation songs—these are kind of sad, as you can imagine. The party continues well into the night. Then, on the morning of the wedding, a child presents the hennaed coin to the groom as a symbol of future prosperity and good fortune.

Unit 8

▶ 70

This mural's been on the wall of a local store in my neighborhood for years. Anyone can write on it. You just have to pick up a piece of chalk and complete the sentence "Before I die, I want to …" This "bucket list" wall isn't the only one of its kind: There are quite a few other walls like it in other cities around the world. The idea was started by a woman in New Orleans, and then it spread.

Sometimes I sit and watch people as they're thinking about what to write on the wall, thinking about the dreams they'd like to come true. Some are goals that are easy to achieve, like "I want to plant a tree"; some just make me laugh, like "I want to fix my kitchen faucet." But others are more personal—people wanting to live up to other people's expectations of them. "I want to be a good parent" was one I found touching. The same things keep coming up, too. A lot of people have an ambition to travel and to learn another language. But, overall, there is an amazing variety of wishes on the wall. I guess some people will fulfill their ambitions and some won't, but this wall shows that most of us are trying to make sense of our direction in life.

▶ 72

1. If the rent were cheaper, I'd take the apartment.
2. What would you have done if you'd been me?
3. So sorry! If I'd known you were here, I'd have asked Jo to get you a coffee.
4. If she had stayed in college, she'd now be a fully qualified journalist.

▶ 73

The National Geographic Explorers' words are spoken by actors.

1. **Albert Lin, Scientist and explorer**
   It's got to be invisibility, right? Like, because if you could be invisible, you could see the entire world in the craziest way.
2. **Laly Lichtenfeld, Big cat conservationist**
   I'd like to be able to fly. It'd help me see the bigger picture.
3. **Andrés Ruzo, Geologist**
   I wish I had the ability to make people magically understand me. You know how frustrating it is, when you wish other people would get what you're trying to say and they just don't. You think, "Goodness, I wish they'd stop looking at me in that confused way!"
4. **Alizé Carrère, Geographer**
   If I had a superpower, it would be to be invisible, so people couldn't see me.
5. **Andrew Thompson, Biologist**
   Teleporting would be pretty cool. I could travel any place I wanted to. I wish I'd had that power earlier in my career. It would have saved me a lot of air miles. I could also use it to transport things I'd forgotten to take with me on my travels.
6. **Catherine Workman, Conservation biologist**
   I would definitely be invisible. I'd go to the White House and listen in on all their conversations.
7. **Neil deGrasse Tyson, Astrophysicist**
   I wish I could read other people's minds. But I would like to be able to turn that power on and off—sometimes you just don't want to know what other people are thinking! Also, I'd want to read not just people's minds, but the minds of animals too, like dogs. I've always wondered what dogs are thinking.
8. **Ricky Qi, Filmmaker**
   Sometimes I think, "If only I could turn anything into any kind of food I wanted." That would be the most awesome superpower.

▶ 74

1. wish
2. shop
3. catch
4. shin
5. watch
6. choose

▶ 76

1
A: Would you like to drive or should I?
B: I'd rather you drove, if you don't mind. I'm feeling kind of tired.
A: No, that's fine. Actually, I prefer driving to being a passenger.

2
A: What would you like for dinner? I could cook some pasta, or we could get some take-out Indian food.
B: Well, if you don't mind cooking, pasta sounds great. I like simple food more than spicy food.

3
A: So what would you like to do tomorrow? We could just take a walk around the old town. Or, if you prefer, we could go to a museum.
B: To be honest, I'd rather not go to a museum. I think the weather's going to be sunny tomorrow, and it seems a pity to be indoors on a nice day.
A: OK. Great. We'll take a walk then.

4
A: What do you feel like doing this weekend? We're thinking either we could go and see the new Matt Damon movie, or there's a music festival in the park, but I'm not sure who's playing. What do you think?
B: Well, if it were up to me, I'd say let's go to the festival in the park. It doesn't matter if the music isn't very good. I think that would probably be more fun.
A: OK. I'd prefer to do that, too.

Unit 9

▶ 78

N = Newsreader, M = Martha Cash

N: And in China, hundreds of parents of first-year students at the University of Wuhan have been sleeping on the floor of the university's gym, so that they can be near their children in their first anxious days at college. As Martha Cash, our China correspondent, reports.

M: For China's many middle-class parents, getting their children—and often it's an only child—into college is an extremely important step in building a better future for their families. Many parents put all their savings into achieving this goal. But being accepted to college is not the end of the story. The parents want to help their child settle into their new college life, and to follow the child's progress through university. The University of Wuhan recognizes this, and it also recognizes that many Chinese families are not particularly well off. Staying in a local hotel during their children's first days at college is not an option for them. So the university offers free accommodation to parents—up to five hundred at a time—in the form of mats in the university gym. As an expression of parental concern, it's certainly impressive.

▶ 80

1
And finally … A refugee in Germany has been called a hero after he handed in €150,000 in cash to the police. He found the money hidden in a wardrobe. In spite of having little money himself, the 25-year-old Syrian—who is believed to have been in Germany for less than a year—decided the right thing to do was to give the money back. The wardrobe was a gift from a charity to help the man furnish his apartment. Local police are now said to be looking for the money's true owner, but they praised the man for his honesty. As well as gaining the respect of the nation, the man will receive a financial reward, since, under German law, he is entitled to three percent of the money found—in this case, around €4,500.

2
And finally … In Naples, Italy, 250 chefs have collaborated to set a Guinness World Record for the world's longest pizza. Measuring 1.8 kilometers long, it took the chefs eleven hours to make. According to Guinness, the pizza makers used 2,000 kilograms of flour, 1,600 kilograms of tomatoes, 2,000 kilograms of mozzarella cheese, and 200 liters of olive oil. Afterwards, everyone in the crowd got a slice to eat, and the rest was given to people in need. The city of Naples has long been synonymous with pizza. It is thought that the first Margherita pizza was baked in Naples in 1889.

3
And finally … A Latvian scientist based in the UK is reported to be close to finding drugs that will help people live to ages of a hundred and beyond. What is more, he is confident that he himself will live to at least 150. Dr. Zhavoronkov is working with US pharmaceutical company The Life Extension Foundation, which hopes to soon be selling a range of products that will slow down the aging process. To reduce the high cost of new drug trials, Dr. Zhavoronkov has been testing the drugs on himself. Now aged 37, he claims to feel much younger than he did a few years ago.

▶ 82

Conversation 1

J = Jess, P = Phil

J: Hi, Phil. How are things?
P: Not bad. But work has been really stressful lately.
J: Yeah, I know what you mean. By the way, did you hear about Liam?

Audioscript 187

Apparently, he's been promoted.

P: Liam? But he's only been here a year!

J: I know. But according to Sarah, he's been given the job of area manager.

P: Area manager? I don't believe it! He's not even that good at his current job.

J: Well, Sarah also reckons that he's going to get a huge pay raise—something like double his current salary.

P: Yeah, well, I'd take that with a grain of salt. I don't think the company has that kind of money to throw around at the moment.

Conversation 2

F = Freddie, C = Caitlin

F: Hi, Caitlin. Hey, you know Dr. Harris at the local clinic?

C: Yes.

F: Well, someone told me that he was fired from his job yesterday. It seems that he's not even a real doctor.

C: What? Who told you that?

F: Tara.

C: Hmm, I wouldn't take too much notice of what Tara says. She tends to exaggerate things.

F: No, I'm pretty sure it's true. Apparently, Dr. Harris—if that's even his real name—has gone from one hospital to another across the country using a fake résumé.

C: Oh my goodness, that's terrible.

F: I know. But actually, that doesn't surprise me. You do hear of things like that happening.

C: Maybe, but I *would* be very surprised. Dr. Harris seemed like a genuine guy to me.

Unit 10

▶ 85

Both the mahout and the elephant start their training at a young age. A mahout generally begins to learn his trade when he's about ten years old. At this age, he is given a baby elephant to look after—they will remain bonded to each other throughout their lives. The job of a mahout is traditionally a family trade, with knowledge of how to care for an elephant passed down from one generation to the next. There are no formal qualifications for the job, but you need to be extremely patient. An elephant will learn as many as 65 commands in its life, depending on what work it's expected to do—some elephants carry logs and other heavy objects, others are trained to carry people. The mahout has to teach his elephant all these commands. He must also develop an understanding of his elephant, so that he knows when it's sick or tired or unhappy. This is something that only comes with time and experience. It's a very physical job and extremely hard work. The elephant must be fed and bathed every day, and watched carefully in case it tries to run away.

▶ 86

This is a photo of the astronaut Buzz Aldrin, taken by the first man on the moon, Neil Armstrong, in 1969. You can see Armstrong taking the photo in the reflection on Aldrin's helmet. It was Armstrong who famously said "That's one small step for man, one giant leap for mankind" when he first stepped onto the moon. Actually, what he really said was "That's one small step for a man, one giant leap for mankind," but no one heard the "a" because of radio interference.

▶ 89

Daniel Kish, **who** has been blind since he was a year old, taught himself to "see" using the technique of echolocation. As he moves around, Kish clicks his tongue and then listens for the echo **that** comes back. If the echo is loud, then he knows that an object is near; if the echo is not so loud, he knows the object is farther away. He has become so skilled at using this technique that he can do many things **that** blind people cannot ordinarily do. By clicking his tongue two or three times a second, he can ride a bicycle, go hiking in the countryside, and play ball games.

Echolocation is a skill **that** is also used in the animal world, **where** it is often key to survival. The best-known example is bats. This has led to Kish being called "the real-life Batman"—a description he welcomes. Just like bats, Kish can tell from the quality of an echo not only how far away an object is, but also its size and its density. A wooden fence, for example, **whose** surface is softer than brick or metal, gives a "warmer" echo than a brick wall. So what can Kish actually "see"? Up close, at about five meters, he can recognize cars and bushes. Houses come into focus at about fifty meters.

Kish now spends a lot of his time training other blind people in his technique, **which** he calls FlashSonar. He says that many blind people already use echolocation in a passive way, but **what** they don't know is how to use it actively. The average person can develop good echolocation skills in about a month if they train for a couple of hours a day. Kish is also looking at the possibility of training fully-sighted people, like firefighters, to use this skill in situations **in which** their vision is limited, like in a smoke-filled building. He is amused by the nickname **for which** he is now famous, but, mostly, he just loves **what** he is doing and sees great potential for it.

▶ 91

S = Sarah, P = Phil

S: So, you're 24 years old, you graduated a year ago, and you're looking for work with a charity. What attracted you to Shelterbox?

P: Well, I'm familiar with your work because I have a friend who volunteered for you last year—packing boxes—and I think it's a fantastic concept. But mainly, I'm very interested in the idea of working in different countries.

S: I see. And what makes you think you'd be suited to that? I see you studied economics at Harvard. Don't you think that's a rather different world?

P: Yes, it's true that I specialized in economics. But actually, I'm good at coping with difficult environments. I spent three months helping to build a school in Chennai in India last summer. And the year before that, I trekked across the Mojave Desert. So I think I'd be suited to the work.

S: OK. But you'd also be spending a good part of the time here in the office doing paperwork.

P: Yeah, that's also fine. I was expecting that. What kind of paperwork is involved?

S: Well, each trip involves a lot of preparation and a certain amount of follow-up, too. Keeping spreadsheets, writing reports. Are you OK doing that kind of thing?

P: Yeah, I'm pretty good with computers. I'm comfortable with all the usual programs—Excel, Word, some financial software.

S: OK. There's just one thing that's worrying me, though. You're clearly a bright person, and you have a good degree. How do we know that you won't just do this job for a few months and then go and get a better-paying job with a bank or consultancy business?

P: That's a good question. It's actually what a lot of my friends from college have done, but I'll tell you why that's not for me. Firstly, I'm serious about wanting to help people in need. Secondly, I think I need to become more knowledgeable about the world, before I use my economics degree to do something else. If you put your faith in me, I will be absolutely committed to doing the best job that I can!

▶ 93

1	clothes	5	folk
2	lengths	6	surface
3	February	7	island
4	receipt	8	thorough

Unit 11

▶ 94

I love this museum. We went to Indianapolis specially to visit it, because we'd heard such great things about it. My kids, who are seven and nine, loved the interactive display of dinosaurs—they could really engage with it. My husband and I learned a lot, too. There was a whole section on Asia—part of the "Take me there" section on foreign cultures. It had so many things I was completely unaware of, like Chinese herbal medicine. The other thing I really liked was the "Children making a difference" section. It included stories of children who had difficult childhoods but have succeeded—like kids who faced prejudice or discrimination. Their stories really inspired me. I'm definitely going to take my kids back to this museum when they're old enough to really get these stories. I think the mixture of visual displays, hands-on stuff, and real-life stories is a great way to acquire knowledge. I guess if I have any criticism of the museum, it's that it's too big—there's too much to take in.

▶ 96

You were about to make a comment in a meeting, and then your mind went blank. You were supposed to send a friend a birthday card, but then you forgot. You recognized someone in the street and would have spoken to them, but you didn't because you couldn't remember their name. You promised to mail a letter for someone, and two days later you found it in your pocket. You were going to write down a great idea you had, but when you found a pen and paper, the idea had gone. I could go on, but I won't because I'm sure everyone recognizes these common failures of memory. Do these situations sound familiar to you? Have any of these things happened to you?

▶ 97

Everyone thinks they would like to remember more, but, actually, would it make us any happier?

I want to tell you the story of a 41-year-old woman from California known in medical literature as "AJ," who remembers almost every day of her life since the age of eleven. She remembers that at 12:34 p.m. on Sunday, August 3rd, 1986, a young man she was attracted to called her on the telephone. She remembers that on March 28th, 1992, she had lunch with her father at the Beverly Hills Hotel. It's a bit like it is for the rest of us when certain smells bring back strong memories. AJ's memory is stimulated in the most intense way by dates.

You'd think that being able to recall facts and knowledge in this way would make us more confident and wiser. But in fact, for AJ, having an incredible memory can be distressing. It is as much a burden as it is a benefit. That's because most people's memories are selective: We remember mostly important things, and mostly good things. AJ remembers every detail, good or bad, important or not. So when we blame our poor memories for forgetting to send a birthday card, actually we should be grateful also for all the things that our memories hide because they don't need to be remembered or thought about.

Technology also helps us. We don't need to remember the precise content of an email or the exact time of a meeting anymore, because it's stored in our computers or our mobile phones. Interestingly, the growth of this technology—which psychologists call our external memory—is having an effect on what and how much we remember. Even our memories of happy events, like parties or holidays, get stored in photo albums on our computers. So our internal memories are probably worse than those of people a hundred years ago. Medical science is trying to address the problem of poor memory, and this is what I want to talk about next.

▶ 98

(This track is repeated from tracks 96 and 97.)

▶ 99

1. I was going to invite Sarah, but I asked Kate instead.
2. She was supposed to be in Cairo this week, but she's sick, so she couldn't go.
3. He would have sent me the original, but he couldn't find it, so he sent me a copy.
4. We were supposed to arrive there by ten o'clock, but the train didn't get in until eleven.
5. He was about to announce his retirement, but now he thinks he'll stay until next year.

▶ 101

L = Liz, A = Ahmad

L: Hello, Rousham Adult Education College. Liz speaking.
A: Hi there. My name's Ahmad, and I'm interested in taking a class at your college—umm, the history of art course.
L: Is that the two-year A-level course?
A: Sorry, what do you mean by "A-level"?
L: The A-level art history course is a two-year pre-university course with examinations at the end of each year.
A: Oh, no, no, no, I don't want to take any exams. It's just for interest.
L: OK. In that case, we have a ten-week art appreciation course.
A: Sorry. Can you speak up a little? I can't hear you very well.
L: Yes, we have a ten-week art appreciation course.
A: Can you explain what the course involves?
L: It's a two-hour class once a week and, basically, it teaches you how to look at art, so that you can appreciate it better.
A: Sorry, I don't understand. Are you saying that it doesn't really deal with the history of art?
L: Umm, there's some history of art involved, but it's mainly learning about the techniques that artists use and what their paintings mean.
A: Could you give me an example of the kind of thing students do in the class?
L: Typically, students look at works of art and comment on them. Then they're told more about the artist, what he or she was trying to achieve, and then they look at the work again, to see if they see it differently.
A: OK. It sounds quite interesting. What was the class called again?
L: Art appreciation.
A: And when is it?
L: Every Tuesday—during the term, that is—from 7 p.m. to 9 p.m., starting on … one minute … yeah, starting on April 5th. The cost is $198, unless you're a registered student.
A: Sorry, I didn't catch the start date. Did you say May 5th?
L: No, April 5th.
A: OK. Well, thanks. I'll think about it, but it sounds interesting.
L: No worries. Bye!

Unit 12

▶ 103

Speaker 1

No, it does matter, absolutely. Because you end up with a divided society instead of a united one—the haves and the have nots, as some people call it. Japan has a much smaller income gap between rich and poor than the US, for example. That's partly because most bosses in Japan don't take huge salaries. They understand that that would be socially irresponsible. It would create feelings of envy and resentment among people who are worse off. The result is that Japan actually has a much more united society than some Western countries, where there are big differences in pay between top and bottom.

Speaker 2
Well, I think it's OK if the rich are getting richer—as long as everyone else's standard of living is rising, too. In other words, if people who aren't earning so much can nevertheless see that their buying power is increasing. Of course, that depends on their wages going up faster than the cost of living. But actually, I think it's how people *see* things that's important. If they think their quality of life is good, then they won't mind if the rich have a better standard of living. On the other hand, if they think they're getting a bad deal and that the rich aren't contributing, then they'll complain.

▶ **105**

1 No, thanks. I'm just looking.
2 Even the most difficult problems have a solution.
3 I'm just going to brush my teeth, then we can leave.
4 Don't worry. It's only money.
5 He's always losing things. He even lost his own wedding ring once.
6 It's only a suggestion—you don't have to follow it.
7 It's only the second time we've met.

▶ **106**

I = Interviewer, D = David Stiles

I: Are we all getting lazier or has economic development just meant that there's now someone available to do any job you want? Forty years ago, the idea of getting someone to hand wash your car was unthinkable—except to the very rich. Either you washed it yourself at home on a Sunday morning, or you took it down to the automatic carwash at your local garage. Nowadays, you can have it washed inside and out by professional car washers for as little as $8. David Stiles, Professor of Economics at Cranford Institute, is here with us to try to explain this phenomenon. What's changed, Professor?

D: Well, first of all, hello and thank you for inviting me onto your program. So, the short answer to your question is "economic development." As society gets richer, people have more money available to buy services, and to get other people to do things that they themselves don't particularly want to do or feel they're not good at doing—like installing a carpet or painting their house.

I: And I suppose it has to do with time, too. We all lead such busy lives.

D: Yes, that's true. It saves time and, of course, the big positive is that it creates a lot of employment. You don't have to be especially rich to have a house cleaner clean your home once a week, or to get your windows cleaned every couple of months. But I think you made a valid point at the beginning about people getting lazier. There are some rich people who take things to the extreme. I'm thinking of people who, for example, employ personal shoppers or who have someone walk their dog every day. When they have a party, they probably get a professional party planner to organize the party. I've even heard of people who get their Christmas tree put up, and then have someone else decorate it for them.

I: That's a bit extreme. Decorating the Christmas tree is supposed to be a fun activity for the family.

D: Well, I tend to agree with you, but I don't think the people who provide the services are necessarily complaining. That's how the economy works. People—particularly the wealthy—pay to have things done for them, and the people who provide the services benefit from that.

▶ **110**

LA = Leasing agent, C = Customer

LA: So, you took a look at the offices. What do you think?
C: Yeah, I think they're absolutely perfect for our needs.
LA: That's great. You'd like to take them then?
C: Well, ideally, yes, I would. But …
LA: But?
C: Well, a key thing for us is the length of the lease.
LA: It's a five-year lease. I think that was in the information I sent you.
C: Yes, that's right. But actually, I was hoping we could negotiate that down because, if you look at it from our point of view, we're a young business and we don't really know how things are going to go over the next few years. Let's face it, five years is a long time. Do you think your client would be willing to move a bit on that?
LA: I doubt it. I'm sure you'll appreciate that my client's main concern is for someone to rent the property for as long as possible. It gives them security. To tell you the truth, that's why the rent is so low. I can ask my client, but I'm not sure we'll get a positive response.
C: Hmm … Isn't there some way around that, maybe?
LA: Not that I can think of. What did you have in mind?
C: Well, perhaps we could sign a five-year lease but with a get-out clause after, say, three years.
LA: I'm afraid that won't work. We do actually have other people interested in the premises, so I'm pretty sure someone will take it on a five-year lease. If I were in your shoes and I found the terms of the lease difficult, I think I'd just walk away. At the end of the day, it has to feel right for you.
C: But it *does* feel right for me. Hang on a minute. I'm just going to call my business partner and see what he thinks.
LA: OK, no problem.

5B
COMBO SPLIT

Life

SECOND EDITION

PAUL DUMMETT
DAVID BOHLKE

Australia • Brazil • Mexico • Singapore • United Kingdom • United States

Contents

Unit 7	Customs and behavior	page 52
Unit 8	Hopes and ambitions	page 60
Unit 9	The news	page 68
Unit 10	Talented people	page 76
Unit 11	Knowledge and learning	page 84
Unit 12	Money	page 92
Audioscripts		page 109

Unit 7 Customs and behavior

7a Child behavior

Listening growing up

1 ▶ 53 Listen to four people talking about growing up and child behavior. Match the speakers (1–4) with the topic they are talking about (a–f). There are two extra topics.

Speaker 1 _____
Speaker 2 _____
Speaker 3 _____
Speaker 4 _____

a Being the youngest in the family
b Being the eldest
c Learning from other children
d Competition between siblings
e Home schooling
f Discipline in the home

> **intervene** (v) /ˌɪntəˈviːn/ get involved
> **sibling** (n) /ˈsɪblɪŋ/ a brother or sister

2 ▶ 53 Listen again. Write the number of the speaker (1–4) next to the view they are expressing.

a The best results are when parents leave children to learn for themselves. _____
b Having to fight to get your parents' attention can have a positive effect. _____
c Children need to mix with lots of other children. _____
d Your position in the family—e.g., first child, second child—is significant. _____

3 Look at the words and phrases in **bold** from the listening and circle the correct definition.

1 Schools don't **stretch** children enough.
   a discipline
   b challenge
   c educate

2 I'm sure they **mean well**, but they're missing the point.
   a have good intentions
   b have good ideas
   c have good qualities

3 Children often **squabble** over toys.
   a have small arguments
   b lose interest
   c make friendships

4 Eldest children are usually **bossy** types.
   a showing leadership qualities
   b independent
   c telling others what to do

5 Younger children are often the **clowns** of the family.
   a ones who aren't taken seriously
   b ones who like to make others laugh
   c the less intelligent ones

6 It's normal just to leave the children to **get on with it**.
   a manage by themselves
   b make friends with each other
   c grow up

Grammar zero and first conditionals

4 Circle the correct option to complete the sentences.

1 In the UK, the law states that you *are / will be* allowed to teach children at home if you *provide / will provide* them with an "efficient, full-time education." The law also says that children *don't / won't* have to be with other children when they *are / will be* taught at home.

2 People who criticize home schooling say children will not learn good social skills, if they *don't / won't* have the company of other children. I agree. If I *decide / will decide* to home school my children, I *make / will make* sure they have plenty of contact with people their own age.

3 There are so many different books for parents. If you *try / will try* to follow all the different psychologists' advice, you *end / will end* up being a very confused parent!

4 I am the youngest child in my family. I don't agree with the experts who say that when you *are / will be* the youngest, you *have / will have* an easier life.

5 Complete the conversations. Use the correct form of the verb in parentheses.

1 A: Can you help me with my homework?
   B: Yes, but you _____ (feel) better about it if you _____ (manage) to do it by yourself.

2 A: Can I borrow your bicycle?
   B: You can, as long as you _____ (promise) to look after it carefully.

3 A: Where are you going to stay?
   B: I _____ (book) a room at the Lido Hotel unless it _____ (be) full.

4 A: The office is so busy with just the two of us here.
   B: Yes, but I'm sure things _____ (get) calmer after everyone _____ (return) from vacation.

5 A: Can I get you a coffee?
   B: No, thanks. I _____ (just / read) the newspaper while I _____ (wait).

6 A: Have you heard anything back from the owners of the house?
   B: No, I haven't. But as soon as I _____ (hear), I _____ (let) you know.

7 A: I think Vicky stands a good chance of winning the short-story competition.
   B: I think so, too. And she says that if she _____ (win), she _____ (take) us all out to dinner.

8 A: What are we going to do for dinner tonight?
   B: I _____ (cook) something if I _____ (get) home early enough.

9 A: Does your sister have children?
   B: Not yet. She says she _____ (not / have) children while she _____ (live) in such a small apartment.

Vocabulary raising children: verbs

6 Complete the sentences using the correct verbs. The first letter is provided.

Hannah: My father worked abroad for most of my childhood, so we were ¹b_____ up by my mother. When my father came home, he used to ²s_____ us, buying us presents and taking us out. He never ³p_____ us if we misbehaved, because he wanted to enjoy his time with us. He left it to my mom to ⁴t_____ us off if we were bad. That was tough on her because we used to ⁵d_____ her a lot—playing outside when she had told us not to.

Laura: It's difficult being a single parent looking after your children. You are always ⁶n_____ them to do things when really you want to enjoy your time with them. My older sister ⁷r_____ against my mom and went to live in L.A. when she was eighteen.

Marco: It isn't easy being a parent. My own kids are always asking me to buy them things, but I try not to ⁸g_____ in to their demands. Of course, when they do something good, I might ⁹r_____ them with a present!

7 Dictation raising children

▶ **54** Listen to a psychologist talking about bringing up children. Complete the text with the words you hear. Which aspect of bringing up children do you agree with most?

Everything depends on _____ _____ .

In other words, what _____ _____ ?

Do you want them _____ _____ ?

If so, _____ _____ , and generally being good citizens.

Or do you want them to be successful individuals? If so, _____ _____ .

Or is it important that they are good family members? Then _____ _____ _____ .

7b Globalization of the food market

Reading global food

1 Read the article. What effect has the globalization of food had?

a Food is now cheaper than it was before.
b The food we eat is now more international.
c Poor people now eat as well as rich people.

2 Read the article again and circle the correct option (a–c).

1 The weekly family menu in Britain 50 years ago:
  a was very boring for those who had to eat it.
  b used food resources carefully.
  c was not very nutritious.
2 The main difference with a weekly family menu in Britain these days is that:
  a people eat food that is in season.
  b people have more money to eat out.
  c there is a greater choice of food.
3 The phrase "standardization of taste" means:
  a we all eat similar things.
  b everything tastes more and more the same.
  c food doesn't taste as good as it once did.
4 The main reason that the price of food has increased globally is:
  a people in fast-developing countries want more Western-style food.
  b climate change has badly affected food production.
  c the general economic depression.
5 Higher food prices have caused people in the West to:
  a eat less meat.
  b not eat in restaurants.
  c reduce the amount they spend on food.

GLOBALIZATION OF THE FOOD MARKET

Globalization has had a huge impact on eating habits all over the world. From the UK to Kenya to China, the food we eat today is determined by global markets and world economic events.

If you go back fifty years, a typical working family in Britain ate the same things every week—not that anyone complained about it. The weekly menu was built around the Sunday roast, when a large piece of meat was served with seasonal vegetables as a treat. On the following days, people used to eat leftovers from this "feast" in a way that clearly avoided waste. On Monday, they would have cold cuts of meat, and on Tuesday, a dish made from the leftovers, such as shepherd's pie. Wednesday and Thursday were less predictable, but Friday was "Fish and Chips" day. Saturday was usually sausage and mash because this was quick and easy, and then it was back to the Sunday roast again.

Look at today's average weekly family menu in Britain and there is no comparison. First, there is no average: the element of predictability has disappeared because what is available now is not just British but international cuisine. Chinese stir-fry on Sunday, Italian lasagna on Wednesday, Mexican tortillas on Thursday. Second, the season is no longer a factor. If you want strawberries in December or asparagus in March, you can buy them even if it's not the season to grow them in the UK, because it is in South Africa or Chile. Eating out is not the treat it used to be. It's normal to eat out at least once a week and to have takeout—maybe curry—when you can't be bothered to cook.

But while globalization may have brought more variety to our table, global food brands have at the same time brought a standardization of taste, particularly in snack foods and fast foods. You can buy a Kit Kat anywhere from Boston to Beijing, and no one is surprised anymore when they see McDonald's in some small town far from the US.

This demand for Western foods—such as hamburgers and pizza—in countries where there is rapid economic development has had a dramatic effect on the price of wheat and other basic foods. Add to this crop failures from bad weather conditions, and the result is that we are all paying more for our food. In the West, this may cause people some inconvenience—eating chicken (which is less expensive) instead of beef, for example, or cutting back on the number of times they eat out; but in under-developed countries, the effect has been much more damaging. For a poor family in Kenya who is used to a diet of corn, rice, and beans, with meat maybe once or twice a week, the choice is not between lamb or chicken, but rather rice with beans or rice without beans.

treat (n) /triːt/ something special to reward people
mash (n) /mæʃ/ mashed potatoes

Grammar *usually, used to, would, be used to,* and *get used to*

3 Circle the correct options according to the article on page 54.

1. Fifty years ago, families in Britain *usually eat / got used to eating / used to eat* the same thing every week.
2. People didn't complain because they *weren't used to seeing / didn't get used to seeing / wouldn't see* food from all over the world.
3. British families *are used to using / got used to using / would use* the Sunday roast to make meals for the next two days.
4. On Fridays, they *usually have / are used to having / would have* fish and chips.
5. Today, people in Britain *are used to eating / get used to eating / used to eat* a variety of international foods.
6. Since food became globalized, people *usually eat / have gotten used to eating / would eat* whatever they want, whether it's in season or not.
7. Nowadays, people *usually see / are used to seeing / got used to seeing* McDonald's everywhere in the world.
8. In the past, people in Kenya *are used to eating / got used to eating / used to eat* rice, corn, beans, and a little meat.
9. Nowadays, in tougher times, they *usually eat / are used to eating / got used to eating* just beans and rice.

4 Read about an English person living 100 years ago. Which of the underlined verbs can be replaced with *used to, would,* or *was/were used to*? Write the alternative. If it can't be replaced, write "–".

"We ¹ didn't cook on a stove because we didn't have one. We ² cooked everything over a fire. For example, if we ³ wanted to cook sausages, we ⁴ hung them on hooks over the fire. But if it ⁵ was a special occasion and we had a lot of things to cook, then we had to take it down the road to the hotel that ⁶ had a proper oven, and for a few pennies they ⁷ cooked it for us. It seems strange now, but we ⁸ did that whenever the whole family got together around the table."

1. *didn't use to cook*
2. _____
3. _____
4. _____
5. _____
6. _____
7. _____
8. _____

5 Pronunciation /juː/ and /uː/

a ▶ 55 Listen to these words. Write the words in the chart.

blue	humanity	humor	lunar	menu
rude	suit	truce	used	usually

/uː/	/juː/

b ▶ 56 Listen and check your answers to Exercise 5a.

Vocabulary food and eating habits

6 Look at what these four people ate for lunch. Which of the following did they have? Write snack food (SF), dairy product (D), protein-rich food (P), fresh fruit and vegetables (F), or soft drinks (SD).

1. **Simon**
   tuna sandwich _____
   bag of chips _____

2. **Kerry**
   yogurt _____
   grapes _____

3. **Will**
   mixed salad _____
   bag of peanuts _____
   can of Cola _____

4. **Katie**
   hamburger _____
   strawberry milkshake _____

Unit 7 Customs and behavior

7c Body language

Listening Desmond Morris

1 ▶ 57 Listen to a description of the work of Desmond Morris. Are the sentences true (T) or false (F)?

1 Desmond Morris trained as a zoologist and a psychologist. T F
2 More than ninety percent of human communication is made using speech. T F
3 The first example describes the body language of Desmond Morris and a radio presenter. T F
4 Postural echo involves imitating someone's facial expressions. T F
5 In the second situation (the job interview), it would be right to use postural echo. T F

2 ▶ 57 Look at the diagrams (a–d) and answer the questions. Then listen again and check.

1 Which diagram shows how Desmond Morris and the presenter are sitting in the first situation? ____
2 Which diagram shows the interviewee sitting in a subordinate position? ____

a  b

c  d

3 ▶ 57 Circle the correct option to complete the sentences. Then listen again and check.

1 Morris's lifelong interest has been human *as much as / rather than* animal behavior.
2 *Unlike / Like* the traditional experts in human behavior, he is not so interested in what people say, but rather in what they do.
3 In fact, he gives *a lot of / little* attention to human speech.
4 In another situation, though, *no / such* postural echo might be inappropriate.

4 Pronunciation unstressed syllables

▶ 58 Look at these words. In each word, the second syllable is unstressed and contains the schwa /ə/ sound. Listen and repeat.

action	common	custom	freedom
human	passion	question	reason

Word focus *same* and *different*

5 Complete the conversations with these expressions.

a difference of opinion	no difference
a different tune	the same boat
the same	the same coin
a different matter	

1 A: Why do you think rich people are often so dissatisfied?
   B: I think that earning more and wanting more are two sides of _____ .
2 A: I spent four years at a teacher's college, but I don't feel any more confident in the classroom.
   B: Learning the theory is one thing, but actually practicing something is _____ .
3 A: What's the difference between a truck and a lorry?
   B: Well, one is American English and one is British English, but in meaning they're one and _____ .
4 A: Did you have an argument with Emilia?
   B: I wouldn't say it was an argument—just _____ .
5 A: Did you find the rooms in the hotel small?
   B: Yes, but it made _____ because we were out sightseeing most of the time.
6 A: Does she still think that golf is easy?
   B: No, now that she's tried it, she's singing _____ .
7 A: They keep giving me more and more work to do. How am I supposed to cope?
   B: Try not to worry about it. We're all in _____ .

7d Wedding customs

Vocabulary weddings

1 Write the words for these definitions.
1. the party after the wedding ceremony: _____
2. a pre-wedding party for men: _____ party
3. a covering for the bride's face: _____
4. a(n) _____ ring showing a promise
5. the man on his wedding day: _____
6. a pre-wedding party for women: _____ party

Real life describing traditions

2 ▶ 59 Listen to the description of the custom of dowry-giving and answer the questions.
1. What is a big dowry a sign of?
   _____
2. Why was a woman's dowry of practical importance?
   _____
   _____
3. Which family normally gives the dowry?
   _____
4. Which family gives the dowry in Nigeria?
   _____
5. What do the guests at a Nigerian engagement ceremony do, as well as dance and have fun?
   _____
6. What two things does a Nigerian dowry consist of?
   _____

> **dowry** (n) /ˈdaʊri/ property or money given to the groom by the bride's family in some cultures

3 ▶ 59 Complete the sentences with the words in the box. Then listen again and check.

bride	customary	marks	occasion
place	rule	symbolizes	traditional

1. Dowry-giving _____ different things, for example, a sign of wealth.
2. As a _____ , brides in the past did not go out to work.
3. It's _____ for a dowry to be given by the bride's family.
4. The engagement ceremony in Nigeria _____ the beginning of the wedding celebrations.
5. The ceremony is an _____ for people to have fun.
6. It takes _____ on the evening or a couple of nights before the wedding itself.
7. It was once _____ for money to be thrown at the couple's feet.
8. On the night of the wedding, the _____ goes back to her own house.

4 Pronunciation the letter *s*

▶ 60 Look at these words. Is the "s" sound /s/ or /z/? Listen and check (✓) the correct box.

		/s/	/z/			/s/	/z/
1	thing*s*	☐	☐	5	cloth*es*	☐	☐
2	hou*s*e	☐	☐	6	*s*uit	☐	☐
3	bride*s*	☐	☐	7	deliver*s*	☐	☐
4	*s*ocial	☐	☐	8	i*s*	☐	☐

5 Listen and respond describing traditions

▶ 61 Listen to some questions about wedding traditions. Respond to each question with your own words. Then compare your response with the model answer that follows.

1. *How does a man ask for a woman's hand in marriage?*

   It's traditional for a man to ask the woman's father for permission to marry her, but these days he usually asks her directly.

Unit 7 Customs and behavior

7e Scarlet sails

1 Writing skill adding detail

Read the description of a festival called Scarlet Sails. Complete the text with the missing details (a–e).

a in which a prince comes for his loved one in a beautiful ship with red sails
b drink and dance
c which is a festival of classical music and dance that runs from May to July
d with bright red sails
e one of the most beautiful cities in the world

2 Read the description again. What adjectives are used to describe these things?

1 Alexander Grin's story:
   _____

2 the ship, *Secret*:
   _____

3 the color of the sails:
   _____

4 the night of the celebration in general:
   _____ , _____ , _____

Writing a description

3 Complete this description of a spring festival in Oxford, in the UK, with the correct verbs and nouns. The first letter of each missing word is provided.

> **May morning**
>
> May morning in Oxford ¹ t_____ p_____ every year on May 1st and ² m_____ the arrival of spring. The celebrations usually ³ b_____ the night before, and many people stay up all through the night waiting for the sunrise. The ⁴ h_____ of the celebrations is when a crowd ⁵ g_____ on a bridge in the city center to listen to a choir singing at the top of Magdalen College tower. At 6:00 a.m., the bells ring and everyone is quiet. Then the silence is broken by the beautiful voices of the choir. When the choir has finished, the celebrations begin again with singing and ⁶ d_____ .

Scarlet sails

Scarlet Sails is a spectacular celebration in St. Petersburg, Russia, ¹_____ . It is a colorful mixture of parades, concerts, and fireworks. It takes place every year in the middle of June, and marks the graduation of students from all over Russia and the end of the academic year. It is part of the summer White Nights festival, ²_____ . Scarlet Sails is named after a romantic fairy tale written in 1917 by the writer Alexander Grin, ³_____ .

The festival begins around 11:00 p.m. with a concert and theatrical performance in St. Petersburg's Palace Square for all the graduating students. The main focus of the festival is the boats that parade along the Neva River, and crowds gather on the waterfront to watch them. As they go past, fireworks are set off in time to classical music by famous Russian composers. The highlight is the appearance of the ship *Secret*, a magnificent sailing ship ⁴_____ . After the parade, celebrations continue with other concerts, and people ⁵_____ until the dawn arrives at four in the morning. It is a magical night.

Wordbuilding word pairs

1 Make matching pairs. Match the words in box A with their "pair" in box B.

A			
this	bride	husband	food
friends	fun	plans	singing
suit	time		

B			
arrangements	dancing	drink	effort
family	games	groom	that
tie		wife	

2 Complete the sentences with matching pairs from Exercise 1.
 1 Karl and Sylvia raised a glass to their new life as ___husband and wife___ .
 2 Planning the wedding took ages, but it was worth all the _____ .
 3 The wedding was lively—there was a lot of _____ .
 4 There was not enough _____ at the reception because of all the uninvited guests.
 5 It was a small wedding. We just invited a few _____ .
 6 The woman usually wears a white dress, and the man wears a _____ .

Learning skills making full use of your teacher

3 Use your teacher as a resource. Read these tips to help improve your English.
 1 Pay attention to the way your teacher pronounces words and phrases and try to imitate them.
 2 Every teacher uses certain idiomatic phrases and expressions. Ask what they mean.
 3 Ask the teacher to correct your mistakes, particularly your pronunciation. Even teachers can feel shy about doing this.
 4 Ask your teacher what they think your main fault in English is and how you can correct it.
 5 Tell your teacher what kinds of books you like to read and ask them to recommend some in English.
 6 Make sure that you have the vocabulary you need (e.g., to describe your job). Ask your teacher to help supply these words.

4 Answer these questions. Then check with your teacher. Does your teacher agree with you?
 1 Can you pronounce these words from Unit 7?
  a disobey
  b dairy
  c future
 2 Which one of these do you think you have most difficulty with?
  a using the right tense
  b amount of vocabulary
  c pronouncing things correctly
 3 What can you do well in English?
  a write texts and emails
  b communicate at work
  c follow the TV news

Check!

5 Complete these phrasal verbs and idiomatic phrases. You can find all the answers in Unit 7 of the Student Book.

Quiz

1 Try not to give _____ to all your children's demands.
2 We don't eat _____ much these days because restaurants are so expensive.
3 It's very rude to stare _____ your phone at the dinner table.
4 Alex and I had a difference _____ opinion.
5 Bringing _____ children is not easy.
6 I don't mind what you do. It's all the same _____ me.
7 The festival begins _____ a big fireworks display.
8 What is it that makes some teenagers rebel _____ their parents?

Unit 8 Hopes and ambitions

8a Fulfilling your dreams

Vocabulary goals and ambitions

1 Complete the sentences about goals and ambitions. Use nouns and verbs. The first letter is provided.

1 They're trying to raise money for charity. Their t_____ is $5,000.
2 I hope your dreams c_____ true one day.
3 It's natural to try to l_____ up to your parents' expectations, but it isn't always easy.
4 I'm sorry, but what exactly is the a_____ of this exercise? I don't see the point.
5 Matt says that I don't h_____ any ambition, but it's just that I don't know yet what I want to do.
6 It took her twenty years, but she finally has a_____ her goal of becoming an author.

Listening ambitions

2 ▶62 Listen to two people talking about their ambitions. Complete the chart.

Speaker	Their ambition	What they were doing before
1 Rhea		
2 Sasha		

3 ▶62 Listen to the speakers again. Circle the correct option (a–c) to complete each statement.

1 Rhea's achievements include:
   a raising children.
   b running a company.
   c building her own home.
2 The aim of the volunteer program in Rwanda was to teach children using:
   a acting and drama.
   b useful work tasks.
   c games and play.
3 Rhea says that before she arrived at the school in Rwanda, the children:
   a didn't learn much.
   b didn't move about much.
   c didn't pay much attention to the teacher.
4 When she left college, Sasha thought that art would probably be:
   a her career.
   b something she did in her free time.
   c her whole life.
5 She moved to Cleveland because:
   a that's where her friends were.
   b it was the center of the art world.
   c it wasn't so expensive to live there.
6 In Sasha's gallery, they have shown:
   a their own work.
   b only local artists' work.
   c some well-known artists' work.

4 Circle the correct definition (a or b) of the words in **bold**.

1 I wanted to help people in a more **meaningful** way.
   a significant   b wanting to do good
2 I was very **fortunate**.
   a happy   b lucky
3 I have found my **calling**.
   a the job that was right for me
   b a job I was good at
4 I had the idea of **setting up** a gallery.
   a building   b establishing
5 It just **took off** from there.
   a became famous   b became successful

Grammar second, third, and mixed conditionals

5 Complete the sentences with the correct form of the verbs in parentheses. Use second, third, and mixed conditionals.

1. If Rhea _____ (feel) that working in insurance was a more meaningful job, she _____ (keep) on doing that job.
2. If Rhea's friend _____ (not / tell) her about the volunteer program, she _____ (not / be) a teacher trainer now.
3. If Cleveland _____ (be) an expensive city to live in, Sasha _____ (not / move) there.
4. If Sasha and her friends _____ (not / find) the old warehouse, they _____ (not / set) up a gallery.
5. If the gallery _____ (not / have) good reviews, it _____ (not / receive) so many visitors now.

6 Rewrite the sentences so they have a similar meaning. Use second, third, and mixed conditionals.

1. She's not an ambitious person. She didn't apply for the job of director.
   If she _____ , she _____ .
2. I met my wife, who is German, and now I am living in Germany.
   If I _____ , I _____ now.
3. I am not a risk-taker. I am not going to invest my own money in the business.
   If I _____ , I _____ .
4. She didn't receive much encouragement. She gave up her plan to become a pilot.
   If she _____ , she _____ .
5. I didn't say anything about the situation, because I am not worried about it.
   If I _____ , I _____ .
6. He left college and became a ski instructor, and now he's very happy with his life.
   If he _____ and _____ , maybe he _____ with his life.

7 Pronunciation contracted or weak forms

▶ 63 Listen to these sentences. Are the underlined verbs pronounced as weak forms (W) or are they contracted (C)? Write *W* or *C*. Then listen again and repeat.

1. If he asked me, I <u>would</u> certainly offer to help him. _____
2. It would have been easier if you <u>had been</u> there. _____
3. If I <u>had</u> known, I would have told you. _____
4. If he <u>was</u> more thoughtful, he would have remembered your birthday. _____
5. If the meeting <u>were</u> an hour earlier, I would be able to come. _____

Word focus *make* and *do*

8 Look at these three expressions used by Sasha when she described her ambition. Circle the correct option to complete the expressions.

1. I already knew it would be difficult to **do / make a living** from my art.
2. My ambition was to **do / make something** in the art world.
3. I still had to **do / make odd jobs** like working as a waiter.

9 Complete the sentences. Use the correct form of *make* or *do*.

1. Before you _____ a decision about the career you want, I think you should _____ some research about job opportunities.
2. Thanks for _____ the translation work that I gave you, but I think you've _____ a couple of small mistakes.
3. I've _____ a list of all the things I'd like to _____ when I'm in London.
4. I don't know how he thinks that sitting around all day and _____ nothing will _____ a difference!

Unit 8 Hopes and ambitions

8b Wish lists

Reading the forget-it list

1 Read the blog. Circle the statement (a–c) that best summarizes why the author is against making wish lists.

a It is a selfish thing to do.
b It won't make you happy.
c It is unrealistic.

2 Read the blog again. Are the sentences true (T) or false (F)? Or is there not enough information (N) to say if the statements are true or false?

1 John Goddard made his list because he was frightened of dying.   T F N
2 Goddard's list was full of things that were difficult to achieve.   T F N
3 Goddard was not able to fulfill all of his wishes.   T F N
4 The author's neighbor had a big party to celebrate her 30th birthday.   T F N
5 The author thinks that we choose some things to put on our wish lists because it will win the respect of people we know.   T F N
6 The author can't afford to take a year off to travel.   T F N
7 The author thinks that he could manage to trek across the Himalayas.   T F N

The forget-it list

In 1940, a fifteen-year-old American boy decided to make a list of everything he wanted to do in his life. John Goddard, who later became an anthropologist, wrote down 127 goals, most of them very ambitious. They included climbing the world's highest mountains, flying a jet, running a mile in five minutes, reading the whole Encyclopedia Britannica, mastering surfing, and visiting the moon. Amazingly, he managed to do most of them and add several more before he died in 2013. He left behind a book about his adventures, but he also left another legacy—the "bucket list." This idea (a list of the things you want to do before you die) was made popular by the 2007 movie *The Bucket List*. Now everyone, it seems, has a bucket list, from Bill Clinton to my neighbor who's just celebrated her thirtieth birthday and feels that life is passing her by.

I have some issues with this. First, why do you need the excuse of dying to have wishes about what you want to achieve? We're all going to die at some point. Second, it becomes rather competitive. Are these really the things that you want to do (for example, become an expert salsa dancer), or are they the things that you would like other people to be impressed by? And finally, what happens if you fail to achieve some of your goals? You will probably be more full of regret than if you had not made a list in the first place.

So I've come up with an alternative idea: the "forget-it list." This is a list of all the wishes you have that are unlikely to come true and all the things that you might think will make you happier or more fulfilled, but may not be so wonderful after all. For example, I wish I was a professional musician. Forget it—I have a good job and great colleagues. I wish I could spend a year traveling around South America. Forget it—I have a family to support—a family I love being with, by the way. I wish I could trek across the Himalayas. Forget it—even though it must be beautiful, it would probably break me physically. What I'm trying to say, in short, is: want what you have, and stop wanting what you don't have.

3 Find words or expressions in the blog on page 62 that mean the following.

1 something left for the benefit of future generations (paragraph 1)
   _____
2 moving too fast to take advantage of (paragraph 1)
   _____
3 a (often poor or false) reason for an action (paragraph 2)
   _____
4 another or different (paragraph 3)
   _____
5 improbable (paragraph 3)
   _____

Grammar *wish* and *if only*

4 Circle the correct verb form to complete these wishes.

1 I wish people *stopped / would stop* making bucket lists.
2 I wish I *can / could* take a year off from my work to do the things I want to do.
3 I wish I *traveled / had traveled* more when I was younger.
4 If only I *were / would be* more satisfied with what I have, then I wouldn't need to write a wish list.
5 I wrote a bucket list some years ago, but I wish I *didn't / hadn't*.
6 I want to go on a cruise, but my husband says they are boring. I wish he *changed / would change* his mind.
7 I bet a lot of people wish John Goddard *didn't start / hadn't started* this trend.
8 My friend said something very funny yesterday. She said, "I wish I *didn't have / wouldn't have* so many regrets."

5 Complete these wishes. Use the correct form of the verbs in parentheses.

1 Oh, no! We're going to be late. I wish we _____ (leave) earlier.
2 I wish you _____ (stop) complaining about the weather.
3 I really want to know how Olivia did at her interview. If only I _____ (have) her number, then I could call her.
4 What would I change about my appearance? Well, I wish I _____ (be) a few centimeters taller, for a start.
5 No one ever listens to my ideas. I wish people _____ (take) me more seriously.
6 I wish the people next door _____ (turn) down that music. I can't concentrate.

6 Pronunciation /s/, /ʃ/, and /tʃ/

▶ 64 Listen to six words. Circle the word you hear.

1 mass   mash   match
2 sip   ship   chip
3 Sue   shoe   chew
4 Swiss   swish   switch
5 sock   shock   chock
6 bass   bash   batch

7 Dictation bucket lists

▶ 65 Listen and complete this opinion of bucket lists with the words you hear.

I am very suspicious of bucket lists now.
They _____ ,
but _____ ,
they have _____ .
In bookstores, _____
100 Places _____
or *100* _____ .
And if your _____
tiger, there are even _____
where they _____ .

8c A cause for hope?

Listening conservation stories

1 ▶66 Listen to three people talking about conservation projects and complete the chart.

	What needs to be protected?	Has the conservation work been successful?
1	The mangrove _____ in _____	
2	The West African _____	
3	The black poplar _____ in _____	

Cancún   West Africa   Poplar tree

2 ▶66 Listen again. Are the sentences true (T), false (F), or is there not enough information (N)?

1 Every inhabitant of Cancún misses the beautiful mangrove forest.   T F N
2 Pollution has badly damaged the coral reef along the Cancún coast.   T F N
3 In West Africa, conservationists needed to find out where the giraffe went for food.   T F N
4 Farmers were killing the giraffes who fed on their land.   T F N
5 People associate the word "conservation" with work in developing countries.   T F N
6 The decrease in the numbers of black poplar trees has been quite sudden.   T F N

3 ▶66 Complete the sentences using these words. Then listen again and check.

| classic | heroic | rarest |
| rotting | sale | small |

1 Today, that forest is buried and _____ underneath 500 hotels.
2 This place is a _____ example of how not to build a tourist resort.
3 Nature is for _____ here.
4 A _____ effort on the part of conservationists has saved the giraffe.
5 But in fact, many conservation efforts are _____ in scale.
6 The black poplar is one of Britain's _____ species of tree.

4 Find words and expressions in Exercise 3 that have these meanings.

1 very typical: _____
2 an area of land with lots of trees: _____
3 placed under the ground: _____
4 you can buy it: _____
5 decaying or going bad: _____

Vocabulary strong feelings

5 Rewrite the text about the black poplar tree. Replace the words in **bold** with a more emotive word from the box.

deprived	exploit	giant
most threatened	overdeveloped	rescue
wonderful		

If you mention the term "conservation efforts," people often think of attempts to [1] **save** endangered animals, or to protect [2] **poor** communities from [3] **big** corporate organizations that are trying to [4] **use** their land. But in fact, many conservation efforts are small in scale, and many have [5] **positive** outcomes. The black poplar tree is one of Britain's [6] **rarest** species of tree, and its numbers have been declining for decades. That's because much of its natural habitat—the floodplain—has been [7] **built on** with new housing.

1 _____   5 _____
2 _____   6 _____
3 _____   7 _____
4 _____

8d Choices

Real life discussing preferences

1 Match the beginnings of the sentences (1–6) with the endings (a–f) to make complete sentences.

1 I prefer walking _____
2 I'd rather walk _____
3 I like walking _____
4 I'd rather we _____
5 I'd rather _____
6 I think it would be better _____

a than cycle.
b walked.
c if we walked.
d to cycling.
e not cycle.
f more than cycling.

2 ▶ 67 Listen to a conversation between friends who are trying to organize a friend's birthday party. Check (✓) the tasks they mention.

☐ buying drinks
☐ decorating the tent
☐ doing shopping
☐ renting a sound system
☐ preparing food
☐ setting tables

3 ▶ 67 Complete the sentences. Then listen to the conversation again and check your answers.

1 I'd _____ any cooking.
2 But if you _____ something else, there are plenty of other things.
3 I don't _____ with the decorations.
4 I could, but I'd rather _____ that.
5 It _____ if I went to get the sound system.
6 OK, and I _____ the decorations anyway, so that's perfect.

4 Complete the sentences so they express the same ideas as the sentences in Exercise 3. Use the word in parentheses.

1 If I had the choice, I _____ any cooking. (prefer)
2 But if you _____ something else, there are plenty of other things. (rather)
3 I'd _____ with the decorations. (happy)
4 I could, but it _____ if someone else did that. (better)
5 I _____ and get the sound system. (rather)
6 I _____ the decorations anyway. (prefer)

5 Pronunciation *do you, would you*

▶ 68 Listen and complete the sentences.

1 _____ a full meal or just something light?
2 _____ to take a short break?
3 _____ we went to the movie another night?
4 _____ Osaka more than Tokyo?

6 Listen and respond talking about preferences

▶ 69 Listen to someone asking you about your preferences. Respond to each question in your own words. Answer in full sentences and give reasons. Then compare your response with the model answer that follows.

1
> I'm going to ask you to explain your preferences for certain things. Ready? Here we go: bath or shower?

> I prefer having a shower. It's quicker and more refreshing.

Unit 8 **Hopes and ambitions** 65

8e A wish for change

Writing an online comment

1 Read the online comment below. Answer the questions.

1 What is the subject of the blog post the writer is responding to?
   _____
   _____

2 Does he agree with the writer of the blog? Why or why not?
   _____
   _____

Sean Thompson (Communications specialist)
Thanks for your interesting blog post and for drawing attention to this topical issue. I am sure a lot of people will agree with you that people who speak loudly on their phones in public places should know better. But I am not convinced that it represents "anti-social behavior."

I was brought up in Brooklyn in New York, where people live close together, and it wasn't unusual to overhear other people's conversations: discussions, family arguments, jokes. Often it was just their everyday business that you heard: a call to someone to get up, a reminder to buy something from the store, asking someone to get out of the bathroom. But I don't see this as anti-social; it's social behavior. Knowing each other's business helps there to be openness between neighbors. Actually, I think it encourages people to talk to each other more.

Of course, some people speak loudly on their phones just to show off. I was on the subway recently where a man was loudly discussing a business deal. As if he thought he hadn't impressed the rest of us enough, halfway through the conversation he switched from English into Chinese! But to have laws against speaking loudly in public, as you suggest, is not the answer.

2 Writing skill giving vivid examples

a Look at the online comment again. Answer the questions.

1 What examples support the writer's argument?
   _____
   _____

2 What example(s) show that there are exceptions to his argument?
   _____
   _____

b Look at this excerpt from another comment posted about the same article. Add examples (1–5) to complete the comment.

Great post. I couldn't agree with you more. People are so inconsiderate in how they use their phones these days: in ¹ _____, ² _____, and especially on ³ _____. And they always talk about the most boring things like ⁴ _____ and ⁵ _____. As if they think the rest of us are interested!

Word focus *better*

3 Underline the phrase with *better* that the writer uses in the comment in Exercise 1. What does the phrase mean (a, b, or c)?
   a have enough sense not to do something
   b improve on the effort of another person
   c be more useful or desirable

4 Complete the sentences using these phrases with *better*.

be better	be better off	know better

1 I'll be in a meeting from 3:00 to 5:00 p.m., so it would _____ to send me a text message.
2 He's always calling me when I'm busy at work. He should _____ .
3 I think we would all _____ if the cell phone had never been invented!

Wordbuilding noun suffixes

1 Write the name of the person who does each of these jobs. Use the correct noun suffix.

1. Someone who sells **flowers** or makes flower arrangements is a _____ .
2. Someone who **translates** documents from one language to another is a _____ .
3. Someone who works in the **banking** sector is a _____ .
4. Someone who specializes in preparing medicines in a **pharmacy** is a _____ .
5. Someone who looks after the books in a **library** is a _____ .
6. Someone who prepares the **accounts** for a company is an _____ .
7. Someone who **specializes** in IT problems is a _____ .
8. Someone who does **surgical** operations on people in a hospital is a _____ .
9. Someone who **consults** with people about their finances is a financial _____ .
10. Someone who does **optical** tests and makes glasses is an _____ .

2 Circle the general name for a person (male or female) with these jobs.

1. someone who sells things: *a salesman / a sales officer / a salesperson*
2. someone who works for the police: *a police operator / a police officer / a police person*
3. someone who works for the fire department: *a firefighter / a fire manager / a fire person*
4. someone who acts: *an actor / an actress / an acting agent*
5. someone who helps passengers on a plane: *a flight agent / a flight operator / a flight attendant*

Learning skills improving your listening

3 ▶ 70 A key to understanding fast native speech is to understand stress and linking in English pronunciation. Listen to this sentence and note the stress and linking in it.

1. **Stress**: Sorry I just don't accept that.
2. **Linking**: Sorry‿I just don't‿accept that.

4 ▶ 71 Look at these sentences. Underline the stressed syllables and indicate where the sounds are linked. Then listen and check.

1. Globalization helps people in rich countries.
2. They can have goods out of season.
3. But to be honest, I don't need flowers imported from Africa in December.

5 ▶ 72 Read these steps (1–5) for improving your listening skills. Listen again to the third speaker from 8c, Exercise 1 and follow the steps.

1. Write down the words you hear.
2. Read your transcript. Does it make grammatical sense?
3. Compare your transcript with the audioscript.
4. Note the words and sounds that have the strongest stress.
5. Note which words are clearly linked. This will help you to distinguish them the next time you hear them.

Check!

6 Complete the crossword. All the answers are in Unit 8 of the Student Book.

Across

2 and 6 form the nickname for a woman who worked as a "computer" at NASA in the 1950s
5 an animal only found in Madagascar
7 Complete this sentence: If I hadn't missed the bus, I would have _____ on time.
9 Complete this sentence: I prefer tea _____ coffee.
10 another expression for "I wish"
11 the superpower most explorers wished they had was to be _____

Down

1 another word for an aim
3 an aim that is usually an amount or a number
4 what you want to achieve (often in your career)
8 If you create a sound, you "make a _____"

Unit 9 The news

9a Photojournalism

Vocabulary reporting verbs

1 Complete the crossword with reporting verbs.

Across
2 He _____ me about the crocodiles in the river.
5 The party was a little noisy, but you didn't need to _____ to call the police!
6 I know you took my pen. Don't try to _____ it.

Down
1 I don't know what to order. What do you _____ ?
3 You always _____ so many questions!
4 I think you've made the wrong choice. I _____ you to think again.

Listening re-touching reality

2 ▶73 Listen to an interview with a journalist talking about altering—or changing—photos. What two examples do they discuss? Complete the descriptions.

1 The _____ of the February _____ edition of *National Geographic* magazine.
2 A _____ of Nancy Reagan and Raisa Gorbachev in *Picture Week* _____ .

3 ▶73 Listen again. Are the sentences true (T) or false (F)?

1 Photo editors changed the size of the Pyramids in the photo. T F
2 An editor said that the changes to the photo were OK because it was a cover photo. T F
3 He also said that technology had made altering images more acceptable. T F
4 Editors have said that it's acceptable to alter covers because they advertise the book or magazine. T F
5 The journalist thinks that there's no difference between manipulating cover images and altering news photos. T F
6 *Picture Week* changed two photos to suggest that the people in them had friendly faces. T F
7 People thought that the *Picture Week* photo was unacceptable. T F

manipulate (v) /məˈnɪpjʊleɪt/ digitally change information or images (on a computer)
digitally enhanced (adj) /ˈdɪdʒɪt(ə)li ɪnˈhɑːnst/ improved using digital technology
touch up (v) /tʌtʃ ˈʌp/ make small changes to improve an image

4 Pronunciation extra long vowel /ō/

▶ 74 Listen to these words. Pay attention to the long /ō/ sound. Then listen again and repeat.

| boat | don't | fellow | going | growing | hotel |
| know | local | opposed | own | photo | soda |

Grammar verb patterns with reporting verbs

5 Rewrite these sentences using the reporting verbs given.

1. People said that the magazine had manipulated reality.
   People **accused** the magazine _____
   _____
   _____ .

2. The editor said they had altered the image.
   The editor **admitted** _____
   _____
   _____ .

3. But he said they hadn't done anything wrong.
   But he **denied** _____
   _____
   _____ .

4. He said modern technology made it easy to alter images.
   He **blamed** _____
   _____
   _____ .

5. The editor told the designer that it was OK to alter the cover image.
   The editor **persuaded** _____
   _____
   _____ .

6. People weren't happy and said that they had been given a false impression.
   People **complained** _____
   _____
   _____ .

7. Some people say, "Don't trust a photo if there's anything important depending on it."
   Some people **warn** you _____
   _____
   _____ .

6 Complete the text with the correct form of the verbs in parentheses. Use prepositions where necessary.

In the past, people criticized photographers ¹_____ (invade) people's privacy or ²_____ (take) pictures that did not reflect the reality of a situation. But nowadays, in the age of digital photography, there is a new problem. How do we know that a photo has not been altered after it has been taken? It would be wrong to blame the photographer ³_____ (manipulate) some of the photos that appear in our newspapers and magazines. A photo editor might be asked ⁴_____ (alter) a photo digitally in order to make a good story. For example, someone might suggest ⁵_____ (use) Photoshop to make a movie star's face look more attractive. Or they might urge the photo editor ⁶_____ (add) an image of a frightened child into a photo of a street protest. You can perhaps forgive the editor ⁷_____ (make) the first alteration, but what about the second? That is a practice people should refuse ⁸_____ (accept).

7 Dictation digital photography

▶ 75 Listen to someone talking about film and digital cameras. Complete the text with the words you hear.

1. Like many of his fellow professionals, photographer Fritz Hoffman _____
   _____ .

2. A digital camera _____
   _____, but a film camera
   _____ .

3. Hoffman also claims _____
   _____
   _____ .

4. That's so that _____
   _____ .

9b News in brief

Reading good-news stories

1 Read the four newspaper stories. Match the headlines (a–d) with the stories (1–4).

a Better to give than to receive
b A sense of community
c A charmed life
d An old secret

2 Write the number of the story (1–4) next to the statements (a–f). More than one answer may be possible.

This story shows that:
a you can help people without spending a lot of money. _____
b there is not one right way of doing something. _____
c you can inspire other people by your actions. _____
d some people are lucky. _____
e good things can come out of bad situations. _____
f people's faith in human nature can be restored. _____

News in brief

1 _____

During the UK street riots of 2011, it was estimated that rioters caused over £100 million worth of damage to their own communities. But when there's a negative, there's often a positive, as the case of Mr. Biber, a London barber, shows. Mr. Biber's barbershop, where he had been cutting hair for forty years, was damaged in the riots, and the 89-year-old thought he had lost everything. But word got around, and a website to support him was set up. Donations raised £35,000—enough to make the necessary repairs. Moreover, the generosity Mr. Biber received encouraged him to continue doing what he loves.

2 _____

Some people believe that the secret to a long life is a glass of red wine every day. For others, it is plenty of exercise. But few people would claim that eating fast food helps. They obviously haven't met 100-year-old Catherine Reddoch from Matamata, New Zealand. Every day, using her walker to support her, she walks a kilometer—a journey which takes her one hour—to her local hamburger café. Here, she eats a cheeseburger and drinks a cup of hot chocolate. Mrs. Reddoch is not concerned about the fat content of the meal. "I eat anything and everything—I like my cheeseburgers," she says. The café owner was reported to have put a plaque on Catherine's usual seat with her name on it.

3 _____

Secret Agent L is the brainchild of one woman, Laura Miller. Laura's mission is to spread kindness around the world. She does this by doing small acts of kindness, like leaving a flower on someone's car windshield or making a nice walking stick for someone to find when they are on a long hike. The idea is that when someone finds these secret gifts, it brightens up their day. It is believed that

Secret Agent L now has over 1,800 followers, all carrying out and sharing their own acts of kindness around the world.

4 _____

A 21-year-old man who drove his car over the edge of the Grand Canyon escaped with only a few minor injuries. Witnesses said that his car had plunged two hundred feet into the mile-deep canyon before hitting a tree, which stopped it from falling further. He is not thought to have been speeding, but the exact cause of the accident remains unknown. Another visitor found him lying on the road after he had apparently climbed back out of the canyon. The emergency services said he was an extremely lucky man.

riot (n) /ˈraɪət/ a violent protest
plaque (n) /plæk/ a small metal sign

3 Find words in the stories on page 70 that mean:
1. gifts of money (story 1): _____
2. a walking aid for old people (story 2): _____
3. an original idea (story 3): _____
4. makes more cheerful (story 3): _____
5. fell or dived (story 4): _____
6. driving too fast (story 4): _____

Grammar passive reporting verbs

4 Underline an example of a passive reporting verb in each story on page 70.

▶ **PASSIVE REPORTING VERBS**

Note how these tenses are transformed from active to passive.

Active	Passive
People say that	It is said that
	(She) is said + infinitive
People have said that	It has been said that
People said that	It was said that
	(She) was said + infinitive / perfect infinitive
People used to say that	It used to be said that

5 Look at the grammar box above. Rewrite the underlined phrases below using passive reporting verbs.
1. People say that the summers are very hot.
   It is said that the summers are very hot.
2. Everyone knows that reading is important.
   Reading _____ to be important.
3. People used to believe that the Earth was flat.
   It _____ that the Earth was flat.
4. People have estimated that the bridge will cost $10 million.
   It _____ that the bridge will cost $10 million.
5. People thought that she was missing.
   She _____ to be missing.
6. People said that she regretted her actions.
   She _____ to have regretted her actions.

6 Rewrite the sentences using passive reporting verbs.
1. People say that there is always a positive side to things.
   It is said that there is always a positive side to things.
2. People hoped that the secret gifts would brighten up someone's day.
   It _____ the secret gifts would brighten up someone's day.
3. Most people don't recommend eating fast food if you want to live longer.
   Eating fast food _____ if you want to live longer.
4. People expect Mr. Biber to continue working.
   It _____ Mr. Biber _____ working.
5. People said that the tree had prevented the car from falling further.
   The tree _____ the car from falling further.
6. People considered the man to be very lucky.
   The man _____ very lucky.

Vocabulary positive adjectives

7 Put the letters in the correct order to make adjectives describing good-news stories.
1. marching _____
2. usaming _____
3. springini _____
4. aggening _____
5. shiningsato _____
6. potisimtic _____

8 Match the adjectives in Exercise 7 (1–6) with these adjectives (a–e) with a similar meaning.
a. hopeful _____
b. funny _____
c. amazing _____
d. pleasant _____ , _____
e. giving hope _____

9 Pronunciation weak forms in verbs

▶ 76 Listen to the auxiliary verbs in these sentences. Notice how they are pronounced using the weak form. Then listen again and repeat.
1. It was estimated that £100 million worth of damage was caused in the riots.
2. It is believed that Secret Agent L has more than 1,800 followers.
3. It was thought that the driver had fallen asleep at the wheel of his car.
4. It was expected that the injured man would make a full recovery.
5. It has been estimated that fifty percent of the population will be overweight by 2025.
6. It had been thought that diet was more important than exercise.

9c Fairness in reporting

Listening balanced reporting

1 ▶ 77 Listen to a journalist talking about balanced reporting. Which statement (a–c) best summarizes the journalist's argument?
   a Broadcasters and journalists often just want to present their own view.
   b It is often a mistake for broadcasters and news writers to try to present both sides of an argument equally.
   c It is very important for broadcasters and news writers to present both sides of an argument equally.

2 ▶ 77 Listen to the report again. Circle the correct option to complete the sentences.
   1 Broadcasters and news writers don't want to be seen as being in favor of *a particular / the stronger* side.
   2 News reports *should / shouldn't* present all the sides of an argument equally.
   3 Most of the scientific evidence supports the view that global warming is *natural / man-made*.
   4 In the 1970s debate about whether smoking was harmful, broadcasters usually presented *only one view / both views*.
   5 Scientists who denied the link between smoking and disease were often *working for tobacco companies / not real scientists*.
   6 People say that the amount of time given to each view should be in proportion to the *number of supporters / amount of real evidence* on each side.

3 Look at the audioscript of Track 77. Find words that mean:
   1 showing favor to one side (adj, paragraph 1):
   _____
   2 basic (adj, paragraph 2):
   _____
   3 very great or strong (adj, paragraph 2):
   _____
   4 gives a false impression of (v, paragraph 4):
   _____
   5 properly corresponding in size (adv, paragraph 4):
   _____

Word focus *word*

4 Look at these expressions with *word* and circle the correct definition (a or b).
   1 The restaurant was popular **from the word go**.
      a from when we had permission
      b from the start
   2 Jamie has been behaving very strangely recently. Can you **have a quiet word with** him?
      a be very strict with   b talk privately to
   3 Please **don't say a word to** Tabitha about the mug I broke. It's her favorite.
      a don't tell   b lie to
   4 He said I would never be successful as a professional artist, but he had to **eat his words**.
      a admit he was wrong   b apologize

5 Complete the sentences using these expressions with *word*.

don't take my word for it	at a loss for words
eat my words	word of mouth
gave his word	one person's word
have the last word	against another's

   1 We get most of our new customers by _____ _____ . We don't really advertise.
   2 I said that there was no way he could win the singing competition. I may have to _____ !
   3 It is just _____ . You'll have to decide who you believe.
   4 If you don't believe me, then _____ _____ . Check the facts for yourself.
   5 He _____ that he would not tell anyone my secret.
   6 I didn't know what to say—I was _____ .
   7 She's very argumentative. She always has to _____ .

9d Spreading the news

Real life reporting what you have heard

1 Complete the sentences. Use a verb in each blank. Do the sentences express belief (B) or disbelief (D)?

1 I wouldn't _____ her word for it.   B D
2 She generally _____ her facts right.   B D
3 I can _____ it.   B D
4 He tends to _____ things.   B D
5 That doesn't _____ me.   B D
6 I'd _____ that with a grain of salt.   B D

2 ▶ 78 Listen to a conversation between two friends, Jane and Annie. Answer the questions.

1 What is the news about Patrick that Annie wants to share?
   _____
   _____

2 Who did she hear this news from?
   _____
   _____

3 What does Annie ask Jane to do with the news?
   _____
   _____

3 ▶ 78 Complete the sentences from the conversation with the words in the box. Then listen again and check.

verbs:	heard	seems	thinks
prepositions:	about	to	
adverbs:	apparently	supposedly	
nouns:	gossip	grain	

1 Did you hear the good news _____ (*preposition*) Patrick?
2 Well, _____ (*adverb*) he was spotted by someone from a big theatrical agency.
3 She _____ (*verb*) it won't be long before we see Patrick on TV.
4 Well, I'd take that with a _____ (*noun*) of salt if I were you.
5 No, according _____ (*preposition*) Kate, it's more than that.
6 I _____ (*verb*) that it's really difficult to get that kind of work.
7 Don't worry. I'm not the type to spread _____ (*noun*). Does the agency take a big fee?
8 It _____ (*verb*) that they only take ten or fifteen percent, _____ (*adverb*).

4 Pronunciation the schwa

▶ 79 Listen to these words. Underline the stressed syllable and circle the schwa /ə/ sounds. Example: sup̲pos̲ed̲ly

1 comedy   4 difficult
2 festival   5 agency
3 apparently   6 theatrical

5 Listen and respond reporting what you have heard

▶ 80 Listen to someone giving you some news about government taxes. Respond each time with your own words. Then compare your response with the model answer that follows.

1 *Did you hear the good news about taxes?*

   Good news about taxes? No, what happened?

9e News article

A
Bama has a higher proportion of people over 100 years old than anywhere else in China. The exact reason for this is not known. Some say it is the mountain air. Others say that strong magnetic fields help improve sleep. ¹_____ , it has attracted a lot of tourists who want to benefit from its healthy environment.
²_____ the tourists increase traffic pollution and also leave their trash behind.
³_____ , the local population who previously lived on simple locally grown food are now eating the less healthy, processed food that tourism has brought with it.

B
⁴_____ a new eco-resort that is now being built will help to reduce this pollution and preserve the old Bama.

C
Bama is a quiet Chinese village in the Guangxi Province with a reputation for well-being and long life. Because of this, it has recently become a popular destination for Chinese "health" tourists.
⁵_____ , with so many people visiting Bama to escape the pollution in Chinese cities, the features that make Bama special are themselves in danger.

D
"It's a paradox," says one local man, aged 84. "In one way, the tourists bring money and jobs for us, but ⁶_____ , they bring pollution."

Writing a news article

1 Read the news article. Put the paragraphs (A–D) in the correct order.

1 _____   2 _____   3 _____   4 _____

2 Look at the article again. Which paragraph:

1. gives the key information? _____
2. gives the details? _____
3. gives a comment on the situation? _____
4. offers a solution? _____

3 Complete the article with these phrases.

at the same time	the problem is that
but now	what is more
it is hoped that	whatever the reason

4 Writing skill using quotations

Complete these quotations. Add quotation marks and other punctuation where necessary.

1. One resident described his life in Bama. I have everything I want here he said. I can go fishing when I want to. I don't have any stress. And then he added why would I want to go and live in the city?

2. Some people come here to take wedding photos said another resident which is fine. But when they leave their trash behind, I get very angry.

3. A health tourist said before I came here I could hardly breathe or speak because the pollution in my city was so bad. He added with a big smile on his face now I sing every day.

Wordbuilding forming adjectives from verbs

1 Complete the sentences using these verbs + *-ing*. More than one answer may be possible.

charm	confuse	depress	inspire
refresh	tire	touch	~~worry~~

1 It is _____worrying_____ that she is so late—she's normally very punctual.
2 The news article was very _____ . You couldn't work out why the daughter had left her family.
3 It's very _____ to hear about a business that doesn't just do things to make money. You don't often hear that.
4 He is a really _____ man—polite, interesting, and kind.
5 The article about two friends overcoming their difficulties was very _____ .
6 Environmental news is often _____ , but in this case, the article offered hope.
7 The news featured the _____ story of a fourteen-year-old girl who got a part-time job to help support her family.
8 It's very _____ to watch a movie with subtitles for three hours.

2 Make adjectives using verbs + *-ive*.

1 good at **inventing** _inventive_ (from *invent*)
2 good at **persuading** _____
3 good at **creating** _____
4 liking to **compete** _____
5 **producing** a lot _____
6 **talking** a lot _____
7 wanting to **protect** _____

Learning skills keeping a learning diary

3 Why is keeping a learning diary a good idea? Compare these reasons with your own ideas.

- to learn from your mistakes and successes
- to track your progress
- to make clear targets for the next stage of your learning
- to record what you have learned

4 Read the following actions that can help you to evaluate and personalize your learning.

Actions

1 Write down your experiences of learning after each lesson: what you found easy, what you found difficult, and what the most important thing you learned was.
2 Note down mistakes that you have made before.
3 Make a note of an excerpt or a sentence that you particularly liked, and try to memorize it.
4 Set yourself a small task based on the language you learned in your last lesson, e.g., write a good news article, or report what someone said to you.

5 Apply the actions (1–4) to Unit 9. Then remember to do it for your next lesson!

Check!

6 Take the quiz. You can find all the answers in Unit 9 of the Student Book.

Quiz Time

1 Add one more reporting verb that is followed by each of these patterns.
   a verb + infinitive: *promise*, *threaten*, _____
   b verb + someone + infinitive: *ask*, *encourage*, _____
   c verb + someone/something + preposition + *-ing*: *criticize*, *thank*, _____

2 Complete these sentences about the characters in Unit 9.
   a Sharbat Gula's photo is one of the most f_____ images of our time.
   b Dr. Zhavoronkov is trying to find drugs that will slow down the a_____ process.
   c The pilot Peter Burkill went from hero to z_____ .

3 Complete the phrases.
   a The best form of advertising is when news travels by word of m_____ .
   b News programs often like to end with a g_____-news story.
   c It's not a good thing to g_____ about people behind their backs.
   d You can usually tell what an article is going to be about by looking at the h_____ .

Unit 10 Talented people

10a The great communicator

Listening

1 ▶ 81 Read the questions. Then listen to the description of Ronald Reagan and complete the answers.

1. Where was Ronald Reagan raised?
   In a _____ .
2. What jobs did he have before he entered politics?
   He worked as a _____ and an _____ .
3. What did people who criticized him say about his speeches?
   He could only _____ .
4. What made him a great communicator?
   His ability to _____ .
5. What other factor worked in his favor as president?
   It was a time of _____ .

2 ▶ 81 Look at the words and phrases in **bold** from the description of Ronald Reagan. Circle the correct meaning (a or b). Then listen again and check.

1. His skills as **an orator** were noticed, and he was persuaded to run for governor of California.
   a a politician
   b a public speaker
2. He was often ridiculed for not being very clever—a **second-rate** actor …
   a not very good
   b slow-speaking
3. Reagan always **gave the impression** that he was listening …
   a made others believe
   b wanted others to think
4. He made people feel that they **mattered**.
   a were lucky
   b were important
5. The economy **thrived** during his presidency.
   a did badly
   b did well
6. Reagan's style of communication **stands out**.
   a is noticeable
   b is old-fashioned

Vocabulary careers

3 ▶ 81 Complete the sentences with the correct verb. Then listen again to the description and check your answers.

1. Ronald Reagan _____ from Eureka College, Illinois, with a degree in economics and sociology.
2. He moved to Los Angeles to _____ a career as an actor in movies and television.
3. After _____ the Republican Party in 1962, his skills as an orator were noticed.
4. He _____ a good job as governor of California.
5. He went on to _____ the president of the United States between 1981 and 1989.

Grammar articles: *a/an*, *the*, or zero article?

4 Complete with *the* or zero article (–).

Countries: _X_ Japan, _The_ United Arab Emirates, _X_ Netherlands, _The_ Thailand
Places: _The_ Amazon River, _X_ countryside, _The_ moon, _The_ Mount Everest
Times: _X_ weekend, _X_ Saturday, _X_ April
Other: _X_ breakfast, _X_ police, _X_ poor, _X_ biology

5 Complete the sentences with *a/an, the,* or zero article (–).

1. After joining _The_ Republican Party in 1962, Reagan's skills as an orator were noticed.
2. Reagan was president of _The_ United States between 1981 and 1989.
3. He remains one of _the_ most popular US presidents of _____ past fifty years.
4. Ronald Reagan understood that it is important to be _a_ good communicator.
5. When he was speaking to you, Reagan always gave _a_ impression that he was listening, too.
6. He looked _____ people in _the_ eye, smiled at them, and made them feel special.
7. He presided over a time of _a_ great economic growth in _The_ United States.
8. _The_ things weren't great for _the_ most Americans, but he gave them _____ hope.
9. It obviously helped that _____ US economy thrived during _the_ time that he was president.
10. If you can connect with _a_ ordinary people, there's very little you can do wrong.

6 Pronunciation linking vowels

a ▶ 82 Listen to these phrases. What sound links the words: /w/ or /j/? Check (✓) the correct box.

	/w/	/j/
1 he often spoke to ordinary people	☐	☐
2 do a good job	☐	☐
3 the beginning of the end	☐	☐
4 look someone in the eye	☐	☐
5 too expensive	☐	☐
6 it's so exciting	☐	☐

b ▶ 82 Listen again and check. Then practice saying each phrase.

7 Dictation careers

▶ 83 Listen to someone talking about job qualifications. Write down the words you hear. Be careful—many of the sentences contain the linking sounds /w/ or /j/.

I was always told _____
_____
_____
_____
_____
_____
_____
_____
_____

Vocabulary qualifications

8 Complete the job interview between an interviewer (I) and an applicant (A) using these words.

| background | experience | knowledge |
| qualifications | qualities | talents |

I: So can you tell me first a little about your ¹ _background_ ?
A: Sure. My mother's French and my father's English. I was brought up in France and …
I: And do you have any previous journalism ² _experience_ ?
A: Yes. At college I was editor of the student magazine, and after that I worked for a local radio station …
I: What ³ _____ do you have?
A: I majored in media studies, with a minor in …
I: What would you say are your best ⁴ _____ ?
A: I'm a very organized person, I'm hardworking, and I think I …
I: Do you have any ⁵ _____ of European politics?
A: Well, I read the papers regularly and I take a great interest in current affairs …
I: And lastly. Do you have any particular ⁶ _____ ? Things that might make you different from other candidates?
A: I'm good at learning languages, and I'm a good photographer.

10b An inspirational scientist

Reading

1 Read the article quickly and underline the part of the text that answers these questions.
1. What is the aim of Hayat Sindi's work?
2. What is the problem with medicines used to fight diseases like hepatitis?
3. What is the tool that can help with this?
4. Why did Sindi move to England?
5. What is her hope for other women like her?

2 Read the article again and answer the questions. Circle the correct option (a–c).
1. Which of the following is NOT a quality of the new tool?
   a small   b powerful   c high-tech
2. Compared to results from a medical laboratory, this tool's results are:
   a more accurate.   b more positive.
   c quicker.
3. Sindi's family was not:
   a rich.   b academic.   c traditional.
4. Sindi studied hard in England because she was afraid of:
   a her parents.   b failure.   c feeling lonely.
5. Sindi would like women to use their education to:
   a go abroad.
   b help their own countries.
   c become scientists.

3 Find these words and phrases in the article. Circle the best definition (a–c).
1. entire (paragraph 1)
   a complete   b modern   c sophisticated
2. detect (paragraph 2)
   a have   b find   c solve
3. low-tech (paragraph 2)
   a cheap   b small   c not sophisticated
4. let (her family) down (paragraph 3)
   a return back to   b disappoint
   c personal
5. overcoming the obstacles (paragraph 3)
   a ignoring the problems
   b doing better than expected
   c dealing with difficulties successfully
6. guidance (paragraph 4)
   a teaching   b comfort   c advice

Something the size of a postage stamp that costs just a penny could be a medical breakthrough that will save millions of lives. According to biotechnology scientist Hayat Sindi, this tiny piece of paper has the same power as an entire medical laboratory. "My mission is to find simple, inexpensive ways to monitor health," Sindi says. She believes that this new technology, created by a team at Harvard University, will make it possible, and so she co-founded the charity "Diagnostics For All" to produce and distribute the innovation.

In the developing world, powerful drugs are used to fight diseases like HIV/AIDS, tuberculosis, and hepatitis. But these can cause liver damage. In developed countries, doctors monitor patients' progress and change the medication if they detect problems. But in isolated corners of the world, no one monitors patients to see what is working and what isn't. The result is that millions are dying from the same drugs that are supposed to cure them. The small piece of paper is a low-tech tool that detects disease by analyzing bodily fluids. Positive results, which show up in less than a minute, are indicated by a change in color on the paper.

Despite coming from a poor background, Sindi moved to England to attend university. She had never traveled outside Saudi Arabia, and did not speak any English. Alone, homesick, and worried that she would fail and let her family down, she prepared for her college entrance exams, for which she studied up to twenty hours a day. (She had learned English by watching the BBC news.) Overcoming the obstacles, she got into Cambridge University and became the first Saudi woman to study biotechnology there. She went on to get a PhD and become a visiting scholar at Harvard University.

Sindi's passion and achievements have made her an inspiration to young women across the Middle East. "I want all women to believe in themselves and know they can transform society. When I speak in schools, the first thing I ask the children attending is to draw a picture of a scientist. 99.9% of them draw an old bald man with glasses. When I tell them I'm a scientist, they look so surprised." A new foundation she has launched gives guidance and money to young women studying abroad, encouraging them to bring the skills they learn back to their homelands.

Grammar relative clauses

4 Read the article on page 78 and find examples of the following.

1. three defining relative clauses using *that* (paragraphs 1 and 2)
   _____
   _____
   _____

2. a defining relative clause with no relative pronoun (paragraph 4)
   _____

3. a non-defining relative clause using *which* (paragraph 2)
   _____

4. a non-defining relative clause that uses a preposition (paragraph 3)
   _____

5. *what* used as a relative pronoun (paragraph 2)
   _____

5 Complete the sentences with the correct relative pronouns. Sometimes, no pronoun is necessary.

1. This is the part of the laboratory _____ we test new drugs.
2. Harvard University, _____ was founded in 1636, is the oldest university in the US.
3. The lecturers, _____ come from all over the world, are highly respected scientists.
4. I think _____ Sindi did in moving to a strange country was very brave.
5. The best teacher _____ I ever had was a woman named Sally Howkins.
6. It's a university _____ reputation has grown enormously in the last ten years.

6 Write sentences using relative clauses. Use the correct relative pronouns, and use commas where necessary.

1. The piece of paper is the size of a postage stamp. It could save millions of lives.
   _____
   _____

2. The charity produces the tool. The charity was co-founded by Sindi.
   _____
   _____

3. The tool will be used in developing countries. It is difficult to find clinics there.
   _____
   _____

4. People say things about existing drugs. I agree with the things they say.
   _____
   _____

5. The results show up on the paper. The paper's color changes if there is a problem.
   _____
   _____

7 Grammar extra **reduced relative clauses**

> **REDUCED RELATIVE CLAUSES**
> We sometimes use a participle in place of a relative clause.
> **Present participle**   *doing*
> She works in Oxford, where she does research. (active)
> **Past participle**   *studied*
> It's a subject which is studied by very few people. (passive)
> Notice that we can't use a reduced relative clause when the relative pronoun is the object of the relative clause.

Look at the grammar box above. Rewrite these sentences with (full) relative clauses.

1. She believes that new technology <u>created</u> at Harvard University will make it possible.
   _____
   _____

2. The first thing I ask the children <u>attending</u> the class is to draw a picture of a scientist.
   _____
   _____

8 Replace the underlined relative clauses in these sentences with reduced relative clauses.

1. Sindi's low-tech tool helps people <u>who are suffering</u> from the negative effects of the drugs.
   _____

2. People <u>who live</u> far away from hospitals and clinics will benefit from this technology.
   _____

3. The same medicines <u>which were designed</u> to fight disease can also harm people.
   _____

4. Sindi, <u>who was determined</u> to succeed, studied up to twenty hours a day.
   _____

Unit 10 Talented people

10c Harriet Tubman

Listening

1 ▶ 84 Check that you understand the meaning of these words. Then listen to a description of the life of Harriet Tubman. Check (✓) the things she was.

☐ a politician ☐ a military officer
☐ an anti-slavery campaigner ☐ a farmer
☐ a spy ☐ a mother
☐ a train driver ☐ a writer
☐ a nurse ☐ a public speaker

2 ▶ 84 Listen to the description again and circle the best option (a–c) to complete each statement.
1 Tubman's disability affected her ability to:
  a concentrate.
  b stay awake.
  c stand upright.
2 Arriving in a Free State was:
  a a painful moment.
  b a confusing moment.
  c a beautiful moment.
3 Tubman worked on the "Underground Railroad" as a:
  a guide to other slaves trying to escape.
  b guard against people who wanted to stop slaves from escaping.
  c keeper of a safe house where slaves could hide.
4 Black people were good spies because most white Southerners didn't think:
  a black people were interested in the war.
  b black people were clever enough to be spies.
  c the Northern states were using spies.
5 Tubman did not receive recognition from the government for her military service until:
  a she retired.
  b she married a second time.
  c she died.

3 Look at the underlined words from the description of Harriet Tubman's life. Explain the meaning in your own words.
1 to escape to a neighboring Free State
   _____
2 "I felt I was in heaven"
   _____
3 She was a determined woman
   _____
4 she had to survive on her husband's pension
   _____
5 campaigning for voting rights for women
   _____

4 **Pronunciation extra** word stress in adjectives ending in *-ive*

a ▶ 85 Listen to the adjectives ending in *-ive*. Underline the stressed syllable in each word.
1 effective   5 persuasive
2 impressive   6 sensitive
3 supportive   7 decisive
4 positive   8 talkative

b What is the rule for words that end with vowel + *-tive*? What is the rule for the other words?

Word focus *self*

5 Complete the expressions with *self*. The first letter is provided.
1 I felt very self-c_____ and nervous standing up there in front of 200 people.
2 She showed a lot of self-c_____ in not losing her temper. I'm sure I would have been very angry.
3 I'm afraid most people vote for what is in their own self-i_____ .
4 My sister is a self-m_____ woman. She set up her business all by herself.
5 Self-h_____ books can be very useful if you are looking for ways to change your life.
6 We try to teach children to be self-c_____ , and to believe in their own abilities.

10d The right job

Real life describing skills, talents, and experience

1 Complete these sentences using the correct prepositions.

1 At college, I specialized _____ photojournalism.
2 I'm very familiar _____ your magazine.
3 I'm good _____ spotting an interesting story.
4 I think I'd be suited _____ working in this kind of environment.
5 I feel very comfortable _____ tight deadlines.
6 I'm very interested _____ the idea of working closely with other journalists.
7 I'm serious _____ wanting to become a full-time photographer.

2 ▶ 86 Listen to three people describing their skills at a job interview. They are applying for the same job. What is it?

_____
_____

3 ▶ 86 Listen again and answer the questions.

1 What are the skills or talents of each applicant?
   Applicant 1
   _____
   _____
   Applicant 2
   _____
   _____
   Applicant 3
   _____
   _____

2 What does each speaker lack experience in?
   Applicant 1
   _____
   _____
   Applicant 2
   _____
   _____
   Applicant 3
   _____
   _____

4 Grammar extra adjective + -ing or + infinitive

> ▶ **ADJECTIVE + -ING or + INFINITIVE**
> Some adjectives can be followed by a preposition + -ing, or by an infinitive.
> I'm interested **in learning** French.
> I'm happy **to show** you how it works.

Look at the grammar box above. Then complete the sentences below. Use the correct form of the verb in parentheses: the -ing form or the infinitive form.

1 I'm serious about _____ (participate) in one of your trial days.
2 I'll be sad _____ (leave) this place.
3 I'm interested in _____ (travel) to new places.
4 I'm excited about _____ (do) field research in India.
5 I'm excited _____ (learn) more about the job.

5 Pronunciation difficult words

▶ 87 Practice saying these pairs of words. Then listen and check your pronunciation.

1 although   also
2 clothes   cloth
3 private   privacy
4 knowledge   know-how
5 suit   sweet
6 island   Iceland
7 receipt   recipe
8 thorough   through

6 Listen and respond describing skills, talents, and experience

▶ 88 Listen to questions at an interview for a job as a journalist with a local newspaper. Respond to each question with your own words. Then compare your response with the model answer that follows.

1 *So what did you study at college?*

   I studied media, but I specialized in newspaper journalism.

10e First impressions

Writing a personal profile

1 Read the personal profiles below. Which profile is written by someone who:
   a wants to do volunteer work? _____
   b is renting out a room? _____
   c is looking for their first job? _____
   d is an experienced professional? _____

1
I'm a young musician and songwriter living in East Nashville, Tennessee. I live in a beautiful house ¹ <u>with</u> a large spare room. I'm a friendly person ² <u>who is very interested in</u> other cultures, and I really enjoy having guests from other parts of the world stay.

2
I am a recent graduate from Michigan State University ³ <u>whose ambition is to work</u> in the sports and leisure industry. I am a hardworking person ⁴ <u>with a passion for</u> sports and healthy living. I am ready to work in any junior position—administrative or operational—so that I can build up my practical knowledge of this industry.

3
An IT consultant ⁵ <u>with specialist knowledge of</u> financial software, I am a flexible individual ⁶ <u>who is experienced in</u> advising both large and small companies.

4
I am an enthusiastic (but administratively overloaded!) teacher looking to take time off to travel abroad, and to use my skills to help children ⁷ <u>who have limited access</u> to education. I am a creative individual ⁸ <u>with a love of teaching</u> younger children (4- to 7-year-olds) using games and physical activities.

2 **Writing skill** using *with*

Look at the profiles again. Rewrite the underlined relative clauses using *with*, and the *with*-phrases using relative clauses.

1 _____
2 _____
3 _____
4 _____
5 _____
6 _____
7 _____
8 _____

Vocabulary personal qualities

3 Match the adjectives (1–6) describing personal qualities in list A with adjectives (a–f) with a similar meaning in list B.

A	B
1 easygoing _____	a intelligent
2 passionate _____	b imaginative
3 adaptable _____	c relaxed
4 creative _____	d (very) interested
5 bright _____	e flexible
6 curious _____	f very enthusiastic

4 Complete this personal profile by writing one word in each blank.

I am a young, ¹ _____ website designer ² _____ six years' industry experience who ³ _____ in creating websites that use video and special effects. I think that most websites aren't very dynamic, and my ⁴ _____ is to create websites ⁵ _____ are more fun and exciting to use.
I have many good recommendations from customers, and you ⁶ _____ see some of the websites I ⁷ _____ created by clicking on the links below.

Wordbuilding verb (+ preposition) + noun collocations

1 In each of these groups, one of the verbs does NOT collocate with the noun on the right. Put a line through this verb.

1	pursue / do / have	a career
2	make / take / attend	a course
3	acquire / learn / get	a skill
4	take / make / pass	an exam
5	get / win / acquire	a promotion
6	gain / win / get	experience
7	possess / own / develop	a talent
8	do / work / get	a job
9	gain / play / get	a qualification
10	join / set up / take	a company

2 Complete the description of someone's career using verbs from Exercise 1. You will need to use the correct form of the verb.

When I was nineteen, I ¹ _____ an exam to get into a drama school in New York, but I was unsuccessful. At that point, I had to decide whether to try to ² _____ a career in acting, or just abandon the idea and ³ _____ a completely different kind of job. All my friends told me that I ⁴ _____ a natural talent for acting and that I didn't need to ⁵ _____ qualifications to prove it. So instead, I ⁶ _____ a small theater company and ⁷ _____ some acting experience that way. Just by working with other actors, I was able to ⁸ _____ new skills. Two years ago, I got my first part in a Broadway play. I haven't looked back since!

Learning skills the language of learning

3 When you learn a language, you often need to ask questions about it. Look at the terms (1–8). Then match the terms with the definitions (a–h).

1 a part of speech _____
2 past participle _____
3 a colloquial expression _____
4 an idiom _____
5 a false friend _____
6 a collocation _____
7 register _____
8 a euphemism _____

a two words that naturally go together
b a phrase whose meaning is not clear from the individual words it is composed of
c the level of formality
d e.g., noun, verb, adjective, adverb, preposition
e a word that looks similar in two languages but has different meanings
f the third form of the verb, e.g., "go, went, <u>gone</u>"
g a word or phrase that expresses an idea more politely or gently
h a phrase used in everyday informal speech

4 Answer the questions below.

1 What is the past participle of *feel*? _____
2 What part of speech is *the*? _____
3 What verb collocates with *knowledge*? _____
4 Is *grab someone's attention* an idiom? _____

Check!

5 Answer these questions. You can find all the answers in Unit 10 of the Student Book.

1 What names are these people known by?

a _____   b _____

2 Which of these places have *the* in front of them?
  a _____ Atlantic Ocean
  b _____ Korea
  c _____ Florida
  d _____ United States
  e _____ moon

3 Read the sentence below. Match the underlined clauses (1 and 2) with the correct type of relative clause (a or b).

Echolocation is a skill ¹ <u>that is also used</u> in the animal world, ² <u>where it is often key to survival</u>.

a a defining relative clause ___
b a non-defining relative clause ___

Unit 11 Knowledge and learning

11a Conserving knowledge

Listening saving languages

1 ▶89 Listen to a description of the work of Dr. K. David Harrison and the "Enduring Voices" team at *National Geographic*. Which aim (a–c) best summarizes their work?

a to help different people in the world to communicate with each other
b to increase the number of languages spoken in the world
c to save dying languages from extinction

2 ▶89 Read the questions. Then listen again and circle the best option (a–c).

1 How many languages will there be in the world in 2050?
  a about 7,000
  b about 3,500
  c about 700

2 Bolivia is used as an example of a country with many languages because:
  a they are so different.
  b it has a large population.
  c it has as many languages as Europe.

3 Yuchi is a language spoken in Oklahoma that:
  a has only 70 speakers.
  b is a dead language.
  c people are trying to revive.

4 According to Dr. Harrison, when we lose a language, we lose a culture's:
  a knowledge of the world.
  b important monuments.
  c historical records.

5 Speakers of Yupik have helped us understand better:
  a the geography of the Arctic.
  b their language and culture.
  c the effects of climate change.

6 The speaker thinks that globalization highlights the importance of:
  a diversity.
  b finding common interests.
  c saving dying languages.

Three women of the Koro group in Kichang Village, India

3 ▶89 Complete the summary of Dr. Harrison's work using the words in the box. Then listen again and check.

| aim | centuries | diversity | express |
| extinct | huge | record | understand |

Dr. Harrison is part of a *National Geographic* project called "Enduring Voices," whose ¹_____ is to document little-known languages that are in danger of becoming ²_____ . The race is on to trace and ³_____ these languages. Dr. Harrison seeks out places—language "hotspots"—where there is a great ⁴_____ of languages. This work is important because when we lose a language, we lose ⁵_____ of thinking. All cultures ⁶_____ their genius through their languages and stories. These languages store knowledge that can be a(n) ⁷_____ benefit to people today. For example, the Yupik language has helped scientists ⁸_____ how climate change is affecting polar ice.

84

Grammar *could, was able to, managed to,* and *succeeded in*

4 Look at these ideas about the Enduring Voices project from the description. Circle the correct option to complete the sentences.

1. Studies in the Oklahoma region of the US *could discover / succeeded in discovering* 26 languages.
2. By highlighting this fact, researchers *could help / were able to help* the community keep this dying language alive.
3. Some ancient cultures *could build / managed to build* large monuments by which we can remember their achievements.
4. A book written a few years ago by Yupik elders and scientists *was able to help / could help* other scientists understand how climate change is affecting polar ice.
5. One of the original arguments for globalization was that it *could bring / managed to bring* us all closer together.

5 Complete the sentences about learning a language using *could, was/were able to, managed to,* or *succeeded in,* and the verb in parentheses. Sometimes more than one answer is possible.

1. The video I got was in Turkish, but I _____ (find) English subtitles on the main menu.
2. My sister is an amazing linguist: she _____ (speak) four languages fluently by the time she was twelve.
3. Esperanto was invented to be a world language, but supporters of it _____ (not / convince) enough people to use it.
4. When I first moved to England, I _____ (not / understand) native speakers because they spoke so quickly.
5. I studied Italian for eight years in school and _____ (get) an "A" in my exams. But when I tried to use it on vacation last year, I _____ (only / remember) the grammar, not the vocabulary.

Vocabulary learning

6 Complete the words to make pairs of verbs with a similar meaning. The number of missing letters is in parentheses.

1. understand and remember = t_____ in (3)
2. pick up = a_____ (6)
3. not know about = be u_____ of (6)
4. understand = g_____ (2)
5. motivate = i_____ (6)

7 Complete the sentences by using the correct form of a verb or expression from Exercise 6.

1. I didn't really learn Arabic while I was in Jordan because most people spoke English, but I _____ a few expressions.
2. She's a great teacher. She really knows how to _____ her students.
3. I used to be completely _____ of how cars work, so I took a basic mechanics course.
4. I don't _____ why we have to memorize the abbreviation of all these chemicals.
5. Sorry, that's too much information to _____ all at once. Can you go through it more slowly?

8 Dictation languages

a ▶ 90 Listen to someone talking about languages, place names, and words. Write the words that they spell.

1. a _____ b _____
2. a _____ b _____
3. _____
4. _____

b ▶ 90 Listen again and match the words from Exercise 8a with the correct meaning (a–d).

a the name of a college in the United States: _____

b a new language found in India: _____

c a word for an animal in a Siberian language: _____

d a very long word in English: _____

Unit 11 **Knowledge and learning** 85

11b Memory loss

Reading memory loss

1 Read the description of three types of memory loss quickly. Match the descriptions (1–3) with the summaries (a–c).

a When you can't recognize people easily _____

b When your mind chooses to forget something it doesn't want to remember _____

c When you have a false memory of something _____

2 Read the descriptions again. Are the sentences true (T) or false (F)? Or is there not enough information (N) to say if the statements are true or false?

1 Lacunar amnesia is when people have had a bad shock and don't remember what happened. T F N

2 With lacunar amnesia, the memory completely disappears from the mind. T F N

3 Sarah only remembers the moment when the truck hit the house. T F N

4 Prosopamnesia is a condition some people inherit from their parents. T F N

5 Philippa was concerned that the man who approached her was William Child. T F N

6 In source amnesia, people intentionally change the source of the memory. T F N

7 The woman wanted her neighbor to be punished for the crime. T F N

1 Lacunar amnesia

This literally means a gap in the memory. People who suffer from this fail to remember a specific event. It usually occurs when a person has suffered a traumatic event and their mind chooses to block it out. The memory is still there, but our psychological defenses stop us remembering the event to protect us from further psychological trauma.

Sarah's story: "When I was a child, something extraordinary happened at our house. My sister and I were about to go to bed, and I was downstairs saying goodnight to our parents. My sister was going to say goodnight to them too, but had gone to the kitchen. At that moment, a truck ran into our house. I only know that because my sister, who was unhurt, told me afterward. All I remember was saying goodnight, and then waking up in the hospital."

2 Prosopamnesia

Prosopamnesia is an inability to remember faces. It is something that many people have in a mild form, but in severe cases, people can forget the faces of even close friends or associates. People can be born with this syndrome, or it can be acquired during their lives.

Philippa's story: "I'm terrible at remembering faces. I recall being at a conference at the University of Berkeley in California. Another academic came up to me and started chatting. I would have asked his name, but knowing my inability to remember faces, I didn't in case he was someone I had met before. Anyway, it turned out that we had a colleague in common. 'Oh yes, I know William Child,' I said. 'We collaborated on a research project last year. He came to dinner at my house many times. How do *you* know him?' 'I *am* William Child,' the man replied."

3 Source amnesia

Source amnesia occurs when a person is unable to recall where, when, or how they learned something. In other words, they remember a fact, but they can't remember the context. A classic example of this is when people "remember" something that happened to them when actually it happened to another person they know.

Jon's story: "I work as a lawyer, and I often come across people who have persuaded themselves of a version of events that may not be true. I had a witness who was going to give evidence in court that her neighbor had thrown a brick at her car. She clearly believed that this had happened, and was determined that her neighbor wasn't going to get away with it. But it turned out that it was not her own memory of events that she was describing, but what another neighbor had told her."

3 Find phrasal verbs in the text on page 86 with the following meanings.

1 ignore something (paragraph 1) _____
2 collided with (paragraph 2) _____
3 approached (paragraph 4) _____
4 became known (paragraph 4) _____
5 find something (without expecting to) (paragraph 6) _____
6 escape without punishment (paragraph 6) _____

Grammar future in the past

4 There are five examples of "future in the past" forms in the text on page 86. Underline the examples. Which other future in the past forms could be used in these sentences? Write them below. Sometimes the answer is "none."

1 *My sister and I were about to go to bed ... or My sister and I were going to go to bed ...*

2 _____
3 _____
4 _____
5 _____

5 Complete the sentences using a future in the past form, and the verb in parentheses. Sometimes more than one form is possible.

1 I'm so sorry. I _____ (write) you a letter, but I lost your address.
2 I _____ (just / book) tickets to visit Munich, but then I remembered that it was Oktoberfest and that all the hotels _____ (be) full.
3 The meeting _____ (last) only an hour, but just as we _____ (finish), Julian remembered that we hadn't discussed the move to our new offices.
4 I _____ (take) my driving test sooner, but I didn't feel ready.
5 That's funny. I _____ (just / ask) you exactly the same question!

6 Pronunciation contrastive sentence stress

a ▶ 91 Circle the words in the first half of each sentence that are most strongly stressed. Then listen and check.

1 I was going to email him, but I decided it would be better to speak face to face.
2 He was supposed to get here early, but he's already ten minutes late.
3 She said she would be pleased if I talked to him, but she seemed really angry.
4 I was about to buy an apartment, but Katie said I could rent hers while she was away.
5 Liz was going to be in charge of the project, but now she's just acting as an adviser.

b ▶ 91 Underline the words in the second half of each sentence in Exercise 6a that are most strongly stressed. Practice saying each sentence. Then listen again and check.

7 Grammar extra future phrases

> ▶ **FUTURE PHRASES**
>
> Notice how the phrases in **bold** are used with other verbs to talk about the future.
> She's **bound to** want to leave early.
> He's **likely to** change his mind.
> You're **unlikely to** find the information here.

Look at the grammar box above. Then read the sentences (1–5) that talk about the future. Match the phrases in **bold** with the correct definition (a–e).

1 I'm sorry, but I always thought it was a terrible idea. It was **bound to** fail. ____
2 The plane was **due to** take off at 7 a.m., but bad weather meant it was delayed. ____
3 We thought that it was **unlikely** to be cold, so we didn't take any warm clothes with us. ____
4 It was **about to** rain, so we decided to eat inside. ____
5 The political situation was **likely** to get worse, so we left the country for our own safety. ____

a not probable
b probable
c certain
d scheduled/expected
e on the point of

Unit 11 Knowledge and learning

11c Intelligent animals

Listening

1 ▶92 Listen to a description of five intelligent animals. Match the name of the animal with the correct picture.

| bonobo monkey | border collie | crow |
| dolphin | scrub-jay | |

1 _____   2 _____

3 _____

4 _____   5 _____

2 ▶92 Listen again. Write the number of the animal (1–5) next to the intelligent behavior that this type of animal is known for (a–e).

a They are good at copying what they see. ____
b They can be taught to communicate with humans using sign language. ____
c They like to follow instructions. ____
d They make plans for the future. ____
e They make tools to get different jobs done. ____

3 ▶92 Listen again and write the number of the animal (1–5) next to the intelligent action each animal did.

a found a clever way to reach some food ____
b did acrobatics in time with one another ____
c kept food in a hiding place ____
d learned to match an image to a real object ____
e cooked himself a treat ____

4 Match these words from the descriptions with the adjectives (1–5) that have a similar meaning.

| expressive inventive mischievous playful smart |

1 intelligent: _____
2 creative: _____
3 fun-loving: _____
4 communicative: _____
5 naughty: _____

Word focus *learn*

5 Complete the sentences using expressions with *learn*.

1 You have to learn to _____ before you can run.
2 It's never too _____ to learn.
3 In life, try to learn from your _____ .
4 I learned a few _____ of the trade.
5 Never again! I've learned my _____ .
6 Just learn to _____ with it!
7 I learned the hard _____ .
8 I learned the whole poem by _____ .

11d Keep learning

Real life getting clarification

1 Complete these sentences with the correct verb.

1. What do you _____ by "difficult"?
2. Can you _____ up a little? I can't hear you.
3. Can you _____ what the exam at the end of this course involves?
4. Are you _____ that learning the historical dates isn't important?
5. Could you _____ me an example of an important historian from the last century?
6. I didn't _____ that last word. Can you repeat it?

2 ▶93 Listen to a conversation between a student and a college lecturer. Answer the questions.

1. What is the student worried about?
2. What is the course?
3. What does the lecturer recommend?

3 ▶93 Listen again and complete the student's questions.

1. Can you explain _____?
2. And are you saying that _____?
3. Could you give me an example of _____?
4. Did you say _____?

4 Grammar extra verbs with indirect objects

> ▶ **VERBS WITH INDIRECT OBJECTS**
>
> Some verbs (e.g., *tell* and *show*) can be followed by an indirect personal object. Other verbs (e.g., *say* and *explain*) don't always need an indirect personal object. If you use an indirect personal object with these verbs, you must put *to* before the object.
>
> He told **me** about the history course.
> I showed **him** a copy of the lecture notes.
> They explained (**to me**) that I missed the deadline.

Look at the grammar box above. Complete these sentences by writing the pronoun *me* where necessary.

1. Can you tell _____ how many hours of study we're expected to do each week?
2. Do you recommend _____ that I read Stephen Hawking's book?
3. She said _____ that I could get most of the books from the library.
4. Can you show _____ how that works?
5. He taught _____ that I didn't always need to write such long essays.

5 Pronunciation linking in question forms

▶94 Practice saying these questions. Then listen and compare your pronunciation.

1. Did you say "Africa"?
2. Could you explain that?
3. What do you mean by "difficult"?

6 Listen and respond getting clarification

▶95 Listen to the comments by a teacher. Respond to each comment with expressions for getting clarification. Then compare your response with the model answer that follows.

1
> *So you wanted to ask me a question about the exam at the end of this course?*

> *Yes. Can you explain what the exam involves?*

Unit 11 Knowledge and learning

11e The wrong course

Writing an email about a misunderstanding

1 These sentences describe a misunderstanding over an application. Match the beginnings of the sentences (1–4) with their endings (a–d).

1 Despite the fact that my application was sent in on time, _____
2 I received an email that I sent in my application late. _____
3 The class is not easy. _____
4 While I appreciate that you have a lot of applicants, _____

a you can't just ignore applications that were sent in early.
b In fact, I sent in my application two weeks before your deadline.
c On the contrary, it's one of the most difficult classes I've ever taken.
d I was told that my application was rejected.

2 Writing skill linking contrasting ideas

Rewrite these sentences from the reply to the emails above using the words in parentheses.

1 We sympathize with your situation, but we are unable to do anything about it. (while)

_____
_____

2 Despite the fact that you submitted your form before the deadline, we had already received too many applications. (although)

_____
_____

3 Most colleges would keep your application fee, whereas we are refunding yours. (but)

_____
_____

4 You say in your email that we have no right to do this, but the college has the right to close the application process anytime before the deadline. (in actual fact)

_____
_____

3 Look at these notes and write an email to a college. Include the following points.

a Reason for writing: you can't attend the presentation skills course this term.
b Misunderstanding: you thought it was an evening class, but it's during the day.
c Effort on your part: you tried to get time off from work, but you can't.
d Apology: probably your mistake, but these things happen.
e Request: you want the college to refund the money you paid for the course fee.

Dear Sir / Madam,

a _____
_____
_____

b _____
_____
_____

c _____
_____
_____

d _____
_____
_____

e _____
_____
_____

I look forward to _____
_____

Yours,

_____

Wordbuilding homonyms

1 Match these homonyms with their meanings.

company   point   room   spare   tip   value

1. a the sharp end of an object
   b purpose ___point___
2. a a business organization
   b being with another person _____
3. a extra money given for good service
   b a piece of advice _____
4. a give something you have enough of (v)
   b extra or additional (adj) _____
5. a available space
   b a part of a building with walls _____
6. a importance of something
   b monetary worth of a thing _____

2 Look at the underlined words in these sentences. Choose the correct meaning (a or b) from Exercise 1.

1. I don't see the point of this homework. __b__
2. There was no room in the hall, so we stood. ____
3. I like her company a lot, but we don't see each other much outside of work. ____
4. Can I give you a tip? Always fill up your car with gas before a long journey. ____
5. Don't underestimate the value of hard work. ____
6. Can you spare some time to help me? ____

Learning skills techniques for memorizing

3 Sometimes you remember better by hearing, sometimes by seeing, and sometimes by doing. It is important to know how you remember things. What do you remember of the following items in Unit 11?

1. The way children learn at the Lumiar School:
   _____
2. How *could* is different from *managed to*:
   _____
3. The intelligence of Alex, the grey parrot:
   _____
4. Useful phrases for getting clarification:
   _____
5. Expressions with the word *learn*:
   _____

4 How did you remember the information in Exercise 3? By hearing, by seeing, or by doing?

5 Look at these tips for memorizing. Check (✓) the one(s) you feel suit you best.

- ☐ Write down five words that you need to learn. Translate them or put them into a sentence. Then listen to them again just before you go to bed at night.
- ☐ Draw pictures of the words that you need to learn. Look at the pictures the following day and see if you can remember the words.
- ☐ Work with another student and simulate a situation that illustrates the meaning of the word. Or think of an action that would help you remember the word.

6 Try to memorize these words and expressions from Unit 11 using the tips in Exercise 5.

| acquire | Can you speak up? | cramming |
| take in | learn your lesson | |

Check!

7 Complete the sentences with words from Unit 11 of the Student Book. Then use the first letter of each missing word in sentences 1–6 to form the name of Character 1. Use the second letter of each missing word in sentences 7–10 to form the name of Character 2.

1. Another way to say "we were able to do" something is "we _____ in doing" it. (9)
2. At the Indianapolis Children's Museum, kids can really _____ with the exhibits. (6)
3. When we have achieved a difficult task, we say we have _____ to do it. (7)
4. "It's never too _____ to learn." (4)
5. "We are more interested in people with practical _____ than academic qualifications." (10)
6. When we "take in" information, we understand and _____ it. (8)

Character 1: __ __ __ __ __ __

7. "Sorry, I didn't _____ your name." (5)
8. "Who's a _____ bird?" (6)
9. If you learn something "by _____," you can repeat it from memory. (5)
10. "Can you _____ what you mean?" (7)

Character 2: __ __ __ __

Unit 12 Money

12a Save or spend?

Listening character and the economy

1 ▶96 Listen to an economist giving his opinion about how character affects our attitude toward money. Answer the questions.

1 What two types of people does the economist describe?
_____

2 Can we apply these characterizations to particular countries? Why or why not?
_____
_____

2 ▶96 Listen to the economist again and circle the best option (a–c) to complete the sentences.

1 People who are careful with money spend it:
  a when they see something they really want.
  b when it's for something of lasting benefit.
  c only on what's necessary.

2 People who are extravagant with money want to:
  a enjoy life while they can.
  b save, but can't.
  c increase their possessions.

3 Some commentators said that certain countries that borrowed money:
  a didn't work hard enough.
  b didn't pay enough tax.
  c weren't careful with the money.

4 A country that lends money risks losing that money and:
  a creating problems for the borrowing country.
  b going out of business.
  c paying more taxes.

5 In most developed and developing economies, people want to:
  a be able to borrow money.
  b live more comfortably.
  c reduce their debts.

6 We need ____ to behave more responsibly.
  a spenders
  b savers
  c spenders and savers

3 Match the words (1–5) with their synonyms.

1 fund ○   ○ careful
2 prudent ○   ○ deal
3 transaction ○   ○ extravagant
4 wages ○   ○ finance
5 wasteful ○   ○ salaries

Vocabulary the economy

4 Find and circle the words in the word search to complete these expressions.

1 the _____ of living
2 the _____ and the have _____
3 the _____ gap
4 the _____ of living
5 people's buying _____
6 _____ of life

S	H	A	V	E	S	B
Q	U	A	L	I	T	Y
U	N	I	T	C	A	P
N	G	I	H	O	N	A
O	R	N	E	S	D	S
T	Y	C	Y	T	A	T
S	P	O	W	E	R	E
N	O	M	I	N	D	N
Y	D	E	L	I	V	E

92

Grammar focus adverbs: *only, just, even*

5 Cross out the focus adverb that is in the incorrect position in these sentences.

1. Let's just consider just people's attitude toward money at its simplest level.
2. Savers also spend only money, but only when they can afford it.
3. People in these countries even would have to work longer hours, pay more taxes, and even accept lower wages.
4. You only not only risk losing the money, but you also risk putting the borrower in a difficult situation.
5. We need both types of people, but only if they lend and borrow only responsibly.

6 Rewrite these sentences with the focus adverbs in parentheses in the correct place. There is sometimes more than one possible answer.

1. Some people keep spending money when they can't afford to. (even)

   _____
   _____

2. You can protect yourself against bad times by putting aside a small amount of money each week. (just)

   _____
   _____

3. If a few people save money, the banks won't have any money to lend to others. (only)

   _____
   _____

4. It's not me who has debts; other people have them, too. (just)

   _____
   _____

5. Most people are careful with money when times are hard. (only)

   _____
   _____

6. Some borrowers admit that they borrow money irresponsibly. (even)

   _____
   _____

Vocabulary money

7 Complete these sentences with the correct noun form of the verbs in parentheses.

1. To buy the car, I had to make _____ of $70 a month for five years. (pay)
2. We need to cut back on our _____ because the cost of living has become so high. (spend)
3. They say that gold is a good _____ at the moment. (invest)
4. We took out a _____ from the bank to finance the purchase of our apartment. (lend)
5. I used my _____ to pay for my vacation. (save)
6. We needed to increase our _____ so that we could build an extension to our house. (borrow)
7. Government workers are protesting because their _____ haven't increased in the last two years. (earn)

8 Dictation money and lifestyle

▶ **97** Listen to someone talking about money and lifestyle. Write down the words you hear.

I think that _____
_____
_____
_____

It's a lifestyle _____
_____
_____
_____

This desire _____
_____
_____
_____

12b Cheap labor

Reading a history of industry

1 Read the article. What is the main message?
   a Cheap labor is a key factor for a country's economic success.
   b Cheap labor is a benefit to the economy only if jobs stay in the country.
   c Businesses use cheap labor as a way of ensuring long-term success.

2 Read the article again. Are these sentences true (T) or false (F)? Or is the information not given (N) in the article?

1 A good exchange rate is the most important ingredient for a successful economy.   T   F   N
2 Britain was still the world's leading industrial power at the end of the 19th century.   T   F   N
3 The American railways were built by people who had migrated to the US from Europe.   T   F   N
4 In recent times, companies have started looking for countries where they can pay people less money to make their goods.   T   F   N
5 It is cheaper to make things abroad partly because the cost of transporting goods is not too high.   T   F   N
6 Making things at low cost abroad is good for the consumer in the short term.   T   F   N
7 Even if some jobs leave a country, better jobs will replace them in that country.   T   F   N

Cheap labor

There are three main ingredients for a successful economy. The first is a good exchange rate with the countries that you want to trade with. No one is going to buy your goods if they are too expensive. The second is technology. In the early 19th century, Britain became the dominant industrial power in the world because the Industrial Revolution started there. Britain was able to benefit from homegrown innovations like the railway and the mass production of goods. By the end of the same century, the US was the dominant power because they took the technological revolution forward with the telephone, the radio, and then the airplane. In the early 20th century, Germany too became a major economy, developing its own new chemical and automobile industries.

Technological innovation was very important for transforming the economies of Britain, the US, and Germany in this period—but their success would not have been possible without the third key ingredient: cheap labor. The history of successful economies has always been a story of cheap labor. If you can get people to work for not much money, your business will be more profitable. In 1830, the United States had only seventy kilometers of railroad, but by 1890 it had over 250,000 kilometers. This was made possible by employing thousands of immigrants on low wages.

These days, you can follow the movement of an industry—textiles and tuna canning are two striking examples—to where the work can be done more cheaply. Improved communications systems have meant that goods can be manufactured where labor costs are lowest. The goods can then be transported, at relatively low cost, to the places (usually richer countries) where they are consumed. UK insurance companies have IT centers in India, French energy companies have call centers in Morocco, and US engineering companies have their machines produced in China and the Philippines.

However, there is a lot of debate about whether this outsourcing of jobs to other countries is a good thing. In the short term, it is profitable for companies to have their products made more cheaply, and it benefits their customers, too. But does this harm their own country's economy in the long term and cause unemployment among their own country's citizens? That is a question that remains to be answered.

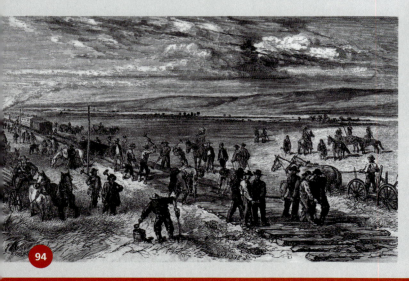

3 Find words or expressions in the article on page 94 with the following meanings.

1. leading or powerful (paragraph 1)
   _____
2. manufacturing in large quantities (paragraph 1)
   _____
3. able to make money (paragraph 2)
   _____
4. salaries (paragraph 2)
   _____
5. bought and used (paragraph 3)
   _____
6. places where large numbers of workers respond to phone calls (paragraph 3)
   _____
7. paying someone outside the company to do the work (paragraph 4)
   _____
8. damage (v) (paragraph 4)
   _____

Grammar causative *have* and *get*

4 Complete the sentences using the correct form of the words in parentheses.

1. It's evident that if you can _____ _____ (get / people / work) for less money, your business is going to be more profitable.
2. Companies are always searching for ways they can _____ (get / their work / do) more cheaply.
3. A lot of Western clothing firms _____ _____ (have / their clothes / make) in India and Bangladesh.
4. A lot of tuna fishing companies _____ _____ (get / their tuna / process) in the Philippines, Vietnam, and Thailand.
5. You can _____ (get / most questions / answer) by a call center operator. If they can't answer you, _____ (get / them / put) you through to a manager.
6. The economic argument for outsourcing is that you can _____ (get / anyone / do) the basic non-skilled jobs, and then you can _____ (have / your own employees / do) the more skilled work.

5 Pronunciation /ʃ/, /tʃ/, /ʒ/, and /dʒ/

a ▶ 98 Listen to the words in the gray box. Notice the pronunciation of the underlined sounds. Then complete the chart.

cheap	decision	ma<u>ch</u>ine	major
revolu<u>t</u>ion	ri<u>ch</u>er	u<u>s</u>ually	wages

/ʃ/	/tʃ/	/ʒ/	/dʒ/
wa<u>sh</u>	wat<u>ch</u>	plea<u>s</u>ure	chan<u>ge</u>

b ▶ 99 Listen and check your answers to Exercise 5a.

Vocabulary getting things done

6 Complete the sentences about house repairs. Use the correct verb in its correct form. The first letter of each missing verb is provided.

1. I asked John to p_____ up new shelves in the living room. He's a professional carpenter.
2. We can d_____ the room ourselves. We don't need to have it done by a professional.
3. The kitchen cabinet came in pieces, and I had to a_____ it by myself.
4. Can you call a roofer? The roof's still leaking, and we need to get it f_____ .
5. You know that guy who t_____ our bathroom walls? He did a terrible job. There are cracks everywhere.
6. I'm going to get someone in to i_____ the new sink. It's just too much work for me.
7. We've just moved into a new apartment, and it's really dirty. I'm going to call the landlord and ask him to get it c_____ .

7 Look at these DIY jobs (1–6). Match each job with the professional (a–f) who does it.

1. fixing a leaky faucet ____
2. rewiring a house ____
3. cutting the grass ____
4. demolishing a wall ____
5. making a wooden cabinet ____
6. choosing wallpaper ____

a. a gardener
b. a plumber
c. a carpenter
d. a general builder
e. a decorator
f. an electrician

12c The world of barter

Listening an interview

1 ▶ 100 Listen to an interview with a member of the Barter Society. What is the advantage of barter, according to him? Circle the correct option (a–c).

a You can exchange goods and services without paying tax.
b It opens up a whole new world of people to do business with.
c You get a much better deal than you would if you used cash.

> **GDP** (n) /ˌdʒiːdiːˈpiː/ gross domestic product
> **spear** (n) /spɪə/ a long, pointed weapon used in hunting

2 ▶ 100 Listen again and circle the best option (a–c) to complete the sentences.

1 The example of barter given by the interviewer is an exchange of a chicken for:
   a an item of clothing.
   b some food.
   c a weapon.
2 Barter is a system of trade that:
   a has always been uncommon.
   b is still used widely today.
   c is primitive.
3 "Exchange barter" is a system:
   a that involves two people exchanging goods with one another.
   b that involves being a member of a club with other barterers.
   c where you exchange goods up to a certain value.
4 Barter exchanges:
   a aren't taxed.
   b are taxed if they are above a certain value.
   c are taxed in some countries.

Vocabulary business words

3 Circle the correct options to complete the description of a hoverboard.

> Hoverboards are two-wheeled motorized boards that you stand and balance on. I don't think they will become very popular—I think they're just a(n) ¹ *upscale / passing* fad. The manufacturers have tried to create a ² *trend / buzz* around them, hoping that they will become the next big ³ *trend / recession*, but I don't think it will work. Part of the problem is the name: It sounds very ⁴ *catchy / upscale*, but hoverboards don't actually hover; they run on wheels. Another problem is the high price. A few people will buy them, but at $300–$400 each, the hoverboard is a(n) ⁵*catchy / upscale* product that most people can't afford.

4 **Grammar extra** *hard* and *hardly*

> ▶ **HARD** and **HARDLY**
>
> The adjective *hard* has two different adverb forms: *hard* and *hardly*.
> I'm trying **hard** to see the advantage of it. (= I'm making a big effort.)
> There **hardly** seems to be any advantage to it. (= There is almost no advantage to it.)
> Notice the position of *hard* and *hardly*: *hard* goes after the main verb, and *hardly* goes before the main verb.

Look at the grammar box and compare the two sentences. Then complete these sentences using *hard* or *hardly,* and the verbs in the correct form.

1 train / hard
   a He _____ . He's very fit.
   b He _____ . He's quite lazy.
2 work / hard
   a She _____ now. She goes to the office once a week, I think.
   b She _____ now. She has a new boss who's very demanding.
3 think / hard
   a I _____ about it. It wasn't an easy decision.
   b I _____ about work when I was away on vacation.
4 try / hard
   a The team _____ . It was as if they didn't care.
   b The team _____ , but they weren't good enough to win.

12d The bottom line

Real life negotiating

1 Match the expressions (1–6) with the phrases (a–f) that have the same meaning.

1 to tell you the truth ____
2 a key thing ____
3 let's face it ____
4 if I were in your shoes ____
5 at the end of the day ____
6 isn't there some way around that ____

a something that's important
b if i were in your position
c after considering everything
d we need to be realistic
e can you see a solution
f to be honest

2 ▶ 101 Listen to two people in a negotiation and answer the questions.

1 What event are they discussing?
   _____

2 What does the client try to negotiate?
   _____

3 ▶ 101 Complete the phrases from the negotiation. Then listen again and check.

1 We want some food, but nothing too fancy, to be _____ .
2 OK, so what did you have in _____ ?
3 Well, I was _____ we could have something more exciting than sandwiches.
4 Yes, that _____ be much more like it.
5 That seems a lot, but let's _____ it, it's an important occasion.
6 If I were in your _____ , I'd put on an event that people would remember.

7 You have to _____ the amount of work involved, setting it up and packing everything away.
8 I see. Well, the _____ thing for us is that it's a nice, relaxing event.

4 Pronunciation long vowel sounds

▶ 102 Listen to the sentences. Which of the underlined vowel sounds are long (L) and which are short (S)?

1 OK, so what did you have in m<u>i</u>nd? ____
2 Maybe if we pr<u>e</u>pared some sushi … ____
3 Yes, that w<u>ou</u>ld be much more like it. ____
4 If I were in your sh<u>oe</u>s, … ____
5 The $10 also covers w<u>ai</u>ting staff. ____
6 You have to appr<u>e</u>ciate the … ____
7 Just let me know ex<u>a</u>ct numbers … ____

5 Grammar extra would

> ▶ **WOULD**
>
> The word *would* helps make what you say sound more polite or diplomatic, so it is often used in negotiations.
> *Yes, that **would** be much more like it.*
> ***Would** that reduce the price?*

Look at the grammar box. Rewrite these sentences using *would* to make the sentences more diplomatic.

1 I'm afraid that will be difficult for me.
   _____
2 Are you willing to negotiate?
   _____
3 Can you give some kind of guarantee?
   _____
4 When do you need to know?
   _____
5 I don't want you to get in trouble.
   _____

6 Listen and respond negotiating

▶ 103 You are hiring a caterer to provide food at a party. Listen to the caterer and respond each time with your own words. Then compare your response with the model answer that follows.

1

> So what kind of food did you have in mind? Some sandwiches?

> I was hoping we could have some hot food, too.

12e Get to the point

1 Writing skill key phrases in report writing

Complete the short report below using these words and phrases.

| as requested | consequently | initially |
| overall | specifically | to sum up |

¹ _____, here are some comments on the Media Hotel as a potential venue for our annual conference.

² _____, the hotel seems like a good choice. It's in a great location—just ten minutes from the seafront and a large number of restaurants. It is extremely comfortable and has very good conference facilities, ³ _____ a large conference hall that seats 300 people, and ten other well-equipped seminar rooms. However, on the weekend that I visited, the hotel had a large group there for a wedding. ⁴ _____, it was very noisy and seemed more like a party venue. ⁵ _____, I thought that this would rule out holding a conference there, but the manager later assured me that on conference weekends, no other functions are allowed in the hotel.

⁶ _____, I think the Media Hotel is a possibility, but I would recommend looking at other options first before making a decision.

Writing a short report

2 Read the short report below about a training course. Where does this information (a–e) go in the report? Two pieces of information are used twice.

a details about the course (2 places)
b an introduction
c a summary of the course (2 places)
d a suggestion for improvement
e a useful fact for future reference

As requested, ¹ _____ on the one-day introductory course to website design that I attended last week at Illinois State Education College.

Overall, it ² _____, although there were one or two things that could be improved. The teacher was very knowledgeable and had lots of experience designing websites. We spent the first two hours looking at different website designs, specifically ³ _____. Initially, I thought this took rather too long, but actually ⁴ _____.

We were then shown the basic tools for constructing a website. There are a lot of very good apps available for this purpose, and the teacher showed us two of his favorites. The apps come with clear instructions. Consequently, it's very easy ⁵ _____. For the last hour of the day, we were able to experiment with using some of these tools.

To sum up, I ⁶ _____. Even if it doesn't tell you everything, it makes the idea of designing a website less frightening. However, I would have liked more ⁷ _____.

3 Complete the report above in your own words. Use your answers in Exercise 2 to help you.

1 _____
2 _____
3 _____
4 _____
5 _____
6 _____
7 _____

Wordbuilding *the* + adjective

1 Write the best adjective for these groups of people in society.

1. People with a lot of money — *the rich*
2. People without a job — _____
3. People with very little money — _____
4. People with nowhere to live — _____
5. People over 80 — _____
6. People who are well-known — _____
7. People who like adventure — _____
8. People who work hard — _____
9. People who don't work hard — _____
10. People who are unwell — _____

2 Look at your answers in Exercise 1. Which do you think describe people in a positive situation (P), a negative situation (N), or neither (X)?

Learning skills using the internet

3 The following ideas are ways you could use the internet to help you learn. Check (✓) the ideas you could use.

- ☐ Listen to or watch the news in English, e.g., on the CNN website. Note down key words as you listen to each story. Check their meaning online or in a dictionary. Then listen again.
- ☐ Search for articles related to your interests on newspaper websites. Read the title and the first paragraph. Note down two questions you would like answered by the article. Then read the article and find the answers.
- ☐ If you are not sure how to pronounce a word, check an online dictionary. Then practice saying it.
- ☐ If you listen to songs in English, search for the lyrics online. Read them as you listen to the song. Look up any words you don't know.
- ☐ Search for interesting quotations, sayings, and anecdotes on websites. Try to memorize them.

4 Use the internet to find:

1. the meaning of the word "spin" in the context of political news.
   _____
2. the opening lyrics to "Big Yellow Taxi" by Joni Mitchell.
   _____
3. a famous quotation on the subject of success.
   _____

Check!

5 Complete these sentences with words from Unit 12 of the Student Book. Then use the first letter of each missing word to spell something that many of us dream of having!

1. The expression "Saving for a _____ day" means saving money in good times in preparation for more difficult times.
2. People use the term "the _____ gap" to refer to the difference in earnings between the rich and the poor.
3. Branding and a _____ name are important for any business. In my town, there is a Chinese restaurant called "Wok and Roll."
4. When we say that another person did a job for us, we use this construction: *get* or _____ + something + past participle.
5. "At the _____ of the day" is a commonly used phrase in negotiations.
6. The opposite of "spend" is "_____."

Word: _____

Unit 7

▶ 53

Speaker 1
People who are in favor of teaching their children at home generally argue that the local schools don't stretch children enough, or that they don't recognize their child's individual needs. I'm sure these people mean well, but I think they're missing the point. Interaction with other children from a range of backgrounds—not just your own siblings—is a key part of learning, and you just don't get that if you're stuck in your own house all day.

Speaker 2
Parents often discipline their children for fighting or being unkind to each other, but there's new evidence to suggest that this kind of behavior may not be a bad thing. Psychologists say that by competing in this way, children are learning valuable social skills. It's common for siblings to squabble over toys or to compete for attention. They will even continue to do this later in life—fight for their parents' approval, that is—but generally, they find a way of working it out so that no one's hurt. That type of negotiation in relationships is important training for later life.

Speaker 3
Where you are in the family clearly has an influence on your behavior more generally. We're all familiar with eldest children who are organizing and bossy types, and middle children who feel ignored. Being the baby of our family, I'm particularly interested in the youngest child syndrome. Certainly you have to fight more for attention—that's why younger children are often the clowns of the family. Parents tend to let you get away with things that your older siblings didn't. You also have the advantage of learning from your older siblings ... and their mistakes.

Speaker 4
I think far too much attention is paid to how parents should bring up children and far too little to how much other environmental factors affect them. Have you ever watched a two-year-old when another slightly older child comes into the room? They're fascinated. They watch what they do, they try to join in—much more than with an adult. What's more, the elder child will quickly take on the role of teacher or parent, explaining pictures in a book, for example. "Look. That's a lion! Can you say 'lion'?" In a lot of societies, it's normal in large families just to leave the children to get on with it. I think parents in the West should do that instead of intervening so much.

▶ 54

Everything depends on what you see as the future role of your children. In other words, what is it that you are raising them to do?

Do you want them to be good members of society? If so, you will teach them values such as obeying the law, cooperating with others, and generally being good citizens.

Or do you want them to be successful individuals? If so, you will help them to be free thinkers and to be independent.

Or is it important that they are good family members? Then you will teach them to respect their elders and to follow family traditions.

▶ 56

/uː/: blue, lunar, rude, suit, truce
/juː/: humanity, humor, menu, used, usually

▶ 57

Desmond Morris trained originally as a zoologist, where he observed the behavior of many different species of animals. However, his lifelong interest has been human rather than animal behavior, and unlike the traditional experts in human behavior—the psychologist, the sociologist, and the anthropologist—he is not so interested in what people say, but rather in what they do. In fact, he gives little attention to human speech because he feels that human actions tell us far more about people than anything they might say. Indeed, it is said that in human communication, as much as ninety percent is non-verbal.

In an interview given some years ago, Morris gave a fascinating example of "postural echo," a type of non-verbal communication. Morris and a presenter were sitting discussing Morris's work in a radio studio. They were both sitting down facing each other across a table. Both had one forearm resting on the table and the other forearm upright, with their chin resting on one hand. Both were leaning forward interestedly as they talked to each other. They had adopted what Morris called *postural echo*: that is to say, because they had a common interest, they were imitating each other's posture.

In another situation, though, such postural echo might be inappropriate. For example, imagine you are being interviewed for a job, and the boss who is interviewing you sits back in his chair and puts his feet up on a stool. His posture is showing that he is in a relaxed and dominant position. Your posture, on the other hand, should show that you are in a subordinate position: in other words, you should be sitting upright, maybe leaning forward a little to show interest, with your hands on your lap. If you were to echo his posture, it would send the message that you felt as relaxed as him, and he is not hiring another boss—he is looking for a subordinate. At best, you would not get the job; at worst, the boss would find it deeply insulting and end the interview immediately.

▶ 59

Dowry-giving—the gift of money or property from one family to another on the occasion of a marriage—is still common in certain parts of the world. It symbolizes different things. For example, it can be a sign of wealth and help increase social status. It can have a historical and practical meaning: as a rule, in the past, brides did not go out to work, so this was her financial contribution to the marriage. It's customary for a dowry to be given by the bride's family to the groom's family, but it can work the other way around, as in Nigeria, where a small dowry is given by the groom's family. The engagement ceremony in Nigeria marks the beginning of the wedding celebrations. It's an occasion for people to celebrate and have fun before the official ceremony, and also to give gifts to the couple. It takes place on the evening or a couple of nights before the wedding itself. During the party, there's a lot of music, and dancing. It used to be traditional for money to be thrown at the couple's feet while they danced, but now people usually bring regular wedding gifts. After the party, the groom's family delivers a kind of dowry to the bride's family's house in the form of a gift of traditional clothes and jewelry. On the night of the wedding, after the reception party is finished, the bride goes back to her own house where she waits until she's claimed by the groom and taken to their new home.

▶ 61

F = Friend, MA = Model answer

1
F: How does a man ask for a woman's hand in marriage?
MA: It's traditional for a man to ask the woman's father for permission to marry her, but these days he usually asks her directly.

2
F: What symbolic acts are there at the wedding ceremony?
MA: The bride walks down the aisle with her father and he brings her to the groom. That symbolizes the handing over of his responsibility for her to the groom.

3
F: What happens after the wedding ceremony?
MA: The bride and groom go to a reception, usually in a special car, where they have a big party with all their friends and family.

4
F: What kinds of gifts are given?
MA: Usually people give the couple things that will be useful in their new home, such as things for their kitchen.

5
F: Is special music played at the reception?
MA: Not really. Once the bride and groom have had their first dance together, everyone usually dances to pop music.

Unit 8

▶ 62

Speaker 1
Rhea: I spent most of my life working for a big insurance company in the US, which is where I come from. I felt I had achieved a lot of things in my life—got a good job, raised a family—but I wanted something more, something with real significance. I felt that insurance was just a money-making business, and I wanted to help people in a more meaningful way. In particular, I wanted to help children get a good education. I was very fortunate because a friend told me about a volunteer program in Rwanda, Africa. The aim of the program was to teach nursery school teachers the value of learning through play. I was trained by the organization, and then I went out to a small village in Rwanda to work with local teachers. The school was in a terrible condition, and the kids sat at desks all day and there was no room to do anything else. But our methods have been a great success. The children love coming to school, and the teachers are really motivated by the new methods. And for me, I have found my calling—helping to educate people who really need and want to learn.

Speaker 2
Sasha: When I left art college seven years ago, I already knew it would be difficult to make a living from my art, so I imagined that art would pretty much be my hobby unless I got lucky. My ambition was not so much to be a professional artist, but just to do something in the art world. I moved to Cleveland in Ohio with a couple of artist friends, because it was cheaper to live there than in Chicago. We found an apartment, and also a space in an old warehouse that had been used for storing wheat which we could use as a studio. But I still had to do odd jobs like being a waiter and working in clubs. Then one of my friends had the idea of setting up a gallery. So we turned the warehouse space into a gallery, and then we got artists from the local art school to exhibit there. Soon, we started to get noticed. We had good reviews in local newspapers and even one art magazine. Then we attracted one or two more well-known artists to exhibit their work there. And it just took off from there—it's going incredibly well. I'm still enjoying painting in my free time, but I feel that in helping to run a gallery, I've found a job where I can be with the people and the things I love.

▶ 64

1 match   4 Swiss
2 ship   5 shock
3 chew   6 bass

▶ 65

I am very suspicious of bucket lists now. They started out as a good idea, but like a lot of things, they have become too commercial. In bookstores, you now find titles like *100 Places You Must Visit Before You Die* or *100 Movies You Should See*. And if your dream is to hold a baby tiger, there are even websites you can visit where they can make your wish come true.

▶ 66

Speaker 1
In the 1970s, Cancún was just a small fishing village—a few huts on the edge of a mangrove forest. Today, that forest is buried and rotting underneath 500 hotels. Only a few inhabitants remember the forest, and the seven million tourists who visit each year don't know it ever existed. This place is a classic example of how not to build a tourist resort. Nature is for sale here. The mangroves are not the only victims. The coral reef all along the coast is also slowly being destroyed by all the tourists' pollution. Very little waste water is treated: it's either pumped into the sea or injected into the land. Up to now, conservationists have failed to stop this development or the pollution it's caused.

Speaker 2
The story of the West African giraffe is a conservation success story. A heroic effort on the part of conservationists has saved the giraffe from extinction—from numbers as low as fifty giraffes twenty years ago to over 200 today. The main job was to track the giraffes' movements, since they travel huge distances looking for food. This was done by fitting them with GPS satellite collars. Once the conservationists knew where the giraffes were going, they could then begin to educate local people about the dangers facing these wonderful creatures, and to compensate farmers when their land had been damaged by them.

Speaker 3
If you mention the term "conservation efforts," people often think of attempts to save endangered animals, like the tiger, or to protect poor communities from big corporate organizations that are trying to use their land. But in fact, many conservation efforts are small in scale, and many have positive outcomes. I'll give you an example: the black poplar tree in Britain. The black poplar is one of Britain's rarest species of tree, and its numbers have been declining for decades. That's because much of its natural habitat—the floodplain—has been built on with new housing. Less floodplain means less protection against flooding. So conservationists persuaded local authorities to stop building on the floodplain and to reintroduce the trees. As a result, black poplar numbers are rising again.

▶ 67

A: So, how are we going to divide these tasks up? Basically, there's the decoration of the main tent to do; there's the sound system to rent from the store; and there's the food to prepare.
B: Oh, I'd rather not do any cooking.
A: It's not cooking, it's just cutting up some pizza and putting out a few chips and things. But if you'd prefer to do something else, there are plenty of other things.
B: No, I'll do that.
A: OK. And what about you, Carla?
C: Well, I don't mind helping with the decorations.
A: Great. And could you help out with that too, Harry?
B: I could, but I'd rather someone else did that. I'm not very good at that kind of thing. It'd probably be better if I went to get the sound system.
A: OK, and I like doing the decorations anyway, so that's perfect. Let's get started then.

▶ 68

1 Would you prefer a full meal or just something light?
2 Do you want to take a short break?
3 Would you rather we went to the movie another night?
4 Do you like Osaka more than Tokyo?

▶ 69

F = Friend, MA = Model answer
1
F: I'm going to ask you to explain your preferences for certain things. Ready? Here we go: bath or shower?
MA: I prefer having a shower. It's quicker and more refreshing.
2
F: Drive or be driven?
MA: I'd rather drive. I feel more in control.
3
F: Tea or coffee?
MA: I like coffee more in the mornings and tea in the afternoon.
4
F: Morning or afternoon?
MA: I prefer the morning to the afternoon. I generally feel fresher in the morning.
5
F: Fancy or casual clothes?
MA: I'd rather wear casual clothes, even at work. It just feels more comfortable.
6
F: Eating in or eating out?
MA: Actually, I prefer eating in, but I'd rather someone else did the cooking!

▶ 72

If you mention the term "conservation efforts," people often think of attempts to save endangered animals, like the tiger, or to protect poor communities from big corporate organizations that are trying to use their land. But in fact, many conservation efforts are small in scale, and many have positive outcomes.

Unit 9

▶ 73

P = Presenter, J = Journalist

P: … that's just one aspect of photojournalism. The question I'd really like to put to you is: When is altering a photo OK, and when is it not?
J: Well, that's a good question. In 1982, *National Geographic Magazine* published on its cover a photo of the Pyramids in Egypt. In order to fit the tops of the two pyramids onto its cover, photo editors digitally decreased the space between them. People said that this was a manipulation of reality and was wrong. Several years later, an associate editor defended the action. He said that although the magazine had altered the image, they hadn't done anything wrong. He said that he was opposed in general to manipulation of images, but that the cover was a graphic item, not a photo in a news story. He also said that photo editors had always touched up photos, but that this practice was now becoming more sophisticated with tools like Photoshop and Scitex.
P: So he said it was the fault of modern technology that people were altering images?
J: No. He was saying that the cover of a magazine was more like a piece of advertising, and it had to look aesthetically pleasing to help the magazine sell.
P: You mean the cover has to look good?
J: Yes, that's right. Other editors have used the same argument to alter images for book covers.
P: And what about cases of manipulation in hard news stories—you know, really serious and important ones?
J: That is, of course, a far more serious thing. Again in the 1980s, there was a case with *Picture Week* magazine. The magazine put together two different photos—one of Nancy Reagan, the other of Raisa Gorbachev—in such a way that they appeared to be great friends. This wasn't actually the case and of course people complained, saying that they had been given a false impression.
P: So what's the rule?
J: Well, some people say, "Don't trust a photo if there's anything important riding on it." Personally, I think that's going too far. We live now in a world of digitally enhanced visual images and alternative realities. But the public's not stupid—they know that, and can make up their own minds about what's real and what's not.

▶ 75

1. Like many of his fellow professionals, photographer Fritz Hoffman recommends using a film camera.
2. A digital camera encourages you to look at the preview before you take the next photo, but a film camera keeps you in the moment.
3. Hoffman also claims that with a digital camera, you need to edit the images after they've been taken.
4. That's so that you can make them look like the image as you saw it.

▶ 77

Most broadcasters and journalists are naturally concerned about being fair in their reporting. They don't want to be seen as biased—that is, in favor of one side of an argument. The solution, they think, is always to present both sides of any argument equally.

So, if a radio station is covering a story about climate change and interviews a scientist who claims that human activity has caused global temperatures to rise to dangerous levels, in order to be fair, they will also interview another scientist who claims that the rise in temperature has nothing to do with human activity, but is all part of the Earth's natural cycle of warmer and colder periods. But there's a fundamental problem with this kind of so-called "fairness," because it leads the listener or reader to think that both arguments have equal weight, when in fact there is an overwhelming amount of scientific evidence suggesting that human activity is responsible for global warming.

Back in the 1970s, reporters used to do something similar when reporting the dangers of smoking. All the evidence clearly showed that smoking was harmful and that it caused various medical conditions such as heart disease and lung cancer. Yet, broadcasters, in the interest of fairness, would always interview other scientists (very often one who was an employee of a tobacco company) who claimed that there was no clear evidence linking smoking to such diseases.

Many people, particularly in the scientific community, think that this kind of journalistic "fairness" often distorts the truth. They say that anyone who shouts their opinions loudly enough these days is given an equal hearing to those who quietly support their views with scientific data. The right way to report any debate, it is claimed, is to give time proportionately, based on the amount of real evidence presented. So, in the case of global warming, 99 percent of the time should be given to the argument that human activity is causing it, and one percent should be given to the view that it is part of a natural cycle, because that is the same proportion of scientific evidence that supports each view.

▶ 78

J = Jane, A = Annie

J: Hi, Annie.
A: Hi, Jane. Did you hear the good news about Patrick?
J: What?
A: Well, you know he was doing a comedy routine …
J: You mean that show that he and his friends took to the Edinburgh Festival?
A: Yes. Well, apparently he was spotted by someone from a big theatrical agency and they want him to sign a contract with them.
J: Really? Who told you about it?
A: Um … Kate. She thinks it won't be long before we see Patrick on TV.
J: Hmm. Well, I'd take that with a grain of salt if I

were you. It could just mean that he'll get some advertising work or something.

A: No, according to Kate, it's more than that. They talked about him getting acting parts on TV.

J: Really? Well, that'd be fantastic. I heard that it's really difficult to get that kind of work.

A: I think it is, which shows he must have really impressed them. But don't tell anyone just yet. I think he wants to keep quiet about it.

J: Don't worry. I'm not the type to spread gossip. Does the agency take a big fee?

A: It seems that they only take ten or fifteen percent, supposedly.

J: That sounds all right. Well, that's great news. Thanks for telling me.

▶ 80

F = Friend, MA = Model answer

1
F: Did you hear the good news about taxes?
MA: Good news about taxes? No, what happened?

2
F: Apparently, the government is going to reduce taxes for all workers.
MA: Really? That doesn't sound very likely. Who told you that?

3
F: Ben told me. It seems that everyone will only pay half the tax they are paying now.
MA: Half? Hmm ... Take no notice of what Ben says.

4
F: Well, maybe he's blown it a bit out of proportion. He said it will be on the news tonight.
MA: OK. Well, I'll watch the news and see.

5
F: What do you think is the truth?
MA: I bet that they've reduced taxes by half a percent or something and Ben misunderstood.

Unit 10

▶ 81

P = Presenter, M = Marjorie Barakowski

P: Ronald Reagan was raised in a small village in Illinois and he graduated from Eureka College, Illinois, with a degree in economics and sociology. He worked for a short time as a radio broadcaster in Iowa, and then moved to Los Angeles to pursue a career as an actor in movies and television. After joining the Republican Party in 1962, his skills as an orator were noticed, and he was persuaded to run for governor of California. He did a good job as governor, and this led to his nomination for Republican presidential candidate in 1980, which he won. He then went on to become the president of the United States between 1981 and 1989. He took a hard line against communism, and his second term in office saw the beginning of the end of communism in Eastern Europe. He was often ridiculed for not being very clever—a second-rate actor who could only read the lines he was given by his advisers— but he remains one of the most popular US presidents of the past fifty years. Why? I put that question to political historian Marjorie Barakowski.

M: Ronald Reagan understood the fundamental essence of leadership: that is, that you have to be able to communicate. Reagan always gave the impression that he was listening when he was speaking to you. It was almost as if it didn't matter what his political views were. He made people feel that they mattered. He looked you in the eye, smiled at you, made you feel special. That is a fantastic quality to have.

I'd also have to say that he presided over a time of great economic growth in the United States. When he came to power, things weren't great for most Americans, but he gave them hope. It obviously helped that the economy thrived during his presidency. But, nevertheless, Reagan's style of communication stands out as a model for all leaders. If you can connect with the ordinary person, there's very little you can do wrong.

▶ 83

I was always told that having good qualifications and the right degree opens doors, but actually it's good communication skills that help you advance in an organization. It's important to understand and be understood by the people you work with.

▶ 84

In 2016, the US Treasury announced that it would put the face of a black woman, Harriet Tubman, on its $20 bill. Unlike former president Andrew Jackson, whose image she has replaced, few people outside the United States have any idea who Harriet Tubman is, or what she did for her country.

Harriet Tubman was born into slavery in Maryland, in the US, around 1820. She had a strange disability called narcolepsy, which meant she could fall asleep at any time without warning. The disability was the result of being struck on the head by an iron weight, which had been thrown at another slave, but which had hit her instead.

In 1851, she used the "Underground Railroad," a system of secret routes and safe houses, to escape to a neighboring Free State. When she realized she had reached freedom, she said she looked at her hands to see if she was still the same person. "The sun came up like gold through the trees," she recalled, "and I felt I was in heaven."

After finding her own freedom, she started trying to help other slaves to escape using the Underground Railroad—first members of her own family, and then others. She became what was known as a "conductor," helping lead almost 300 other slaves to freedom over a fifteen-year period. She was a determined woman—it is said that she threatened to shoot any of the escapees who said they wanted to turn back.

During the Civil War between the Northern and Southern states of America, Harriet Tubman became a spy for the Northern forces. Black people were effective as spies because many white Southerners did not think they had the intelligence to do such work. Tubman also worked as a nurse in the war, and even acted as a military officer, leading a force of 300 free black soldiers to liberate seven hundred slaves in South Carolina.

In spite of her brave service to her country, Tubman never received a pension from the government—she had to survive on her husband's pension. (She was married twice, and had one adopted child.) After the war, she wrote her story with the help of a biographer. She also traveled across the eastern United States giving public speeches about her experiences and campaigning for voting rights for women. She died of pneumonia in 1913 and only then received the recognition that her impressive career deserved, when she was given a full military funeral at Auburn cemetery.

▶ 86
Speaker 1
Well, I'd be interested to know a little more about the job, because although I'm very interested in the idea of working with young people—people are always telling me that I'm very good with children—I actually don't have much direct experience with this age group.

Speaker 2
I specialize in canoeing and various other water sports, but I feel comfortable with most outdoor activities, really—as long as you're not going to expect me to lead a climbing expedition up a glacier or anything. I haven't done mountaineering. But I have led groups before, so I have organizational skills

Speaker 3
I think I'd be very well suited to this job, actually. Although I haven't led expeditions as such, I've been working as a physical education teacher at my local high school for the last four years. I'm good at a number of sports, in fact. But when I saw your advertisement, I thought, "This could be just the thing for me." I'm familiar with your organization, and I really like the fact that you run these activities for kids from poor backgrounds.

▶ 88
I = Interviewer, MA = Model answer
1
I: So what did you study at college?
MA: I studied media, but I specialized in newspaper journalism.
2
I: And what attracted you to our newspaper?
MA: I want to pursue a career in journalism, and I'm very interested in local news.
3
I: How do you feel about working under very tight deadlines?
MA: I think I'm good at working under pressure. I had a lot of experience with that at college.
4
I: Have you had any experience writing for a newspaper before?
MA: Not really, but I think I write well and I'm very eager to learn.
5
I: If you get the job, don't you think you might become bored just dealing with local news stories?
MA: No. I'm serious about wanting to become a professional journalist, and this would be a perfect place to start.

Unit 11
▶ 89
Dr. K. David Harrison believes that language diversity is just as important as biodiversity. He's part of a *National Geographic* project called "Enduring Voices," whose aim is to document little-known languages that are in danger of becoming extinct. It's estimated that over half the world's 7,000 languages will disappear by 2050, and so the race is on to trace and record these languages, and also to help keep them alive.

Diversity doesn't depend on the size of a territory or country. In Bolivia, which only has a population of twelve million, there are 37 different languages, belonging to eighteen language families. This is the same number as the whole of Europe.

Dr. Harrison seeks out these language "hotspots"—places where there is a great diversity of languages spoken and where some are in danger. Studies in the Oklahoma region of the US succeeded in discovering 26 languages, one of which—Yuchi—had as few as seven speakers. By highlighting this fact, researchers were able to help the community keep this dying language alive.

Why is this work important? According to Harrison, "When we lose a language, we lose centuries of human thinking about time, seasons, sea creatures, reindeer, edible flowers, mathematics, landscapes, myths, music—the unknown and the everyday." Some ancient cultures managed to build large monuments by which we can remember their achievements, but all cultures express their genius through their languages and stories. We would be shocked if the Great Pyramid of Giza disappeared; we should be equally concerned when we lose a language.

These languages store knowledge that can be a huge benefit to people today. The Yupik language is spoken in parts of Siberia and Alaska. A book written a few years ago by Yupik elders and scientists, in which they described the changing conditions of the ice in the Arctic, was able to help other scientists understand how climate change is affecting polar ice.

One of the original arguments for globalization was that it could bring us all closer together. And in some ways, this is true. But that doesn't mean we all have to do the same things—eat the same food or speak the same language. If anything, globalization has reminded us how important differences and diversity are. While he couldn't save Ubykh (a language spoken near the Black Sea) from extinction, or Kakadu (an Australian aboriginal language), Dr. Harrison and his team aim to save as many languages as they can.

▶ 90

1 David Harrison is a linguist at Swarthmore College (S-W-A-R-T-H-M-O-R-E) in Pennsylvania (P-E-N-N-S-Y-L-V-A-N-I-A).
2 In 2008, the Enduring Voices project found a new language in Arunachal Pradesh (A-R-U-N-A-C-H-A-L) in India called Koro (K-O-R-O).
3 *Chary* is a word from the Siberian language Tofa. Spelled C-H-A-R-Y, it means a four-year-old domesticated reindeer.
4 The longest non-scientific word in the English language is *floccinaucinihilipilification*, which means the habit of regarding something as unimportant. I'll spell it: F-L-O-C-C-I-N-A-U-C-I-N-I-H-I-L-I-P-I-L-I-F-I-C-A-T-I-O-N.

▶ 92

1 Meg is a border collie, a smart breed of dog used by farmers because they understand instructions well and like to be helpful. Their usual job is to round up and direct sheep. You can show Meg a picture of a toy and tell her its name (like a duck or a frisbee), and then ask her to go and find it in a room full of toys. Once she has found it once and learned the name, all you have to do the next time is to ask her to fetch the duck or the frisbee from the room, and she will go and find it.
2 Betty is a New Caledonian crow. These animals are pretty inventive tool makers. In the wild, for example, they use sticks to get insects out of trees. But researchers also discovered that in the lab, these birds were able to make tools from materials that they had never used before. Experimenters placed a piece of meat in a little basket and put it in a tube. Betty looked at the problem, and found a solution. She took a straight piece of wire, bent it into the shape of a hook using her beak, and lifted the basket out of the tube.
3 Maya is a dolphin. I think most people know that dolphins have incredible imitative abilities. They can see an action performed and then repeat it when asked to. They also seem to understand spoken directions from humans very well. So you can get two of them to leap out of the water and turn a somersault at the same time. In fact, dolphins do these kinds of synchronized tricks all the time in the wild anyway because they're naturally playful creatures. But no one really understands how they communicate with each other to get the timing so perfect.
4 Kanzi is a bonobo monkey who has been taught sign language so that he can communicate with humans. One anecdote about his intelligence is that on a walk in the woods, Kanzi indicated that he wanted marshmallows and a fire. He was given the marshmallows and some matches. He found some twigs, broke them into pieces, and lit them with the matches. And then, most amazingly, he toasted the marshmallows on a stick over the fire. Bonobos are known to be expressive and intelligent, but even experts who had studied them were surprised by this behavior.
5 Psychobird is a western scrub-jay. These birds are known for being mischievous—they play tricks all the time. They're also supposed to be the only non-mammals that plan ahead. They hide food that they're storing up for future use. Their large memories allow them to remember as many as 200 hiding places. In a lab, Psychobird hid food so carefully that none of the experimenters could work out where she had put it.

▶ 93

S = Student, L = Lecturer
S: Hi, do you have a minute? I just wanted to ask a little more about this course.
L: Sure, how can I help?
S: Well, first of all, thanks for the interesting lecture. It was a lot to take in, though, and I don't really have as much background knowledge as some of the other students.
L: Don't worry—I think a lot of people find it difficult at first. Things will become clearer.
S: Well, can you explain what the course is going to be about? I thought it was going to be about Roman history, mainly.
L: Well, it's a mixture of Roman and Greek history—mainly Hellenistic.
S: Sorry, I didn't catch that word—Helle-something?
L: Hellenistic—Alexander the Great and so on.
S: Oh, yeah, OK. And are you saying that no previous knowledge of ancient history is needed?
L: Well, a little understanding of the geography of the eastern Mediterranean is very helpful. And if you've heard of or read about some of the Greek myths and legends, that helps too.
S: Do you mean stories like the war at Troy and so on?
L: Exactly.
S: OK, well, could you give me an example of a book I could read before the next lecture?
L: Um, you could have a look at some texts by Herodotus. He was a historian of the fifth century B.C., and his writing reads a lot like a good bedtime story!
S: Did you say Herodotus?
L: That's right, H-E-R-O-D-O-T-U-S.
S: OK, thanks. I'll do that.

▶ 95

T = Teacher, MA = Model answer

1
T: So you wanted to ask me a question about the exam at the end of this course?
MA: Yes. Can you explain what the exam involves?
2
T: Yes, there's a two-hour written exam and then a short oral exam afterward.
MA: Sorry, did you say "oral exam"?
3
T: Yes, you'll be asked some simple questions about what you have written.
MA: Could you give me an example of the questions?
4
T: Well, they might ask you to explain your reasons for an argument. But this part only carries a small proportion of the total grade.
MA: I'm sorry, I don't understand.
5
T: What I mean is that the oral exam is only fifteen percent of the total grade.
MA: Did you say fifteen or fifty percent?

Unit 12

▶ 96

How does national character affect economics? Well, let's just consider people's attitude toward money at its simplest level. There are basically two types of people—savers and spenders—and we all know people who fit these descriptions. Savers are prudent and careful, never wasteful. Of course they spend money too, but only when they can afford it, and only if it's a wise or long-term investment. On the other side, we have the spenders, the more extravagant types. For them, life is too short to worry about saving a little money here and there.

So, can you apply such simple stereotypes on a national scale? During the 2010–2011 global debt crisis, some commentators tried to do exactly that, saying that certain countries had been irresponsible with the money that they had borrowed from banks and governments in more prudent countries. As a result, people in these "irresponsible countries" would have to work longer hours, pay more taxes, and even accept lower wages if they wanted to receive any more loans.

The question these commentators failed to ask was whether it was irresponsible of the so-called "prudent countries" to lend the money in the first place. Because when you lend money, you take two risks: you risk losing the money, but you also risk putting the borrower in a difficult situation. In such a transaction, both parties have a similar motive—to get more money—and so both have a shared responsibility.

To portray one country as a nation of extravagant spenders and another as a nation of prudent savers is too simplistic. What drives economies in most developed or developing countries is the desire to have a better standard of living. And that goes for all of us, spenders and savers alike. For some people, it will mean spending money that they don't have at the moment—taking out a loan to get a new car, for example. For others, it will mean saving money to earn interest on it. And in order for the economy to function successfully, we need both types of people, but only as long as they lend and borrow responsibly.

▶ 97

I think that people often get into debt because they want a lifestyle that they can't really afford.

It's a lifestyle that is sold to them constantly through advertisements that appear on TV and in magazines. This desire to have a better lifestyle can affect some governments, too. They try to give their citizens the lifestyles that they see in these advertisements in order to win votes.

▶ 99

/ʃ/: wash, machine, revolution
/tʃ/: watch, cheap, richer
/ʒ/: pleasure, decision, usually
/dʒ/: change, major, wages

▶ 100

I = Interviewer, R = Rick Castro

I: Most of us will be familiar with the concept of barter from our notions of how primitive societies work: you have a chicken I want, and I've just made a new hunting spear that you need. So let's do a deal. But is barter, as a system of buying and selling goods and services, coming back into fashion? With me is Rick Castro of the Barter Society. Rick, is this a serious alternative to current systems of trade or just a romantic notion?
R: The first thing I'd say is that barter never went out of fashion. People have been using barter as a way of exchanging goods for a lot longer than they have been using money. It is, as you've said, a feature of almost every society, past and present. But it's also very much a feature of the modern economy. People are making bartering arrangements all the time. It's just that conventional economic statistics—GDP figures and so on—don't record it. How could they?
I: Can you give us an example of that?
R: Yes, but first we should make an important distinction between direct barter—like the example you gave of two people exchanging a chicken for a spear—and "exchange barter," which is when you belong to a barter group and make more indirect exchanges.
I: What does that mean?
R: Well, imagine I'm a yoga teacher and you're a car mechanic. I want to get my car serviced, and I'm ready to offer you a month of yoga classes in return. But you don't want to do yoga. What happens then? Well, if we belong to a barter exchange group, like "Bartercard" …
I: "Bartercard"? You're not serious …
R: Perfectly serious. If I belong to a group like that, I

can sell my yoga classes for "trade credits." These can then be spent buying the goods or services of over 75,000 other members—restaurants, sporting good stores, almost anything. So if you're a member, I can buy your mechanic services with my credits.
I: Hang on, though. This is just a tax dodge, isn't it? Normally I'd have to pay tax on my mechanic's bill, wouldn't I? And you should charge tax on your yoga classes, too.
R: Of course these exchanges are liable to tax—at least that's the law in most developed countries.
I: So what's the advantage then? I'm trying hard to see one. Why not just use money?
R: Well, because if you belong to a group like that, it gives you access to a new market—a big circle of new contacts, who will potentially become regular customers and, possibly, your friends, too!

▶ 101
A = Client, B = Caterer
A: So there'll be about sixty of us. We want some food, but nothing too fancy, to be honest. I imagine a lot of people will be going home and having dinner later anyway.
B: OK, so what did you have in mind? Some sandwiches?
A: Well, I was hoping we could have something more exciting than sandwiches.
B: Maybe if we prepared some sushi, some smoked salmon, or a few samosas?
A: Yes, that would be much more like it. Is that going to be very pricey?
B: About $10 per person.
A: Mmm … that seems a lot, but let's face it, it's an important occasion. It's a going-away party for someone who's been working with us for 37 years, so we don't want it looking cheap.
B: That makes sense. If I were in your shoes, I'd put on an event that people would remember. By the way, the $10 also covers waiting staff for the two hours.
A: Oh, we don't need that. We can just help ourselves. Would that reduce the price?
B: No, I'm sorry. You have to appreciate the amount of work involved, setting it up and packing everything away. But since we're there, we're happy to help serve the guests, too.
A: I see. Well, the key thing for us is that it's a nice, relaxing event, so we'll go with that, I guess.
B: Great. Just let me know exact numbers when you have them.

▶ 103
C = Caterer, MA = Model answer
1
C: So what kind of food did you have in mind? Some sandwiches?
MA: I was hoping we could have some hot food, too.
2
C: OK. We could provide a few hot pastries as well. How does that sound?
MA: Yes, that would be great.
3
C: That would be about $10 per person.
MA: That seems a lot. Could you move a little on that price?
4
C: Sorry. You have to appreciate it's a lot of work for us. We could do it more cheaply, but the food would have to be much more basic.
MA: No. The key thing for us is that the food is nice.
5
C: Well, if I were in your shoes, I would go for the more expensive menu.
MA: I suppose you're right. OK, then. We'll do that.

Life Combo Split 5B, 2nd Edition
Paul Dummett, John Hughes,
Helen Stephenson, David Bohlke

Vice President, Editorial Director:
  John McHugh

Publisher: Andrew Robinson

Senior Development Editor: Derek Mackrell

Associate Development Editor: Yvonne Tan

Editorial Assistant: Dawne Law

Director of Global Marketing: Ian Martin

Senior Product Marketing Manager:
  Caitlin Thomas

Media Researcher: Rebecca Ray,
  Leila Hishmeh

Senior IP Analyst: Alexandra Ricciardi

IP Project Manager: Carissa Poweleit

Senior Director, Production:
  Michael Burggren

Production Manager: Daisy Sosa

Content Project Manager: Beth McNally,
  Tan Jin Hock

Manufacturing Planner:
  Mary Beth Hennebury

Art Director: Brenda Carmichael

Cover Design: Lisa Trager

Text Design: emc design ltd.

Compositor: DoubleInk Publishing Services

American Adaptation: Kasia McNabb

© 2019 National Geographic Learning, a Cengage Learning Company

ALL RIGHTS RESERVED. No part of this work covered by the copyright herein may be reproduced or distributed in any form or by any means, except as permitted by U.S. copyright law, without the prior written permission of the copyright owner.

"National Geographic", "National Geographic Society" and the Yellow Border Design are registered trademarks of the National Geographic Society
® Marcas Registradas

> For product information and technology assistance, contact us at
> **Cengage Learning Customer & Sales Support, cengage.com/contact**
> For permission to use material from this text or product,
> submit all requests online at **cengage.com/permissions**
> Further permissions questions can be emailed to
> **permissionrequest@cengage.com**

Combo Split 5B + App: 978-1-337-90819-1
Combo Split 5B + App + My Life Online: 978-0-357-04799-6

National Geographic Learning
20 Channel Center Street
Boston, MA 02210
USA

National Geographic Learning, a Cengage Learning Company, has a mission to bring the world to the classroom and the classroom to life. With our English language programs, students learn about their world by experiencing it. Through our partnerships with National Geographic and TED Talks, they develop the language and skills they need to be successful global citizens and leaders.

Locate your local office at **international.cengage.com/region**

Visit National Geographic Learning online at **NGL.Cengage.com/ELT**
Visit our corporate website at **www.cengage.com**

STUDENT BOOK CREDITS
Although every effort has been made to contact copyright holders before publication, this has not always been possible. If notified, the publisher will undertake to rectify any errors or omissions at the earliest opportunity.
Text: p87 Sources: "Universals and cultural variation in turn-taking in conversation" by Tanya Stivers et al., April 2, 2009; "Cultural Variations in Personal Space: Theory, Methods, and Evidence" by Mark Baldassare and Susan Feller, Ethos 3.4, October 28, 2009; "The Incredible Thing We Do During Conversations" by Ed Yong, January 4, 2016; p94 Source: "The Secret History of the Women Who Got Us Beyond the Moon" by Simon Worrall, National Geographic, May 8, 2016; p96/p187 Source: "What superpower do you wish you had?", http://www.nationalgeographic.com. Reproduced by permission; p99 Source: "Madagascar's Pierced Heart" by Robert Draper, http://ngm.nationalgeographic.com/; p105 Source: utstudentsandnews.blogspot.co.uk; p106 Source: "A life revealed" by Cathy Newman, April 2002, www.ngm.nationalgeographic.com; p123: "The King Herself" by Chip Brown, www.ngm.nationalgeographic.com. Reproduced by permission; p130 Source: "Innovation in education for work: The Lumiar schools, Sao Paolo, Brazil" by Leonie Shanks, Innovation Unit, October 2012; p135: "Animal minds" by Virginia Morell, March 2008, www.ngm.nationalgeographic.com. Reproduced by permission; p147: "How One Korean Taco Truck Launched an $800 Million Industry" by David Brindley, www.ngm.nationalgeographic.com. Reproduced by permission.
Cover: © JOSEP LAGO/AFP/Getty Images.
Photos: 6–7 ©National Geographic Maps. DATA SOURCES: Shaded relief and bathymetry: GTOPO30, USGS EROS Data Center, 2000. ETOPO1/Amante and Eakins, 2009. Land cover: Natural Earth. naturalearthdata.com. Population Density: LandScan 2012 Global Population Database. Developed by Oak Ridge National Laboratory (ORNL), July 2013. Distributed by East View Geospatial: geospatial.com and East View Information Services: eastview.com/online/landscan. Original copyright year: 2015; 6 (t) © danielcastromaia/Shutterstock.com; 6 (m) © Carsten Peter/National Geographic Creative; 6 (b) © Michael Nichols/National Geographic Creative; 7 (t) imageBROKER/Alamy Stock Photo; 7 (bl) © Aleksandr Lukjanov; 7 (br) © sippakorn/Shutterstock.com; 8 (tl) © Shivji Joshi; 8 (tm) © pikselstock/Shutterstock.com;

Printed in China
Print Number: 02   Print Year: 2020

8 (tr) © Jing Wei; 8 (mtl) © Alejandra Brun/AFP/Getty Images; 8 (mtm) © StockLapse/Getty Images; 8 (mtr) © Peter Boehi; 8 (mbl) © Harrison Liu; 8 (mbm) Randy Duchaine/Alamy Stock Photo; 8 (mbr) © Stringer China/Reuters; 8 (bl) © Jody MacDonald/National Geographic Creative; 8 (bm) © David R. Frazier Photolibrary, Inc./Alamy Stock Photo; 8 (br) © DlightSwitch/Barcroft Media/Getty Images; 81 © Harrison Liu; 82 © Charles Eshelman/FilmMagic/Getty Images; 84 © Yva Momatiuk and John Eastcott/National Geographic Creative; 87 © Tom Merton/OJO Images/Getty Images; 88 © James L. Stanfield/National Geographic Creative; 89 ZUMA Press, Inc./Alamy Stock Photo; 90 © danielcastromaia/Shutterstock.com; 91 (tl) Roberto Nistri/Alamy Stock Photo; 91 (tr) © nhungboon/Shutterstock.com; 91 (ml) © corlaffra/Shutterstock.com; 91 (mr) Papilio/Alamy Stock Photo; 91 (bl) © Mark Bridger/Shutterstock.com; 91 (br) © chaipanya/Shutterstock.com; 92 RosaIreneBetancourt 10/Alamy Stock Photo; 93 Randy Duchaine/Alamy Stock Photo; 94 NASA Archive/Alamy Stock Photo; 96 (tl) © Albert Yu-Min Lin/National Geographic Creative; 96 (tr) Courtesy of Laly Lichtenfeld; 96 (mtl) © Andres Ruzo/National Geographic Creative; 96 (mtr) © Alize Carrere/National Geographic Creative; 96 (mbl) © Andrew Thompson; 96 (mbr) © Jen Shook; 96 (bl) © Rick Kern/WireImage/Getty Images; 96 (br) © Ricky Qi; 99 © Nazzu/Shutterstock.com; 100 Ashok Tholpady/Alamy Stock Photo; 102 © sippakorn/Shutterstock.com; 104 © oversnap/Getty Images; 105 © Stringer China/Reuters; 106 dpa picture alliance/Alamy Stock Photo; 108 © Mario Laporta/AFP/Getty Images; 111 © 1000 Words/Shutterstock.com; 114 © Jason Edwards/National Geographic Creative; 116 (left col) © Kyodo News/Getty Images; 116 (right col: l) dpa picture alliance/Alamy Stock Photo; 116 (right col: r) © Cate Gillon/Getty Images; 117 © Jody MacDonald/National Geographic Creative; 118 © NASA; 120 © Marco Grob/National Geographic Creative; 123 (t, b) © Kenneth Garrett/National Geographic Creative; 124 © Shelterbox; 126 © Photo-Loci/Alamy Stock Photo; 128 © Bjoern Bertheau; 129 © David R. Frazier Photolibrary, Inc./Alamy Stock Photo; 130 © Paulo Friedman; 132 © Christopher Pledger/eyevine/Redux; 135 © cheetahok/Shutterstock.com; 138 © Michael Nichols/National Geographic Creative; 140 (l) © David R. Frazier Photolibrary, Inc./Alamy Stock Photo; 140 (r) © Paulo Friedman; 141 © DlightSwitch/Barcroft Media/Getty Images; 142 © Luka Tambaca/National Geographic Creative; 144 Peter Horree/Alamy Stock Photo; 145 © giuseppe carbone/Shutterstock.com; 146 Phil Wills/Alamy Stock Photo; 147 © Gerd Ludwig/National Geographic Creative; 149 © Dougal Waters/Getty Images; 150 © The Farmery (TheFarmery.com); 152 © Lynn Koenig/Getty Images; 153 Motoring Picture Library/Alamy Stock Photo; 155 Motoring Picture Library/Alamy Stock Photo.

WORKBOOK CREDITS
Although every effort has been made to contact copyright holders before publication, this has not always been possible. If notified, the publisher will undertake to rectify any errors or omissions at the earliest opportunity.
Text: p78 source: 'Hayat Sindi, Science Entrepreneur', National Geographic, http://www.nationalgeographic.com/explorers/; p84/p112 source: 'Disappearing languages', National Geographic, http://travel.nationalgeographic.com/, https://livingtongues.wordpress.com/national-geographic-enduring-voices-project/.
Photos: 52 © rossario/iStockphoto; 55 © Steve Raymer/National Geographic Creative; 57 © mary delaney cooke/Corbis Historical/Getty Images; 58 © Vitaly Ilyasov/Shutterstock.com; 60 © Adriano Castelli/Shutterstock.com; 62 © Vixit/Shutterstock.com; 63 © Anan Kaewkhammul/Shutterstock.com; 64 (l) © woraput/iStockphoto; 64 (m) © lilly3/iStockphoto; 64 (r) © vesilvio/iStockphoto; 65 © Syda Productions/Shutterstock.com; 68 © Gordon Gahan/National Geographic Creative; 70 © Joyce Dale/National Geographic Creative; 72 © FloridaStock/Shutterstock.com; 73 © pierredesvarre/iStockphoto; 74 © Dmitry Kalinovsky/Shutterstock.com; 76 WDC Photos/Alamy Stock Photo; 78 Courtesy of Hayat Sindi; 80 © Pantheon/SuperStock; 83 (l) © Jody MacDonald/National Geographic Creative; 83 (r) © Marco Grob/National Geographic Creative; 84 © Chris Rainier; 86 FirePhoto/Alamy Stock Photo; 88 (tl) © Andraž Cerar/Shutterstock.com; 88 (tr, mbr) © Steve Byland/Shutterstock.com; 88 (mt) © L. S. Luecke/Shutterstock.com; 88 (mbl) © Robbie Taylor/Shutterstock.com; 88 (b) © Steve Noakes/Shutterstock.com; 92 © PeskyMonkey/iStockphoto; 94 North Wind Picture Archives/Alamy Stock Photo; 96 (l) maurice joseph/Alamy Stock Photo; 96 (r) © ERainbow/Shutterstock.com; 97 © Stefano Viola/Shutterstock.com; 98 © August_0802/Shutterstock.com; 99 © XPacifica/National Geographic Creative.
Illustrations: 56 Kevin Hopgood/Kevin Hopgood Illustration.

ACKNOWLEDGEMENTS
The *Life* publishing team would like to thank the following teachers and students who provided invaluable and detailed feedback on the first edition:
Armik Adamians, Colombo Americano, Cali; Carlos Alberto Aguirre, Universidad Madero, Puebla; Anabel Aikin, La Escuela Oficial de Idiomas de Coslada, Madrid; Pamela Alvarez, Colegio Eccleston, Lanús; Manuel Antonio, CEL – Unicamp, São Paulo; Bob Ashcroft, Shonan Koka University; Linda Azzopardi, Clubclass; Éricka Bauchwitz, Universidad Madero, Puebla; Paola Biancolini, Università Cattolica del Sacro Cuore, Milan; Laura Bottiglieri, Universidad Nacional de Salta; Richard Brookes, Brookes Talen, Aalsmeer; Maria Cante, Universidad Madero, Puebla; Carmín Castillo, Universidad Madero, Puebla; Ana Laura Chacón, Universidad Madero, Puebla; Somchao Chatnaridom, Suratthani Rajabhat University, Surat Thani; Adrian Cini, British Study Centres, London; Andrew Clarke, Centre of English Studies, Dublin; Mariano Cordoni, Centro Universitario de Idiomas, Buenos Aires; Monica Cuellar, Universidad La Gran Colombia; Jacqui Davis-Bowen, St Giles International; Nuria Mendoza Dominguez, Universidad Nebrija, Madrid; Robin Duncan, ITC London; Christine Eade, Libera Università Internazionale degli Studi Sociali Guido Carli, Rome; Leopoldo Pinzon Escobar, Universidad Catolica; Joanne Evans, Linguarama, Berlin; Juan David Figueroa, Colombo Americano, Cali; Emmanuel Flores, Universidad del Valle de Puebla; Sally Fryer, University of Sheffield, Sheffield; Antonio David Berbel García, Escuela Oficial de Idiomas de Almería; Lia Gargioni, Feltrinelli Secondary School, Milan; Roberta Giugni, Galileo Galilei Secondary School, Legnano; Monica Gomez, Universidad Pontificia Bolivariana; Doctor Erwin Gonzales, Centro de Idiomas Universidad Nacional San Agustin; Ivonne Gonzalez, Universidad de La Sabana; J Gouman, Pieter Zandt Scholengemeenschap, Kampen; Cherryll Harrison, UNINT, Rome; Lottie Harrison, International House Recoleta; Marjo Heij, CSG Prins Maurits, Middelharnis; María del Pilar Hernández, Universidad Madero, Puebla; Luz Stella Hernandez, Universidad de La Sabana; Rogelio Herrera, Colombo Americano, Cali; Amy Huang, Language Canada, Taipei; Huang Huei-Jiun, Pu Tai Senior High School; Nelson Jaramillo, Colombo Americano, Cali; Jacek Kaczmarek, Xiehe YouDe High School, Taipei; Thurgadevi Kalay, Kaplan, Singapore; Noreen Kane, Centre of English Studies, Dublin; Billy Kao, Jinwen University of Science and Technology; Shih-Fan Kao, Jinwen University of Science and Technology, Taipei; Youmay Kao, Mackay Junior College of Medicine, Nursing, and Management, Taipei; Fleur Kelder, Vechtstede College, Weesp; Dr Sarinya Khattiya, Chiang Mai University; Lucy Khoo, Kaplan, Singapore; Karen Koh, Kaplan, Singapore; Susan Langerfeld, Liceo Scientifico Statale Augusto Righi, Rome; Hilary Lawler, Centre of English Studies, Dublin; Eva Lendi, Kantonsschule Zürich Nord, Zürich; Evon Lo, Jinwen University of Science and Technology; Peter Loftus, Centre of English Studies, Dublin; José Luiz, Inglês com Tecnologia, Cruzeiro; Christopher MacGuire, UC Language Center; Eric Maher, Centre of English Studies, Dublin; Nick Malewski, ITC London; Claudia Maribell Loo, Universidad Madero, Puebla; Malcolm Marr, ITC London; Graciela Martin, ICANA (Belgrano); Erik Meek, CS Vincent van Gogh, Assen; Marlene Merkt, Kantonsschule Zürich Nord, Zürich; David Moran, Qatar University, Doha; Rosella Morini, Feltrinelli Secondary School, Milan; Judith Mundell, Quarenghi Adult Learning Centre, Milan; Cinthya Nestor, Universidad Madero, Puebla; Peter O'Connor, Musashino University, Tokyo; Cliona O'Neill, Trinity School, Rome; María José Colón Orellana, Escola Oficial d'Idiomes de Terrassa, Barcelona; Viviana Ortega, Universidad Mayor, Santiago; Luc Peeters, Kyoto Sangyo University, Kyoto; Sanja Brekalo Pelin, La Escuela Oficial de Idiomas de Coslada, Madrid; Itzel Carolina Pérez, Universidad Madero, Puebla; Sutthima Peung, Rajamangala University of Technology Rattanakosin; Marina Pezzuoli, Liceo Scientifico Amedeo Avogadro, Rome; Andrew Pharis, Aichi Gakuin University, Nagoya; Hugh Podmore, St Giles International; Carolina Porras, Universidad de La Sabana; Brigit Portilla, Colombo Americano, Cali; Soudaben Pradeep, Kaplan; Judith Puertas, Colombo Americano, Cali; Takako Ramsden, Kyoto Sangyo University, Kyoto; Sophie Rebel-Dijkstra, Aeres Hogeschool; Zita Reszler, Nottingham Language Academy, Nottingham; Sophia Rizzo, St Giles International; Gloria Stella Quintero Riveros, Universidad Catolica; Cecilia Rosas, Euroidiomas; Eleonora Salas, IICANA Centro, Córdoba; Victoria Samaniego, La Escuela Oficial de Idiomas de Pozuelo de Alarcón, Madrid; Jeanette Sandre, Universidad Madero, Puebla; Bruno Scafati, ARICANA; Anya Shaw, International House Belgrano; Anne Smith, UNINT, Rome & University of Rome Tor Vergata; Suzannah Spencer-George, British Study Centres, Bournemouth; Students of Cultura Inglesa, São Paulo; Makiko Takeda, Aichi Gakuin University, Nagoya; Jilly Taylor, British Study Centres, London; Juliana Trisno, Kaplan, Singapore; Ruey Miin Tsao, National Cheng Kung University, Tainan City; Michelle Uitterhoeve, Vechtstede College, Weesp; Anna Maria Usai, Liceo Spallanzani, Rome; Carolina Valdiri, Colombo Americano, Cali; Gina Vasquez, Colombo Americano, Cali; Andreas Vikran, NET School of English, Milan; Mimi Watts, Università Cattolica del Sacro Cuore, Milan; Helen Ward, Oxford; Yvonne Wee, Kaplan Higher Education Academy, Singapore; Christopher Wood, Meijo University; Yanina Zagarrio, ARICANA.